Welcome Home Cookbook

450 Comfort Food Recipes for the Slow Cooker, Stovetop, and Oven

Hope Comerford

PHOTOS BY
CLARE BARBOZA

Good Books
New York, New York

Good Books books may be purchased in bulk at special discounts for sales promotion, corporate gifts, fund-raising, or educational purposes. Special editions can also be created to specifications. For details, contact the Special Sales Department, Good Books, 307 West 36th Street, 11th Floor, New York, NY 10018 or info@skyhorsepublishing.com.

Good Books is an imprint of Skyhorse Publishing, Inc.®, a Delaware corporation.

Visit our website at www.goodbooks.com.

10 9 8 7 6 5 4 3 2 1

Library of Congress Cataloging-in-Publication Data is available on file.

Cover design by Jane Sheppard
Cover photo by Clare Barboza

Print ISBN: 978-1-68099-329-5
Ebook ISBN: 978-1-68099-331-8

Printed in China

To my Meme. You have always been, and will always be, my inspiration to cook and create recipes. I'm grateful every day for the gifts you've passed on to me. I love you!

Table of Contents

About *Welcome Home Cookbook*

Whether you're the most novice of cooks, or the most experienced, this book is for you! We've covered all the bases for you, from appetizers and breakfast to main courses, desserts, and breads. This book contains hundreds of tried-and-true recipes you can confidently cook for your family, bring to a potluck, take to your church banquet, or make for a party.

When I was a little girl, I used to stand by my Meme's (grandma's) counter and watch her cook. I would pull up a chair from the kitchen table and sit on my knees so I could get in on the action. When I was very young, she started letting me stir the cookie or cake batter, or sprinkle the seasoning on the pork chops. When I got a little older, she began letting me measure out the flour, sugar, butter, etc. When I was older still, she let me chop the onions, celery, carrots, etc. She rarely cooked from a recipe, but the ones she did use were well-loved and usually written in her mother's handwriting.

Over the years, I've compiled many recipes from my Meme. I've gained many more from my own cooking experiences, but my most favorite recipes are from her. They're the comfort food of my past! They are how my love of cooking began. The recipes in this book are collected from home cooks across the country—they are the best recipes from grandmas and grandpas, moms, dads, and beloved friends, the kind you pass from generation to generation—and each recipe has been tested by everyday folks too. These are the favorite casserole recipes served when the kids come home from college, the cookies remembered from grandma's cookie jar, the macaroni and cheese recipe that will take you back to your childhood. Food brings us together and preserves special memories like few things can.

As you begin journeying through this book, I always suggest reading from cover to cover. I can't tell you the good recipes I've passed over in the past by not following this advice. Don't become overwhelmed. Bookmark or dog-ear the pages of the recipes that interest you the most as you go through. Then, when you've looked at everything, go back to those marked pages and pick two or three to start with. Maybe you'll try the recipes that remind you of your own grandma or maybe you'll be inspired to try something entirely new. Don't be surprised if you discover a new favorite dish to share with your loved ones, creating new memories that will be passed down through the generations.

Appetizers

Appetizers

Shrimp Appetizer Platter

**Tammy Smith,
Dorchester, WI**

Makes 5 cups
Prep. Time: 15 minutes
Chilling Time: 1 hour

8 oz. cream cheese, softened

½ cup sour cream

¼ cup salad dressing or mayonnaise

1-2 4-oz. cans broken shrimp, drained and
   rinsed

1 cup cocktail sauce

2 cups shredded cheese

1 pepper, chopped

1 tomato, chopped

3 green onions, chopped

crackers of choice

1. Beat together cream cheese, sour cream,
and salad dressing.

2. Put on a 12-inch platter.

3. Layer rest of ingredients in order given.

4. Cover and chill at least 1 hour. Serve
with crackers.

Hot Artichoke and Spinach Dip

Jennifer Archer,
Kalona, IA

Makes 2½ cups
Prep. Time: 10–15 minutes
Baking Time: 20–25 minutes

6-oz. jar marinated artichoke hearts, drained

9-11-oz. pkg. frozen creamed spinach, thawed

¼ cup mayonnaise

¼ cup sour cream

½ cup grated Parmesan cheese

1 garlic clove, minced, *optional*

tortilla or pita chips

1. Chop artichoke hearts and place in small bowl. Stir in spinach.

2. Fold in mayonnaise and sour cream.

3. Mix in Parmesan cheese, and garlic if you wish.

4. Spoon into a small baking dish. Bake at 350°F for 20–25 minutes, or until bubbly.

5. Serve warm with tortilla or pita chips.

Hot Reuben Dip

**Leona Miller,
Millersburg, OH**

Makes 12 servings
Prep. Time: 10 minutes
Baking Time: 35 minutes

8-oz. fat-free cream cheese, softened

½ cup fat-free sour cream

2 Tbsp. ketchup

½ lb. deli lean corned beef, finely chopped

1 cup sauerkraut, chopped, rinsed, and
   drained

1 cup reduced-fat shredded Swiss cheese

2 Tbsp. onion, finely chopped

rye melba toast or crackers

1.   In a mixing bowl, beat cream cheese, sour cream, and ketchup until smooth.

2.   Stir in corned beef, sauerkraut, Swiss cheese, and onion until blended.

3.   Transfer to a greased 1-quart baking dish.

4.   Cover and bake at 375°F for 30 minutes. Uncover and bake 5 minutes longer or until bubbly.

5.   Serve warm with melba toast or crackers.

Buffalo Chicken Dip

**Deb Martin,
Gap, PA**

Makes 8 cups
Prep. Time: 15 minutes
Cooking Time: 20-60 minutes

10-oz. can chunk chicken, drained

¼ cup Frank's RedHot sauce

2 8-oz. pkgs. cream cheese, softened

1 cup ranch dressing

1½-3 cups shredded cheddar jack cheese, *divided*

tortilla chips

1. Heat chicken and hot sauce in a large frying pan over medium heat until heated through.

2. Stir in cream cheese and ranch dressing. Cook, stirring until well blended and warm.

3. Mix in half of shredded cheese.

4. Transfer the mixture to a small slow cooker. Sprinkle the remaining cheese over the top.

5. Cover and cook on Low setting until hot and bubbly. Serve with tortilla chips.

Variation:
Replace hot sauce with 1 cup buffalo wing sauce. Spread cream cheese in bottom of small shallow baking dish. Layer with shredded chicken, buffalo wing sauce, ranch dressing, and shredded cheese. Bake at 350°F for 20 minutes or until cheese is melted.
—Donna Treloar,
Muncie, IN

Party-Starter Bean Dip

**Leona Yoder,
Hartville, OH**

Fills a 9-inch pie pan (about 15 servings)
Prep. Time: 15 minutes
Baking Time: 20 minutes

16-oz. can refried beans

8-oz. pkg. cream cheese, softened

12-oz. jar salsa, *divided*

slices of jalapeño peppers, *optional*

1. Preheat oven to 350°F. Spread beans into bottom of a greased 9-inch pie pan or ovenproof dish.

2. Beat cream cheese until creamy in a medium-sized mixing bowl. Add ⅔ cup salsa and beat until smooth.

3. Spread cream cheese mixture over beans. Bake 20 minutes.

4. Let cool 5 minutes.

5. Spread remaining salsa over hot dip and garnish with jalapeño slices, if you wish.

6. Serve with tortilla, pita, or other sturdy chips.

Easy Layered Taco Dip

**Lindsey Spencer,
Morrow, OH
Jenny R. Unternahrer,
Wayland, IA**

Makes 8–10 servings
Prep. Time: 15 minutes

8-oz. cream cheese, softened

8-oz. sour cream

8-oz. taco sauce or salsa

shredded lettuce

chopped tomato

chopped green pepper, *optional*

shredded cheese, cheddar or Mexican blend

tortilla chips

1. Blend cream cheese and sour cream until smooth.

2. Spread in bottom of a 9x13-inch dish.

3. Layer salsa over sour cream mixture, then lettuce, tomato, green pepper (if using), and cheese.

4. Serve with tortilla chips.

Variations:

1. Instead of salsa, use 1-oz. packet of taco seasoning to mix with the cream cheese and sour cream.
—Virginia Graybill, Hershey, PA

2. Add a layer of chopped onion.
—Barbara J. Bey, Hillsboro, OH

TIP

If you can, add the lettuce, tomato, and cheese at the last minute so the lettuce doesn't get soggy.
—Jenny R. Unternahrer, Wayland, IA

Hummus from Scratch

**Melanie Thrower,
McPherson, KS**

Makes 24 servings
Prep. Time: 10 minutes
Soaking Time: 8 hours, or overnight
Cooking Time: 1½ hours

16-oz. bag dried chickpeas (garbanzo beans)

⅔ cup lemon juice

3 cloves garlic

⅔ cup peanut butter, or tahini (sesame seed paste)

½ cup chopped cilantro

2-3 Tbsp. ground cumin

1 Tbsp. olive oil

1. Place chickpeas in large stockpot. Cover with water. Let stand overnight.

2. In the morning, drain chickpeas and discard soaking water.

3. Cover chickpeas with fresh water.

4. Cover and cook 1–1½ hours over low-medium heat, or until tender.

5. Drain off any liquid. Pour beans into food processor.

6. Add all other ingredients, except olive oil, to processor.

7. Blend until smooth. Add additional lemon juice and cumin to suit your taste.

8. Place hummus in serving dish. Drizzle with olive oil.

Serving Suggestion:
Serve as a dip with cut-up fresh vegetables, baked chips, or pita bread. Or use as a spread on a sandwich with vegetables.

TIP

You can freeze the hummus and use it up to a week later.

Dill Weed Dip for Vegetables

**Hannah D. Burkholder,
Bridgewater, VA**

Makes 1 cup
Prep. Time: 15 minutes

⅔ cup sour cream

⅔ cup mayonnaise

1 Tbsp. fresh chopped parsley

1 Tbsp. grated onion

1 Tbsp. dried dill weed

¼ tsp. dry mustard

carrots and celery, cut into sticks

1. Mix all ingredients together; then refrigerate until ready to serve.

2. Serve with cut-up fresh vegetables.

TIP

If you think of it, prepare this a day or two before you plan to use it. The flavors are enhanced by some time together.

Fresh Salsa

**Barbara Kuhns,
Millersburg, OH**

Makes 3 cups
Prep. Time: 20 minutes

3 tomatoes, chopped

½ cup chopped green bell peppers

¼ cup chopped onions

1 tsp. garlic powder

1 tsp. cumin

¼ tsp. ground red pepper

2 tsp. vinegar

1 tsp. olive oil

2 tsp. lemon juice

1. Combine vegetables.

2. Add remaining ingredients and mix well.

Guacamole

**Joyce Shackelford,
Green Bay, WI**

Makes 5 cups
Prep. Time: 15 minutes

3 avocados

¼ cup onion, minced

¾ tsp. garlic powder

½ tsp. chili powder

2 Tbsp. lemon juice

1 large ripe tomato, chopped

1. Cut avocados in half and remove seeds. With spoon scoop out insides and put in medium bowl. Add onion, garlic, and chili powders, and lemon juice.

2. With a masher, squash avocados until creamy.

3. Fold in tomato, mixing everything together well.

Serving Suggestion:
Serve as a dip, sandwich filling, or garnish.

Cheese and Olive Spread

Suzanne Yoder,
Gap, PA

Makes 2 cups
Prep. Time: 15 minutes
Chilling Time: 1 hour

8-oz. pkg. shredded mild cheddar cheese

8-oz. pkg. cream cheese, softened

½ cup mayonnaise

¼ cup stuffed green olives, chopped

¼ cup chopped green onions

2 Tbsp. lemon juice

¼ tsp. ground red pepper or to taste

Ritz crackers

1. Mix all ingredients except crackers.

2. Refrigerate at least an hour. Serve with Ritz crackers.

Fruit Dip

**Linda Eberly Miller,
Harrisonburg, VA
Stacy Stoltzfus,
Grantham, PA
Diane Eby,
Holtwood, PA
Janet L. Roggie,
Lowville, NY**

Makes 1½–2 cups
Prep. Time: 5–10 minutes

oz. marshmallow cream

-oz. pkg. cream cheese, softened

Tbsp. orange juice concentrate, not
   reconstituted

½ tsp. grated orange zest

ssorted fruit, cut into bite-sized pieces

1. Beat the ingredients together with an electric beater. Chill.

2. Serve with fresh fruit.

TIPS

1. You can change the flavor of this dip by substituting other fruit juices for the orange juice: strawberry, lime, blueberry, peach, cherry, and so on. Or add herbs and/or spices to complement your selection of fruit: ground ginger, ground cinnamon, chopped mint and/or lemon verbena, and others.
2. If you cut the fruit in advance of serving, dip apples (and any other fruit that may turn brown) in lemon juice.
3. Keeps 1 week or more in the refrigerator.

Zesty and Fruity Cream Cheese Block

Hope Comerford,
Clinton Township, MI

Makes 1 cup
Prep. Time: 30–35 minutes

2 tsp. olive oil

¼ cup minced shallot or onion

1-2 chipotle peppers in adobo sauce
(depending on the level of heat you like),
minced

1 cup strawberry preserves (or any other flavor
you like)

8-oz. cream cheese block

rice crackers or other crisp crackers

1. In a small sauté pan, heat the oil over medium heat.

2. Sauté the shallots and chipotle peppers until the shallots are translucent. Add the strawberry preserves and heat until the mixture has thickened.

3. Let the preserves mixture cool for about 10–15 minutes.

4. Place the cream cheese block on a serving plate or platter and pour the preserves mixture over the top.

5. Serve with crisp crackers, such as rice crackers.

Party Pinwheels

Della Yoder,
Kalona, IA

Makes 36 pieces
Prep. Time: 20–25 minutes
Chilling Time: 2 hours

1-oz. packet Original Hidden Valley Ranch Dressing Mix

2 8-oz. pkgs. cream cheese, softened

2 green onions, minced

4 12-inch flour tortillas

4-oz. jar diced pimentos, drained

4-oz. can diced green chilies, drained

2¼-oz. can diced black olives, drained

1. Mix together ranch mix, cream cheese, and green onions. Spread onto tortillas.

2. Sprinkle equal amounts of vegetables over cream cheese mixture.

3. Roll up tortillas tightly. Refrigerate for at least 2 hours.

4. Cut tortillas into 1-inch slices. Discard ends. Serve with spirals facing up.

Feta Bruschetta

Lena Sheaffer,
Port Matilda, PA

Makes 10 servings
Prep. Time: 15 minutes
Baking Time: 20 minutes

sp. butter, melted

cup olive or vegetable oil

ices French bread, cut 1-inch thick

pkg. crumbled feta cheese

garlic cloves, minced

sp. chopped fresh basil, or 1 tsp. dried
sil

ge tomato, seeded and chopped

Combine butter and oil. Brush on both
of bread. Place on baking sheet.

Bake at 350°F for 8–10 minutes, or until
ly browned.

3. Combine feta cheese, garlic, and basil.
Sprinkle over toast. Top with tomato.

4. Bake 8–10 minutes longer, or until
heated through. Serve warm.

Variation:
Mix chopped red pepper into Step 3, along
with any of your other favorite herbs.

Veggie Pizza

**Jean Butzer,
Batavia, NY
Julette Rush,
Harrisonburg, VA**

Makes 18 servings
Prep. Time: 20–30 minutes
Cooking Time: 9–12 minutes
Chilling Time: 30 minutes

2 8-oz. pkgs. refrigerated crescent rolls

8-oz. pkg. fat-free cream cheese, softened

½ cup fat-free mayonnaise

1 tsp. dill weed

½ tsp. onion salt

¼–1 cup broccoli florets

¼–1 cup finely chopped green pepper or
mushrooms

¼–1 cup finely chopped tomato, membranes
and seeds removed

½ cup sliced ripe olives

¼ cup finely chopped sweet onion or red
onion

¼ cup finely shredded cheddar cheese,
optional

1. Separate dough into 4 rectangles.

2. Press onto bottom and up sides of
10x13-inch jelly roll baking pan to form crust.

3. Bake 9–12 minutes or until golden
brown. Cool.

4. Mix cream cheese, mayonnaise, dill,
and onion salt until well blended.

5. Spread over cooled crust, but not too
thickly. About ¼ cup mixture should be left
over.

6. Top with chopped vegetables and
optional cheese.

7. Press down lightly into cream cheese
mixture.

8. Refrigerate. Cut into squares to serve.

TIPS

1. Add veggies depending on your preference and availability.
2. Do not put the cream cheese mixture on too thick. As noted, there may be ¼ cup left
   after spreading it on the crescent rolls. This can be saved to use as a dip with any
   leftover vegetables you have.

Cucumber Bites

Hope Comerford,
Clinton Township, MI

Makes 25–30 servings
Prep. Time: 25 minutes

8 oz. cream cheese, softened

1 tsp. garlic powder

1 tsp. onion powder

¼ tsp. parsley flakes

¼ tsp. dill

¼ tsp. salt

⅛ tsp. pepper

2 seedless cucumbers, sliced about ¼-inch
thick

8 oz. thinly sliced smoked salmon

1¼ oz. capers

1. In a bowl, mix together the softened
cream cheese, garlic powder, onion powder,
parsley flakes, dill, salt, and pepper.

2. Lay the cucumber slices on a large
platter or two in a single layer. Spread about
½ tsp. of the cream cheese mixture on each
slice of cucumber.

3. Cut the salmon into approximately
½ × ½-inch pieces. Place a single piece on
top of each cucumber slice and press gently
in the middle of each piece to create a very
small divot.

4. Place 3 capers into each little divot on
top of each slice of salmon.

Apricot Wraps

Doyle Rounds,
Bridgewater, VA

Makes about 4½ dozen wraps
Prep. Time: 10 minutes
Baking Time: 25 minutes

14-oz. pkg. dried apricot halves

½ cup whole almonds

1 lb. sliced bacon

¼ cup plum, or apple, jelly

2 Tbsp. soy sauce

1. Fold each apricot around an almond.

2. Cut bacon strips into thirds vertically. Wrap a strip around each apricot and secure with a toothpick.

3. Spread out over two ungreased 10x15-inch baking pans.

4. Bake uncovered at 375°F for 15 minutes. Turn each wrap over. Continue baking 10 more minutes, or until bacon is crisp.

5. While wraps are baking, combine jelly and soy sauce in a small saucepan. Cook and stir over low heat for 5 minutes, or until warm and smooth.

6. Remove apricots to paper towels and drain. Serve with sauce for dipping.

Basic Deviled Eggs

Joanne Warfel,
Lancaster, PA

Makes 12 halves
Prep. Time: 30 minutes
Cooking Time: 20 minutes

6 large eggs

¼ cup light mayonnaise

1 tsp. vinegar

1 tsp. prepared mustard

⅛ tsp. salt

sprinkle of pepper

paprika, for garnish

parsley sprigs, for garnish, *optional*

To hard-boil eggs:

1. Place eggs in a single layer in a lidded pan.

2. Fill the pan with cold water to just cover the eggs.

3. Bring to a full boil over high heat, covered.

4. As soon as the water begins the full boil, immediately turn the heat down to low for a simmer. Allow to barely simmer for exactly 8 minutes.

5. Pour off hot water. Run cold water and/or ice over the eggs to quickly cool them.

To make deviled eggs:

1. Cut eggs in half lengthwise. Gently remove yolk sections into a bowl.

2. Discard two yolks. Mash remaining yolk sections together with a fork. Stir in remaining ingredients with yolk mixture until smooth.

3. Fill empty egg whites. The filling will make a little mound in the egg white. Garnish, if desired.

4. Refrigerate.

Stuffed Jalapeños

Barbara Walker,
Sturgis, SD

Makes 12 servings
Prep. Time: 20 minutes
Baking Time: 45 minutes

12 fresh jalapeño peppers, halved lengthwise and seeded

8-oz. pkg. cream cheese, softened

12 slices bacon

1. Preheat oven to 400°F.

2. Use rubber gloves to seed and slice peppers. Keep hands away from your face; the liquid and seeds from the peppers can burn your eyes.

3. Stuff each pepper half with cream cheese.

4. Wrap half a slice of bacon around each stuffed pepper.

5. Place in single layer on baking sheet.

6. Bake for 45 minutes, or until bacon is done.

Bacon-Wrapped Water Chestnuts

**John D. Allen,
Rye, CO**

Makes 10–12 servings
Marinating Time: 1 hour
Prep. Time: 45 minutes
Baking Time: 30 minutes

1 can water chestnuts, drained

¼ cup soy sauce

1 lb. bacon

½ cup brown sugar

1. Soak the water chestnuts in soy sauce for 1 hour.

2. Cut bacon strips in half crosswise. Fry until limp but not crisp.

3. Roll the chestnuts in brown sugar.

4. Wrap bacon around the chestnuts and secure with toothpicks. Place on a baking sheet.

5. Bake at 350°F for 30 minutes.

Crab-Stuffed Mushrooms

Kim Stoll,
Abbeville, SC

Makes 6 servings
Prep. Time: 30 minutes
Baking Time: 15 minutes

12 large, fresh mushrooms

½ cup crabmeat, chopped fine

¼ cup cream cheese, at room temperature

½ cup grated Monterey Jack cheese

dash of pepper

¼ tsp. garlic powder

1 tsp. melted butter

1. Clean mushrooms and remove stems.

2. Mix remaining ingredients except melted butter together in a bowl.

3. Dip mushrooms in melted butter and place each one in a muffin tin cup, bottom up.

4. Fill mushrooms with crab-cheese mixture.

5. Bake at 400° for 15 minutes.

Variations:

1. You can substitute other cheese for the Monterey Jack, such as Colby or mozzarella.

2. Instead of using mushroom caps, cut slices of bread into quarters, dip in the melted butter, and push down into the individual cups in a mini-muffin pan. Fill the center of each bread cup with the crab mixture. Bake according to directions above.

Party Kielbasa

**Mary C. Wirth,
Lancaster, PA**

Makes 8-10 servings
Prep. Time: 35 minutes
Baking Time: 1½-2 hours

3 lbs. kielbasa or smoked sausage

1 cup ketchup

½ cup chili sauce

½ cup brown sugar, packed

2 Tbsp. Worcestershire sauce

1 Tbsp. lemon juice

¼ tsp. prepared mustard

1. Cut kielbasa or smoked sausage into 6 or 9 large pieces. Lay in a large saucepan of water.

2. Simmer 20 minutes. Drain.

3. Cool slightly. Cut into bite-sized pieces.

4. Mix all other ingredients in 9x13-inch baking dish.

5. Add kielbasa. Toss to coat with sauce.

6. Bake at 325°F for 1½–2 hours, stirring occasionally.

TIP

You can keep this warm in a slow cooker or chafing dish.

TIPS

1. It's easy to double the recipe to share, or freeze. You can also make this as a meatloaf.
   —Carla Koslowsky, Hillsboro, KS
2. Bring the sauce to a boil and boil 2 minutes. Reserve a little before pouring over the meatballs. Then, at the end of baking and just before serving, brush on the reserved sauce.
3. You can also bake these meatballs for 2 hours at 300°F. Cover with foil the first hour, then uncover.
   —Sherry Kreider, Lancaster, PA

Smoky Barbecue Meatballs

**Carla Koslowsky,
Hillsboro, KS
Sherry Kreider,
Lancaster, PA
Jennie Martin,
Richfield, PA**

Makes 10 servings
Prep. Time: 30 minutes
Baking Time: 1 hour

1½ lbs. 90%-lean ground beef

½ cup quick oats

½ cup fat-free evaporated milk or milk

¼ cup egg substitute

¼–½ cup finely chopped onion, *optional*

¼ tsp. garlic powder

¼ tsp. pepper

¼ tsp. chili powder

1 tsp. salt

Sauce:
1 cup ketchup

3 Tbsp. Splenda Brown Sugar Blend

¼ cup chopped onion

¼ tsp. liquid smoke

1. Mix ground beef, oats, milk, egg substitute, onion, garlic powder, pepper, chili powder, and salt together. Form 10 balls, each weighing about 2 oz. Place in 9x13-inch baking dish.

2. Bake at 350°F for 40 minutes. Mix the sauce ingredients while the meatballs bake. Set aside.

3. Pour off any grease from the meatballs. Pour sauce over meatballs.

4. Bake meatballs and sauce an additional 10–20 minutes, until bubbling and heated through.

Tangy Cocktail Franks

Linda Sluiter,
Schererville, PA

Makes 8–10 servings
Prep. Time: 15 minutes
Cooking Time: 15 minutes

12-oz. jar red currant jelly

¼ cup mustard

3 Tbsp. dry sherry

¼ tsp. ground allspice

20-oz. can pineapple chunks, drained

12-oz. pkg. cocktail franks

1. In saucepan, melt jelly. Add mustard, sherry, and allspice.

2. Add pineapple and cocktail franks to the pan.

3. Cook on medium heat about 10 minutes.

Breakfast and Brunch

Breakfast and Brunch

Veggie Quiche

Hope Comerford,
Clinton Township, MI

Makes 4-6 servings
Prep. Time: 25 minutes
Cooking Time: 1 hour

1 prepared piecrust

1 tsp. prepared mustard

½ cup chopped asparagus

½ cup chopped zucchini

½ cup chopped summer squash

½ cup chopped mushrooms

½ cup chopped onions

1 Tbsp. olive oil

3-4 eggs

1 tsp. garlic powder

1 tsp. onion powder

½ tsp. salt

½ tsp. pepper

10 oz. shredded Monterey Jack cheese

1. Preheat the oven to 325°F.

2. Press the prepared crust into the bottom of a pie plate. Brush it with the prepared mustard.

3. Sauté the asparagus, zucchini, summer squash, mushrooms, and onions in the olive oil until they are tender.

4. In a bowl, beat the eggs with the garlic powder, onion powder, salt, and pepper. Add in the sautéed veggies and Monterey Jack cheese.

5. Pour the egg/veggie mixture into the prepared crust. Bake for 1 hour.

6. When the egg is set in the middle, the quiche is done. Let it cool for about 10 minutes before slicing and serving.

Mom's Heavenly Quiche

**Barbara Forrester
Landis, Lititz, PA**

Makes 6-8 servings
Prep. Time: 15 minutes
Baking Time: 40-50 minutes

6 eggs, or equivalent amount of egg substitute

2 Tbsp. flour

2 cups cottage cheese

1 cup shredded cheddar cheese

½ stick (4 Tbsp.) butter, melted

4-oz. can diced green chilies, undrained

1. In a good-sized mixing bowl, beat eggs or pour in egg substitute.

2. Stir in flour.

3. When well mixed, stir in cottage cheese, shredded cheese, butter, and chilies.

4. Pour into greased 10-inch pie plate.

5. Bake 40–45 minutes, or until set in center. Insert blade of knife in center. If it comes out clean, the quiche is finished. If it doesn't, bake for 5 more minutes. Test again, and continue baking if needed.

6. Let stand 10 minutes before cutting to allow cheeses to firm up.

TIPS

1. You can use any kind of flour. I use whole wheat.
2. You can use any kind of cottage cheese. I use low-fat.
3. This is delicious eaten cold the next day if there's any left.
4. If you have leftover cooked veggies in your fridge, place them in the bottom of the pan and cover with egg mixture as a variation.

Overnight Breakfast Casserole

Hannah D. Burkholder,
Bridgewater, VA
Esther S. Martin,
Ephrata, PA

Makes 8–10 servings
Prep. Time: 45 minutes
Chilling Time: 8 hours, or overnight
Baking Time: 1 hour

1 lb. fresh bulk sausage

4 cups cubed day-old bread

2 cups shredded sharp cheddar cheese

1 tsp. dry mustard

10 eggs, slightly beaten

4 cups milk

1 tsp. salt

freshly ground pepper, to taste

¼ cup chopped or grated onion

½ cup peeled, chopped tomatoes, *optional*

½ cup diced green and red peppers, *optional*

½ cup sliced fresh mushrooms, *optional*

1. Cook the sausage in a skillet until browned. Drain and break up the meat into small pieces. Set aside.

2. Place bread in buttered 9x13-inch baking dish. Sprinkle with cheese.

3. Combine the next six ingredients. Pour evenly over the bread and cheese.

4. Sprinkle cooked sausage and chopped tomatoes, peppers, and mushrooms (if using) over the top.

5. Cover and chill in refrigerator for 8 hours, or overnight.

6. Preheat oven to 325°F. Bake uncovered for 1 hour. Tent with foil if top begins to brown too quickly.

Elegant Scrambled Eggs

**John D. Allen,
Rye, CO**

Makes 6–8 servings
Prep. Time: 15 minutes
Cooking Time: 10 minutes

12 eggs

½ tsp. salt

⅛ tsp. pepper

2 Tbsp. butter

2 Tbsp. whipping cream

1. Combine the first three ingredients in a large bowl. Beat until well mixed.

2. Melt butter in a skillet, making sure the bottom is covered. Add eggs. Set the heat at medium.

3. Stir constantly until eggs firm up but are not dry. Remove from heat.

4. Stir in the cream. Serve immediately.

Southwestern Egg Casserole

Eileen Eash,
Lafayette, CO

Makes 12 servings
Prep. Time: 20–30 minutes
Baking Time: 35–45 minutes
Standing Time: 5–10 minutes

10 eggs

½ cup flour

1 tsp. baking powder

⅛ tsp. salt

⅛ tsp. pepper

4 cups shredded Monterey Jack, or cheddar, cheese

2 cups cottage cheese

1 stick (8 Tbsp.) butter, melted

2 4-oz. cans chopped green chilies

1. Beat eggs in a large mixing bowl.

2. In a smaller bowl, combine flour, baking powder, salt, and pepper.

3. Stir flour mixture into eggs. Batter will be lumpy.

4. Add shredded cheese, cottage cheese, butter, and chilies to batter.

5. Pour into greased 9x13-inch baking dish.

6. Bake at 350°F for 35–45 minutes, or until knife inserted near center comes out clean.

7. Let stand 5–10 minutes before cutting.

TIPS

1. This is a great recipe for brunch. I usually put it together the night before and then refrigerate it.
2. To take to a potluck after baking it, I transport it in an insulated carrier, which I wrap in an old mattress pad. It stays hot for at least an hour.

Breakfast Casserole (Eggless)

Jean Butzer,
Batavia, NY

Makes 4–6 servings
Prep. Time: 20 minutes
Cooking Time: 1 hour

1 lb. bulk sausage

30-oz. pkg. frozen shredded hash browns, thawed

16-oz. container French onion dip

2 cups sour cream

2 cups shredded cheddar cheese, *divided*

1. Brown the sausage in a skillet. Drain.

2. In a large mixing bowl, combine the browned sausage, hash browns, French onion dip, sour cream, and 1 cup shredded cheese.

3. Spread mixture in a greased 9x13-inch baking pan. Bake at 350°F for 45 minutes.

4. Sprinkle with remaining cheese and bake an additional 15 minutes.

Breakfast Pizza

Jessica Hontz,
Coatesville, PA

Makes 8 servings
Prep. Time: 10 minutes
Baking Time: 20-25 minutes

z. refrigerated pizza crust

gs

ıp milk or cream

ces bacon, cooked crisp and crumbled

ɔs shredded cheddar, or Monterey Jack,
ıeese

Unroll pizza crust onto baking sheet.

Bake at 425°F for 10 minutes.

Whisk together eggs and milk in a large
ng bowl.

4. Cook in skillet until eggs start to congeal, about 3–4 minutes. Spoon onto crust.

5. Top with bacon and cheese.

6. Bake an additional 10 minutes until eggs are set and crust is golden brown.

Potato-Bacon Gratin

Valerie Drobel,
Carlisle, PA

Makes 6 servings
Prep. Time: 15 minutes
Baking Time: 1 hour

6-oz. bag fresh spinach

1 clove garlic, minced

1 Tbsp. olive oil

4 large potatoes, peeled or unpeeled, *divided*

6 oz. Canadian bacon slices, *divided*

6 oz. grated Swiss, cheddar, or Gruyère cheese, *divided*

1 cup chicken broth

1. In large skillet, sauté spinach and garlic in olive oil just until spinach is wilted.

2. Cut potatoes into thin slices.

3. In 2-qt. baking dish, layer ⅓ the potatoes, half the bacon, ⅓ the cheese, and half the wilted spinach.

4. Repeat layers ending with potatoes. Reserve ⅓ cheese for later.

5. Pour chicken broth over all.

6. Cover and bake at 350°F for 45 minutes.

7. Uncover and bake 15 more minutes. During last 5 minutes, top with remaining cheese.

8. Allow to stand 10 minutes before serving.

TIP

Leftovers are delicious. Make two of these bakes at a time and freeze one.

Gold Rush Brunch

Trish Dick,
Ladysmith, WI

Makes 12 servings
Prep. Time: 2 hours
Baking Time: 40-45 minutes
Standing Time: 10 minutes

4 large potatoes, peeled or unpeeled

½ stick (4 Tbsp.) butter, *divided*

2 Tbsp. chopped onion

2 Tbsp. parsley

1 lb. sausage, ham, or bacon

8 eggs, beaten

1 lb. shredded cheddar cheese, *divided*

White Sauce:
½ stick (4 Tbsp.) butter

¼ tsp. salt

1¾ cups milk

¼ cup cornstarch

1 cup sour cream, *optional*

1. Boil potatoes until just soft. Cool to room temperature. Then refrigerate until chilled through.

2. When potatoes are cold, grate.

3. Melt 2 Tbsp. butter in large skillet. Stir potatoes and onion into skillet. Cook until lightly browned. Toss in parsley.

4. Spread in well-greased 9x13-inch baking pan.

5. Brown sausage, ham, or bacon in same skillet. Drain off drippings.

6. Crumble over potato layer in baking pan.

7. Melt 2 Tbsp. butter in skillet. Pour eggs into skillet. Cook, stirring up from the bottom until eggs are scrambled and just set.

8. Layer eggs over meat.

9. Sprinkle with half of shredded cheese.

10. Make white sauce by melting 4 Tbsp. butter in saucepan.

11. Stir in salt, milk, and cornstarch. Stir continually with a wooden spoon until bubbly and thickened.

12. Remove from heat. Stir in sour cream if you wish.

13. Pour white sauce over egg layer in pan.

14. Sprinkle with remaining shredded cheese.

15. Bake at 350°F for 40 minutes. Insert knife blade in center. If it comes out clean, the dish is finished. If it doesn't, continue baking another 5 minutes. Test again with knife blade. Continue cooking—and testing—as needed.

16. Allow to stand 10 minutes before cutting and serving.

Country Brunch

Esther J. Mast,
Lancaster, PA
Barbara Yoder,
Christiana, PA
Ruth Ann Gingrich,
New Holland, PA
Lafaye Musser,
Denver, PA

Makes 12-15 servings
Prep. Time: 30 minutes
Chilling Time: 8 hours, or overnight
Baking Time: 45-60 minutes
Standing Time: 10-15 minutes

16 slices firm white bread

1⅔-2 lbs. (2½ cups) cubed ham or browned sausage, drained

1 lb. (3 cups) shredded cheddar cheese

1 lb. (3 cups) shredded mozzarella cheese

8 eggs, beaten

3½ cups milk

½ tsp. dry mustard

¼ tsp. onion powder

½ tsp. seasoning salt

1 Tbsp. parsley

Topping:
3 cups uncrushed cornflakes

1 stick (8 Tbsp.) butter, melted

1. Trim crusts from bread and cut slices in half.

2. Grease a 10x15-inch baking dish.

3. Layer ingredients in this order: cover bottom of pan with half the bread, top with half the ham, then half the cheddar cheese, and then half the mozzarella cheese.

4. Repeat layers once more.

5. In large mixing bowl, combine eggs, milk, dry mustard, onion powder, seasoning salt, and parsley. Mix well and pour over layers.

6. Cover and refrigerate for 8 hours, or overnight.

7. Remove from refrigerator 30 minutes before baking.

8. Combine cornflakes and butter and sprinkle over casserole.

9. Cover loosely with foil to prevent over-browning. Bake at 375°F for 45 minutes.

10. Remove from oven and let stand 10–15 minutes before cutting into squares.

Breakfast Pie

Darlene Bloom,
San Antonio, TX

Makes 6 servings
Prep. Time: 20 minutes
Baking Time: 30 minutes
Standing Time: 5–10 minutes

8 oz. lower-sodium ham

1 cup chopped onions

1 cup chopped bell pepper, red or green

1 cup 75%-less-fat shredded cheddar cheese

½ cup reduced-fat buttermilk baking mix

1 cup fat-free milk

2 eggs

1. Brown meat, onion, and bell pepper in skillet on stove until done. Drain off drippings.

2. Place cooked ingredients in a greased 9-inch pie plate.

3. Top with layer of shredded cheese.

4. In a mixing bowl, whisk baking mix, milk, and eggs together. Pour over ingredients in pie plate.

5. Bake at 400°F for 30 minutes.

6. Allow to stand 5–10 minutes before cutting and serving.

TIPS

1. Double this recipe and prepare in a 9x13-inch baking pan. I take this to potlucks all the time (warm) out of the oven.
2. You can use ground turkey or beef as your choice of meats and add 1 envelope taco seasoning mix to the skillet as you cook. I call this version Taco Bake and often make it for dinner.

Baked Oatmeal

Lena Sheaffer, Port Matilda, PA
Susie Nissley, Millersburg, OH
Esther Nafziger, Bluffton, OH
Katie Stoltzfus, Leola, PA
Martha Hershey, Ronks, PA
Annabelle Unternahrer, Shipshewana, IN

Makes 4–6 servings
Prep. Time: 10 minutes
Baking Time: 30 minutes

½ cup oil

1 cup honey or brown sugar

2 eggs

3 cups rolled or quick oats, uncooked

2 tsp. baking powder

1 cup milk

½ tsp. cinnamon or nutmeg, *optional*

1 cup chopped nuts, raisins, apples, or
   other fruit*

Variation:

For a lower calorie version, use only 1 egg
and ½ cup sugar, use skim milk, and use
½ cup applesauce instead of ½ cup oil.

—Evie Hershey, Atglen, PA

1. Combine oil, honey or brown sugar, and
eggs in a large mixing bowl.

2. Add dry oats, baking powder, and milk.
Add spice if using. Mix well.

3. Add nuts and/or fruit. Mix well.

4. Pour into a greased 8-inch-square
baking pan.

5. Bake at 350°F for 30 minutes.

6. Serve hot, cold, or at room temperature
with milk.

*Add any or all of these: ½ cup dried
cherries, ½ cup dried cranberries, ½ cup
cut-up apricots.

Light Buttermilk Pancakes

Mary Lynn Miller,
Reinholds, PA

Makes 4 servings
Prep. Time: 10 minutes
Cooking Time: 10–15 minutes

1 cup flour

1 Tbsp. sugar

1½ tsp. baking powder

½ tsp. salt

½ tsp. baking soda

1 Tbsp. oil

1 cup buttermilk

1 egg, beaten

1. Combine dry ingredients in mixing bowl.

2. Combine oil, buttermilk, and egg in a separate bowl. Add to dry ingredients, stirring just until flour mixture is moistened.

3. Fry on griddle until bubbly on top. Flip and continue cooking until bottom is lightly browned.

TIP

If you don't have buttermilk, make your own by placing 1 Tbsp. lemon juice in a 1-cup measure. Fill cup with milk. Mix well.

—Linda E. Wilcox,
Blythewood, SC

Oatmeal Pancakes

**Barbara J. Bey,
Hillsboro, OH**

Makes 6 pancakes
Prep. Time: 5 minutes
Cooking Time: 10 minutes

½ cup flour

½ cup dry oats, rolled or quick-cooking

1 Tbsp. sugar, or Splenda

1 tsp. baking powder

½ tsp. baking soda

¾ cup buttermilk

¼ cup milk

2 Tbsp. vegetable oil

1 egg, beaten

1. Stir together flour, oats, sugar, baking powder, and baking soda in a large mixing bowl.

2. In a separate bowl, blend buttermilk, milk, oil, and egg until smooth.

3. Stir wet ingredients into dry ingredients, just until moistened.

4. Drop by scant half-cupfuls into skillet or onto griddle.

5. Cook until small bubbles form on top.

6. Flip and cook until lightly browned.

Fast, Friendly French Toast

**Donna Barnitz,
Rio Rancho, NM**

Makes 4 servings
Prep. Time: 15 minutes
Soaking Time: 1–24 hours
Baking Time: 15 minutes

1 loaf French bread, cut in 1-inch thick slices

1½ cups milk

4 eggs

½ cup orange juice

¼ cup sugar

1 Tbsp. vanilla extract

cinnamon, *optional*

confectioners' sugar

1. Arrange bread slices in a 9x13-inch baking pan.

2. In a mixing bowl, beat milk, eggs, orange juice, sugar, and vanilla together until well blended.

3. Pour over bread.

4. Cover and refrigerate 1–24 hours, according to your schedule.

5. Transfer bread to greased 10x15-inch pan, making sure slices don't touch. Dust with cinnamon, if you wish.

6. Bake 15 minutes at 400°F, or until puffy and lightly browned.

7. Dust with confectioners' sugar just before serving.

Strawberry Pancakes

Becky Frey,
Lebanon, PA

Makes 15 medium-sized
pancakes, or 4–5 servings
Prep. Time: 10–15 minutes
Cooking Time: 10 minutes

2 eggs

1 cup buttermilk

1 cup crushed strawberries

¼ cup oil

1 tsp. almond extract

2 cups whole wheat (or white) flour

2 Tbsp. brown sugar

2 tsp. baking powder

1 tsp. baking soda

1. In large mixing bowl beat eggs until fluffy.

2. Stir buttermilk, strawberries, oil, and almond extract into eggs.

3. In a separate bowl, combine flour, brown sugar, baking powder, and baking soda. Add to wet ingredients. Beat together with whisk just until smooth.

4. Heat skillet or griddle until a few drops of water sizzle when sprinkled on top. Fry pancakes until bubbly on top. Flip and continue cooking until browned. Strawberries can scorch, so keep checking to make sure they're not burning. Turn the heat lower if necessary.

NOTES

1. I have a tough time getting small pancakes to turn out nicely. I make one "plate-size" pancake at a time. It can easily be cut into wedges to serve to those with smaller appetites.

2. Top finished pancakes with vanilla yogurt and fruit sauce and serve for breakfast, brunch, a light lunch or supper, or as a dessert.

TIP

You can use fresh or frozen berries. If frozen, thaw them and drain them well before mixing into batter.

Baked French Toast

Susan Wenger,
Lebanon, PA
Nancy Funk,
North Newton, KS

Makes 8 servings
Prep. Time: 20 minutes
Chilling Time: 4 hours, or overnight
Baking Time: 35-45 minutes

1 stick (8 Tbsp.) butter

1 cup brown sugar

2 tsp. molasses

peanut butter, *optional*

8-10 slices sturdy white bread

5-6 eggs

1½-2 cups milk

1 tsp. cinnamon

1. In a saucepan, heat butter, brown sugar, and molasses together until sugar is dissolved and butter is melted. Stir occasionally to prevent sticking. When melted and blended together, pour into a 9x13-inch baking pan.

2. If you wish, spread peanut butter on one side of each slice of bread and then lay the bread on the syrup, peanut butter side down. If you don't include peanut butter, simply lay the bread in a single layer on top of the syrup.

3. In a mixing bowl, mix eggs, milk, and cinnamon together, and then pour on top of bread.

4. Cover and refrigerate for at least 4 hours, or overnight.

5. Bake at 350°F for 35–45 minutes, or until browned.

Variations:

1. Instead of 1 cup brown sugar and 2 tsp. molasses, use ½ cup brown sugar and ½ cup pure maple syrup.

2. Immediately after Step 1, sprinkle ½–1 cup coarsely chopped pecans over the syrup. (Omit the peanut butter in Step 2.)

3. Instead of milk, use half-and-half. And add 1 tsp. vanilla extract to Step 3.
    —Esther Nafziger, Bluffton, OH

4. After Step 1, add a layer of the following mixture, tossed lightly together: 3 tart apples, peeled, cored, and thinly sliced; ½ cup raisins; 2 tsp. cinnamon. Continue with Step 2, without the peanut butter.
    —Diann J. Dunham, State College, PA

Blueberry French Toast

Stacie Skelly,
Millersville, PA

Makes 12 servings
Prep. Time: 30 minutes
Chilling Time: 6–12 hours
Baking Time: 1 hour

12-15 slices day-old bread

8-oz. pkg. cream cheese

1 cup frozen blueberries

12 eggs

2 cups milk

⅓ cup honey

Sauce:

1 cup sugar

2 Tbsp. cornstarch

1 cup water

1 cup blueberries

1. Grease 9x13-inch baking pan.

2. Cube bread and spread in pan.

3. Cube cream cheese. Distribute evenly over bread.

4. Sprinkle blueberries on top.

5. In a mixing bowl, blend eggs, milk, and honey.

6. Pour over pan contents.

7. Cover. Refrigerate 6–8 hours, or overnight.

8. Remove from refrigerator 30 minutes before baking.

9. Bake, covered, at 350°F for 30 minutes.

10. Uncover. Bake 30 more minutes. Serve with sauce.

To make sauce:

1. Mix sugar, cornstarch, and water in a saucepan. Bring to a boil.

2. Stir in blueberries.

3. Reduce heat, cooking until blueberries burst.

4. Serve warm over French toast.

Breakfast Bread Pudding

**Jean H. Robinson,
Cinnaminson, NJ**

Makes 6–8 servings
Prep. Time: 10 minutes
Standing Time: 20 minutes–8 hours
Baking Time: 1 hour

½ loaf French bread, cut into 16 slices 1-inch thick

6 large eggs

2½ cups milk, or half-and-half

½ cup honey

2 Tbsp. orange zest

maple syrup, *optional*

1. Spray a 9x12-inch baking pan with nonstick cooking spray.

2. Lay bread slices flat in the baking pan.

3. In a large mixing bowl, beat together eggs, milk, honey, and orange zest. Pour over bread slices and allow bread to absorb liquid for 20 minutes, or overnight if that's more convenient for you. (Cover the bread and refrigerate it if it will be standing overnight.)

4. Bake for 60 minutes at 350°F.

5. Allow to stand for 10 minutes before serving. Serve with maple syrup as a topping, if you wish.

Cranberry Buttermilk Scones

**Edwina Stoltzfus,
Narvon, PA**

Makes 12-16 servings
Prep. Time: 20 minutes
Baking Time: 15-20 minutes

3 cups flour

⅓ cup plus 2 Tbsp. sugar, *divided*

2 tsp. baking powder

¾ tsp. salt

½ tsp. baking soda

1½ sticks (12 Tbsp.) cold butter

1 cup buttermilk

1 cup dried cranberries

1 tsp. grated orange peel

1 Tbsp. milk

¼ tsp. ground cinnamon

1. In a bowl, combine flour, ⅓ cup sugar, baking powder, salt, and baking soda.

2. Cut in butter, using a pastry cutter or two knives, until mixture resembles small peas.

3. Stir in buttermilk, just until combined.

4. Fold in cranberries and orange peel.

5. Turn dough onto floured surface. Divide dough in half.

6. Shape each portion into a ball. Pat each into a 6-inch circle.

7. Cut each circle into 6–8 wedges. Place on lightly greased baking sheet.

8. Brush tops with milk.

9. In a small bowl, combine 2 Tbsp. sugar with cinnamon. Sprinkle on top of wedges.

10. Bake at 400°F for 15–20 minutes, or until golden brown. Serve warm.

TIPS

1. These freeze well after baking.
2. I make my own orange peel by grating the peel of 1 whole orange and then freezing it. It's handy for whenever I need it.

Banana Oat Breakfast Cookies

**Mary Ann Lefever,
Lancaster, PA**

Makes 12 cookies
Prep. Time: 15 minutes
Baking Time: 14–16 minutes,
per baking sheet

1 large banana, mashed (about ½ cup)

½ cup chunky natural (unsalted and unsweetened) peanut butter, or regular chunky peanut butter

½ cup honey

1 tsp. vanilla extract

1 cup uncooked rolled oats

½ cup whole wheat pastry flour

¼ cup nonfat dry milk powder

2 tsp. ground cinnamon

¼ tsp. baking soda

1 cup dried cranberries, or raisins

1. Preheat oven to 350°F. Lightly coat two baking sheets with nonstick cooking spray. Set aside.

2. In large bowl, stir together banana, peanut butter, honey, and vanilla.

3. In a small bowl, combine oats, flour, milk powder, cinnamon, and baking soda.

4. Stir oat mixture into banana mixture until combined.

5. Stir in dried cranberries.

6. Using a ¼-cup measure, drop dough into mounds 3 inches apart on prepared baking sheets.

7. With a thick spatula dipped in water, flatten and spread each dough mound into a 2¾-inch round, about a ½-inch thick.

8. Bake, one sheet at a time, 14–16 minutes, or until cookies are lightly browned.

9. Transfer cookies to wire racks to cool completely.

10. Store in airtight container or resealable plastic bag for up to three days, or freeze for up to two months. Thaw before serving.

Blueberry Streusel Corn Bread

Mary Lynn Miller,
Reinholds, PA

Makes 9 servings
Prep. Time: 20–30 minutes
Baking Time: 45–50 minutes

2 8½-oz. pkgs. corn muffin mix

2 eggs

⅔ cup milk

2 Tbsp. flour

2 cups fresh blueberries

Streusel Topping:
3 Tbsp. butter or margarine, softened

¾ cup sugar

½ cup flour

¾ tsp. cinnamon

1. Mix corn muffin mix, eggs, milk, and flour in a medium-sized mixing bowl for 30–60 seconds, using an electric mixer.

2. Fold in blueberries. Pour into greased 9x9-inch baking dish.

3. In a small mixing bowl, using a pastry blender, combine streusel topping ingredients until mixed into fine crumbs. Spoon over corn bread mixture in pan.

4. Bake at 350°F for 45–50 minutes, or until a toothpick stuck into the center comes out clean. Serve warm.

Cinnamon Coffee Cake

**Janice Burkholder,
Richfield, PA**

Makes 16 servings
Prep. Time: 15 minutes
Baking Time: 70 minutes

2 sticks (16 Tbsp.) butter or margarine, softened

2¾ cups sugar, *divided*

2 tsp. vanilla extract

4 eggs

3 cups flour

2 tsp. baking powder

1 tsp. baking soda

1 tsp. salt

2 cups (16 oz.) sour cream

2 Tbsp. cinnamon

½ cup chopped walnuts

1. In a large mixing bowl, cream butter and 2 cups sugar together with a mixer until fluffy. Blend in vanilla.

2. Add eggs one at a time, beating well after each addition.

3. Combine flour, baking powder, soda, and salt in a separate bowl and add to egg mixture, alternating with sour cream.

4. Spoon ⅓ of the batter into a greased 10-inch tube or Bundt pan.

5. Combine cinnamon, nuts, and remaining sugar. Layer ⅓ of this mixture over batter. Repeat layers two more times.

6. Bake at 350°F for 70 minutes, or until toothpick inserted in center of cake comes out clean.

7. Remove from pan and cool on a wire rack.

Maple Twists

Marcella Heatwole,
North Lawrence, OH

Makes 16-18 servings
Prep. Time: 2 hours
Rising Time: 2½-3 hours
Baking Time: 18-22 minutes

Dough:

¾ cup milk

½ stick (4 Tbsp.) butter

2¾-3 cups flour, *divided*

3 Tbsp. sugar

½ tsp. salt

1 pkg. yeast

1 tsp. maple extract

1 egg

¾ cup butter, melted, *divided*

Filling:

½ cup brown sugar

⅓ cup nuts

1 tsp. cinnamon

1 tsp. maple extract

Glaze:

2 Tbsp. butter, melted

1 Tbsp. milk

½ tsp. maple extract

1 cup confectioners' sugar

1. In small pan, heat milk and butter until it just reaches the boiling point.

2. In large electric mixer bowl, blend warm liquid, 1 cup flour, 3 Tbsp. sugar, salt, yeast, 1 tsp. maple extract, and egg at low speed until moistened. Beat 2 minutes at medium speed.

3. By hand, add remaining flour to form soft dough.

4. Place on floured surface and knead until smooth and elastic. Place dough in greased bowl. Cover and let rise until double, about 1½–2 hours.

5. Grease 12-inch pizza pan. Divide dough into 3 balls. Roll out 1 ball of dough to cover pan. Brush with ¼ cup melted butter.

6. Sprinkle with ⅓ of filling, made by combining brown sugar, nuts, cinnamon, and maple extract in a small bowl.

7. Repeat two more layers: rolled-out dough, melted butter, and filling. (Press last layer of filling down into dough to prevent it from falling off during Step 8.)

8. With scissors, mark 16 or 18 evenly spaced wedges in the circle. Cut from outside edge of circle into wedges. Carefully twist each wedge 5 times.

9. Lay twists on a jelly roll pan. Cover. Let rise for 45–60 minutes, or until almost double in size.

10. Bake at 375°F for 18–22 minutes.

11. Cool to room temperature. Drizzle with glaze made by combining 2 Tbsp. melted butter, milk, ½ tsp. maple extract, and confectioners' sugar. Add 1 Tbsp. more milk if needed to make of pouring consistency.

Sticky Buns

**Elaine Rineer,
Lancaster, PA**

Makes 12 servings
Prep. Time: 20 minutes
Chilling Time: 8 hours, or overnight
Baking Time: 35 minutes

1 stick (8 Tbsp.) butter, *divided*

½ cup brown sugar

½ cup corn syrup

¼ cup plus 2 Tbsp. sugar

2 Tbsp. cinnamon

2 loaves frozen bread dough, thawed

1. Melt ½ stick (4 Tbsp.) of butter on stovetop or in microwave. Stir in brown sugar and corn syrup until well blended. Pour into a 9x13-inch baking pan.

2. Melt remaining ½ stick (4 Tbsp.) butter in microwave or on stovetop. Set aside.

3. In a small mixing bowl, combine sugar and cinnamon.

4. Break off golf-ball-sized pieces of bread dough, 12 per loaf. Dip each in melted butter and then roll in sugar-cinnamon mixture. Place coated balls in baking pan.

5. Cover and refrigerate for 8 hours, or overnight.

6. Remove from refrigerator and let stand for 30 minutes before baking.

7. Bake uncovered at 325°F for 35 minutes. Turn out of pan immediately onto serving platter.

Variation:
Add ½–¾ cup chopped pecans to mixture in pan (Step 1).

Breads

Breads

Homemade White Bread

**Cathy Farren,
Bridgewater, VA**

Makes 5 loaves
Prep. Time: 30 minutes
Rising and Standing Time: 3–4½ hours
Baking Time: 45 minutes

2 Tbsp. yeast

5 cups lukewarm water

12 cups flour, *divided*

¾ cup sugar

2 Tbsp. salt

3 Tbsp. shortening

1. Dissolve yeast in water in a large mixing bowl.

2. Add 3 cups flour. Mix to make a soft dough.

3. Add sugar, salt, and shortening. Mix well.

4. Stir in remaining flour. Knead dough until smooth and elastic.

5. Place in greased bowl. Let rise until double in size, about 1–1½ hours.

6. Knead well and let rise again until double in size, about 1–1½ hours.

7. Form into 5 loaves. Place in greased 8x5-inch or 9x5-inch loaf pans. Let rise until double in size, about 1–1½ hours.

8. Bake at 325°F for 45 minutes.

Breads

The Best Honey Whole Wheat Bread

**Pamela Metzler,
Gilman, WI**

Makes 4 loaves of bread
Prep. Time: 20-30 minutes
Rising Time: 3-4 hours
Baking Time: 25 minutes

Breads

1 cup dry rolled oats

3 cups water

3 cups whole wheat flour

¾ cup soy flour

¾ cup ground flaxseed, or flaxseed meal

3 Tbsp. flaxseed

3 Tbsp. sesame seeds

3 Tbsp. poppy seeds

4½ Tbsp. yeast

1 Tbsp. sea salt

1 cup unsweetened applesauce

½ cup honey

¼ cup olive oil

about 5 cups unbleached white flour

1. In microwave-safe bowl, microwave oats mixed with water to about 120–130°F, about 45 seconds.

2. In mixer bowl of a heavy stand mixer with dough hook, combine whole wheat flour, soy flour, ground flaxseed or meal, seeds, yeast, and salt. Stir to mix.

3. Add applesauce, honey, and oil. Mix by hand.

4. Add hot water with oatmeal. Mix by hand.

5. When blended, start mixing with dough hook of mixer and continue for about 3 minutes.

6. Slowly add white flour until dough comes away from sides of bowl and becomes smooth and elastic.

7. Cover dough in bowl and place in a warm spot. Let rise until about double in size, about 1½–2 hours.

8. Punch dough down. Turn onto countertop. Divide evenly into 4 pieces.

9. Shape into 4 loaves. Place in 2½x4½x8½-inch loaf pans that have been generously sprayed with nonstick cooking spray.

10. Cover and place in a warm spot. Allow to rise until nearly double in size, about 1½–2 hours.

11. Bake at 350°F for 25 minutes, or until tops of loaves are golden.

12. Remove from pans and cool on rack.

TIP

This is not a fast, easy recipe, but if you like to make a nutritious bread, this is for you. Making good bread takes practice, so keep trying. Be sure to knead it long enough. Like most baked goods, this bread is great right out of the oven.

Breads

No-Knead French Bread

**Naomi Ressler,
Harrisonburg, VA**

Makes 2 loaves
Prep. Time: 1½ hours
Baking Time: 20 minutes

2 Tbsp. shortening

2 Tbsp. sugar

2 tsp. salt

1 cup boiling water

1 cup cold water

2 ¼-oz. pkgs. yeast

1 scant Tbsp. sugar

½ cup warm water

6 cups flour

1. Dissolve shortening, sugar, and salt in boiling water.

2. Add cold water to shortening mixture.

3. Dissolve yeast and sugar in warm water. Add to the shortening mixture.

4. Add flour. Do not beat. Stir with big spoon every 10 minutes, 4 or 5 times, for approximately an hour.

5. Divide dough in half. Flour dough board or counter and hands and pat each section into rectangle shape about ½-inch thick.

6. Roll lengthwise in jelly roll fashion and tuck in ends.

7. Cut slits diagonally 2–3 inches apart (shallow) on top of loaves.

8. Put on lightly greased baking sheet. Let rise until double, about 20–30 minutes depending on temperature of room.

9. Bake at 375–400°F for approximately 20 minutes.

TIPS

1. You may wish to brush butter or margarine on top of loaf after baking.
2. Delicious with any meal but especially with pasta.
3. Dough will be stiff/thick and difficult to stir, but do the best you can!

Whole Wheat Rolls

Faye Pankratz,
Inola, OK

Makes 2 dozen rolls, 1 roll per serving
Prep. Time: 25 minutes
Cooling Time: 20 minutes
Rising Time: about 2 hours
Baking Time: 20 minutes

2 pkgs. dry yeast

½ cup warm water

¼ cup plus 1 tsp. sugar, *divided*

1¾ cups fat-free milk, scalded

1 Tbsp. salt

3 Tbsp. all-vegetable shortening

2 cups whole wheat flour

3 egg whites

3 cups white flour, or more

1. Combine yeast and warm water in small bowl. Sprinkle 1 tsp. sugar over yeast and water. Set aside.

2. Pour scalded milk over ¼ cup sugar, salt, and shortening in large bowl. Cool until lukewarm. Add yeast mixture and stir well.

3. Add whole wheat flour and egg whites. Beat well and gradually add white flour until you have soft dough.

4. Turn onto floured surface and knead until dough is elastic, about 5–7 minutes. Place in greased bowl, turning dough to grease top. Cover with clean cloth and let rise until doubled in bulk.

5. Punch down and shape into rolls. Place on greased cookie sheets and let rise until double (about 2 hours).

6. Bake at 350°F for 20 minutes or until lightly browned.

Italian Bread

**Tabitha Schmidt,
Baltic, OH**

Makes 6 servings
Prep. Time: 25 minutes
Rising Time: 20 minutes
Baking Time: 15 minutes

2½ cups flour

1 tsp. salt

1 tsp. sugar

1 Tbsp. dry yeast

1 cup warm (120–130°F) water

1 Tbsp. oil

Topping:

¼–⅓ cup Italian salad dressing

¼ tsp. salt

¼ tsp. garlic powder

¼ tsp. dried oregano

¼ tsp. dried thyme, *optional*

dash of pepper

1 Tbsp. grated Parmesan cheese

½ cup grated mozzarella cheese

1. In a large mixing bowl, combine flour, salt, sugar, and yeast.

2. In a separate bowl, mix water and oil together. Add to flour mixture.

3. Stir well. Add more flour, if needed, to form soft dough.

4. Place dough on lightly floured surface, and knead for 1–2 minutes, or until smooth. Place in a greased bowl. Cover and let rise for 20 minutes.

5. Knead dough down. Then place on a 12-inch pizza pan. Roll or pat into a 12-inch circle.

6. Brush with salad dressing.

7. Combine seasonings and sprinkle over top. Sprinkle with cheeses.

8. Bake at 450°F for 15 minutes, or until golden brown. Cover with foil tent to prevent over-browning if necessary.

9. Cut into narrow wedges and serve warm.

Breads

Sour Cream Corn Bread

**Ida H. Goering,
Dayton, VA**

Makes 12 servings
Prep. Time: 10–15 minutes
Baking Time: 20–22 minutes

¾ cup yellow cornmeal

1 cup flour

1 tsp. baking soda

1 tsp. cream of tartar

1 tsp. salt

3 Tbsp. sugar

1 egg, well beaten

1 cup sour cream

½ cup milk

3 Tbsp. butter, melted

1. Preheat oven to 400°F.

2. Grease a 9x9-inch, or 7x11-inch, baking pan.

3. Measure cornmeal into a mixing bowl and sift into it the flour, baking soda, cream of tartar, salt, and sugar.

4. In a separate bowl, beat egg well, and then add sour cream, milk, and melted butter.

5. Pour wet ingredients into flour mixture. Stir just until well mixed.

6. Pour into baking pan.

7. Bake for 20–22 minutes, or until tester inserted in center of bread comes out clean.

8. Serve hot.

TIPS

1. Leftovers can be split into pieces, buttered lightly, and placed under the broiler until browned. Delicious!
2. For breakfast, serve the corn bread with sausage gravy and fried apples on the side. For a main meal, serve it with smoked sausage, steamed cabbage, pinto beans, and applesauce.

Breads

Homemade Rolls

**Ruth S. Weaver,
Reinholds, PA**

Makes 20 servings, 1 roll per serving
Prep. Time: 25 minutes
Rising Time: 2 hours
Baking Time: 15–20 minutes

5¾-6 ¾ cups bread flour, *divided*

⅓ cup instant nonfat dry milk solids

¼ cup sugar

1 Tbsp. salt

2 pkgs. dry yeast

5 Tbsp. margarine, softened, plus melted
    margarine for brushing

2 cups warm (120-130°F) water

1. In large bowl mix 2 cups flour, milk solids, sugar, salt, and yeast. Add 5 Tbsp. softened margarine.

2. Gradually add water and beat 2 minutes at medium speed with a mixer. Add 1 more cup flour and beat 2 minutes on high speed. Stir in enough flour to make a stiff dough.

3. Turn out onto a lightly floured board and knead about 8–10 minutes. Place in greased bowl, turning to grease top of dough.

4. Cover with a kitchen towel and let rise in warm place until doubled in bulk (about 45 minutes). Punch down and allow to rise again for 20 minutes.

5. Divide dough in half and cut each half into 10 equal pieces. Form into rolls and place on greased baking sheet about 2 inches apart. Cover and let rise again about 1 hour.

6. Bake at 375°F for 15–20 minutes. Remove from baking sheet and brush with melted margarine.

TIP

Not many other people bring homemade bread or rolls to a church potluck, and I always bake them several days before the fellowship meal so I have no last-minute rush.

Bread Sticks

**Janice Burkholder,
Richfield, PA**

Makes 6 servings
Prep. Time: 15 minutes
Rising Time: 1–1½ hours
Baking Time: 10–15 minutes

1½ cups warm (120–130°F) water

1 Tbsp. dry yeast

1 Tbsp. oil

1 Tbsp. salt

1 Tbsp. sugar

3 cups whole wheat flour

1 cup all-purpose flour

¼ cup butter, melted

3 Tbsp. vegetable or olive oil

3 Tbsp. Parmesan cheese

1 tsp. garlic powder

2 Tbsp. dried parsley

1 tsp. dried oregano

1. In large mixing bowl, dissolve yeast in warm water.

2. Add oil, salt, and sugar.

3. In separate bowl mix flours together.

4. Stir flour into wet ingredients until dough becomes stiff.

5. Place dough on lightly floured surface and knead in flour, if some remains, for several minutes until smooth and elastic.

6. Place dough in greased bowl. Turn dough to grease all over, and then cover. Allow to rise until double in size, about 1–1½ hours.

7. On a flat, lightly floured surface, roll dough out into a 15-inch square.

8. Cut in half with a pizza cutter, and then cut each half into 1-inch strips. Lay strips on a lightly greased cookie sheet.

9. In a small bowl, combine butter, oil, Parmesan cheese, garlic powder, parsley, and oregano. Brush strips of dough with the mixture.

10. Bake at 400°F for 10–15 minutes or until golden brown.

11. Serve with cheese dip or warm pizza sauce.

Cheddar Garlic Biscuits

Mary Jane Hoober, Shipshewana, IN
Jolene Schrock, Millersburg, OH
Darla Sathre, Baxter, MN
Ruth Shank, Monroe, GA
Elaine Patton, West Middletown, PA
Joyce L. Moser, Copenhagen, NY
Shari Ladd, Hudson, MI
Amber Swarey, Honea Path, SC
Denae Villines, Whitewater, KS
Marsha Sabus, Fallbrook, CA

Makes 12 servings
Prep. Time: 5–10 minutes
Baking Time: 8–10 minutes

2 cups buttermilk baking mix

⅔ cup milk

½–1 cup shredded cheddar cheese, according to your taste preferences

2 Tbsp. melted butter

⅛–¼ tsp. garlic powder, according to your taste preference

1 Tbsp. parsley flakes, *optional*

1. Preheat oven to 450°F.

2. In a medium-sized mixing bowl, mix the buttermilk baking mix, milk, and shredded cheddar to form a soft dough.

3. Drop by spoonfuls onto ungreased cookie sheet.

4. Bake 8–10 minutes.

5. Mix butter, garlic powder, and parsley flakes, if you wish, in a small bowl. Brush over warm biscuits.

TIP

There are always variations that could be added or exchanged with the ingredients listed above: bacon bits added for breakfast muffins; minced onion, finely chopped garlic cloves, crisp-cooked carrot bits, and/or cooked chopped ham for anytime!

Quick Pizza Dough

Becky Frey,
Lebanon, PA

Makes 2 10-inch pizza crusts
Prep. Time: 10 minutes
Rising Time: 5 minutes
Baking Time: 20 minutes

1 Tbsp. yeast

1 cup warm water

1 Tbsp. sugar

½ tsp. salt

2 Tbsp. canola oil

1¼ cups all-purpose flour

1¼ cups whole wheat flour

1. In a good-sized bowl, dissolve yeast in water.

2. Stir in sugar, salt, and oil.

3. Add enough of each flour to make a fairly stiff dough.

4. Cover bowl and set in warm place. Let dough rise 5 minutes.

5. Turn dough onto countertop. Knead until smooth and elastic, using whatever you need of remaining flour.

6. Spray 2 10-inch pizza pans with nonstick cooking spray. Press dough onto pans, stretching as needed.

7. Spread with your favorite low-calorie toppings.

8. Bake at 400–425°F for about 20 minutes, or until lightly browned.

TIP

We like to top our pizzas with caramelized onions and bell pepper. Slice 2 large onions and chop a large red or green pepper. Put 1 Tbsp. or less olive oil in a large nonstick skillet. Stir in onion and pepper. Cook on low heat, covered, for 45–60 minutes. Stir occasionally. When onions are golden and as tender as you like them, remove from heat and season with a bit of balsamic vinegar. Spread over pizza crust.

Bagels

Bob Litt,
London, OH

Makes 32 servings, 1 bagel per serving
Prep. Time: 30 minutes
Rising Time: 2–2½ hours
Baking/Cooking Time: 45 minutes

2 Tbsp. active dry yeast

¼ cup sugar plus 1 tsp. sugar, *divided*

1½ cups warm water

4–4½ cups flour, *divided*

2 eggs

cornmeal

egg whites, *optional*

chopped onion or poppy seeds, *optional*

1. Dissolve yeast and 1 tsp. sugar in warm water. Let stand until foamy.

2. Add ¼ cup sugar, 2 cups flour, and eggs. Beat until well mixed, approximately 200 strokes.

3. Slowly add remaining flour to make soft dough. Turn out onto lightly floured surface. Knead dough until smooth and elastic, approximately 8–10 minutes.

4. Place dough in greased bowl, turning to coat top of dough. Cover and let stand in warm place until doubled in size, approximately 1½ hours.

5. Punch down and divide into 32 pieces (cut in half, then in half again, and so on).

6. Shape each piece into a ball and punch finger through each piece to make a bagel shape. Let rise until double in size (about an hour).

7. Bring a large pot of water to boil. Boil each bagel for 2 minutes, turning after first minute.

8. Grease baking pan and coat with cornmeal. Place bagels on pan. Brush each bagel with egg white and top with either onion or poppy seeds if you wish. Bake at 375°F for 25–30 minutes.

Breads

Banana Bread

**Maxine "Meme" Phanuef,
Washington Township, MI**

Makes 1 loaf of bread
Prep. Time: 10 minutes
Baking Time: 1 hour

Breads

1½ sticks (12 Tbsp.) unsalted butter, room temperature

1½ cups sugar

2 eggs, beaten

1 tsp. vanilla extract

1½ cups mashed banana

2 cups flour

¼ tsp. salt

1 tsp. baking powder

1 tsp. baking soda

½ cup milk

1. Preheat oven to 325°F.

2. In a stand mixer, cream together the butter and sugar.

3. Blend in eggs and vanilla. Next, mix in the mashed banana.

4. Slowly add the flour, a little at a time. Mix in the salt and baking powder.

5. In a small bowl, add the baking soda to the milk and stir until well mixed. Add this mixture to the rest of the ingredients and mix well.

6. Grease a loaf pan and then pour the banana bread mixture into the loaf pan.

7. Bake for 1 hour. The bread is done when a toothpick inserted in the center comes out clean.

Zucchini Bread with Cranberries

**Renita Denlinger,
Denver, PA**

Makes 8 servings
Prep. Time: 20 minutes
Baking Time: 12–19 minutes

½ cup sugar

½ cup shredded zucchini

⅓ cup skim milk

1 Tbsp. corn oil

egg substitute equivalent to 1 egg, or 2 egg
    whites

1 cup whole wheat flour

2 tsp. baking powder

½ tsp. cinnamon

½ tsp. ground cloves

½ cup dried cranberries

1. Preheat oven to 400°F.

2. In a large bowl, combine sugar,
zucchini, milk, oil, and egg substitute. Mix
well.

3. In a separate bowl, combine dry
ingredients except cranberries.

4. Add dry ingredients to zucchini
mixture.

5. Fold in dried cranberries.

6. Spoon into bread pan that has been
generously sprayed with nonstick cooking
spray.

7. Bake for 12–19 minutes, or until tester
inserted in center comes out clean.

Pumpkin Bread

Joanne Warfel,
Lancaster, PA

Makes 2 or 3 larger loaves, or 8 small loaves
Prep. Time: 15–20 minutes
Baking Time: 25–70 minutes, depending on size of loaves

⅔ cup cooking oil

2⅔ cups sugar

4 eggs

16-oz. can (2 cups) pumpkin

⅔ cup water

3⅓ cups flour

2 tsp. baking soda

1 tsp. salt

½ tsp. baking powder

1 tsp. cinnamon

½ tsp. cloves

½ tsp. nutmeg

1 cup raisins

⅔ cup chopped nuts

1. In large bowl, cream oil and sugar until fluffy.

2. Blend in eggs, and then pumpkin and water.

3. In a separate bowl, sift together flour, baking soda, salt, baking powder, cinnamon, cloves, and nutmeg.

4. Stir sifted dry ingredients into pumpkin mixture.

5. Stir in raisins and nuts.

6. Pour into two greased 5x9-inch loaf pans or three 4½x8½-inch loaf pans, or eight 3x6-inch loaf pans. Bake at 350°F for 60–70 minutes for larger loaves; 25–30 minutes for small loaves. Test that bread is done by inserting toothpick into center of loaves. If pick comes out clean, bread is finished baking. If it doesn't, continue baking 3–5 minutes more. Test again.

7. Allow to cool in pans 10 minutes. Remove from pan and allow to cool another 30 minutes or so before slicing and serving.

TIPS

1. I like to use garden-grown butternut squash for this recipe. I use 2 cups cooked and mashed squash instead of the 16-oz. can pumpkin. I like the texture of butternut squash better than cooked pumpkin.
2. I make the small loaves so I have them for gifts. They freeze well, and people have told me it's the best pumpkin bread they've ever had.

Holiday Almond Ring

Christina Ricker,
Gordonville, PA

Makes 12 servings
Prep. Time: 30 minutes
Rising Time: 3½ hours
Baking Time: 35 minutes

Breads

2 pkgs. yeast

2 cups scalded milk, cooled to lukewarm

½ cup sugar

2 tsp. salt

2 eggs, well beaten

7-7½ cups flour, *divided*

½ cup melted shortening, cooled

Filling:

1½ cups brown sugar

1½ cups flour

1½ sticks (12 Tbsp.) butter, cold

1½ tsp. almond extract

Icing:

1½-2 cups confectioners' sugar

2-3 Tbsp. warm milk

1. In a large mixing bowl, add yeast to cooled (lukewarm) scalded milk. Add sugar and salt. Stir until dissolved.

2. Stir in beaten eggs and 3½ cups flour. Beat until smooth.

3. Beat in cooled, melted shortening. Add remaining flour and stir until you've blended it as well as you can.

4. Turn dough out onto floured surface. Cover with bowl and let rest for 10 minutes.

5. Knead dough until smooth and elastic.

6. Place in large greased bowl, cover with towel, and let rise for 2 hours.

7. Punch down, cover, and let rise again for 45 minutes.

8. While dough is rising, make filling. In mixing bowl, mix sugar and flour together. Cut in butter with pastry cutter until mixture becomes crumbly. Gently stir in almond extract. Set aside.

9. After dough has risen for 45 minutes, punch it down again, shape it into a ball, and then divide it into 3 equal parts.

10. On lightly floured surface, roll each piece into a large circle and spread with ⅓ of the filling. Roll up into a long roll.

11. Place each in a pie pan, forming a ring Seal the ends together by using a few drops of water. Repeat for each ring.

12. Let rise for 35 minutes. Bake at 350°F for 35 minutes.

13. While rings are baking, mix together icing ingredients in a small bowl until of spreading consistency.

14. Remove baked rings from oven and, while they are still warm, drizzle with icing.

TIP

This takes time, but it's worth it!

Monkey Bread

Sheila Heil,
Lancaster, PA

Makes 12 servings
Prep. Time: 20 minutes
Baking Time: 28–32 minutes
Cooling Time: 10 minutes

½ cup sugar

1 tsp. cinnamon

3 7½-oz. cans refrigerated buttermilk biscuits

1 cup brown sugar

1½ sticks (12 Tbsp.) butter or margarine, melted

1. Preheat oven to 350°F. Lightly grease a 12-cup fluted tube, or Bundt, pan.

2. Mix sugar and cinnamon together in plastic bag.

3. Separate dough into 30 biscuits. Cut each into quarters.

4. Shake 3 or 4 biscuit pieces at a time in the bag to coat.

5. Arrange coated pieces in pan.

6. In a small mixing bowl, mix brown sugar and butter together and pour over biscuit pieces.

7. Bake 28–32 minutes, or until golden brown and no longer doughy in center.

8. Cool in pan for 10 minutes.

9. Turn upside down onto a serving plate. Serve warm, allowing each person at the table to pull off pieces to eat.

Breads

Apple Cranberry Muffins

**Judy Buller,
Bluffton, OH**

Makes 12 servings
Prep. Time: 20 minutes
Baking Time: 15 minutes
Cooling Time: 5–10 minutes

1⅓ cups whole wheat pastry flour

⅓ cup brown sugar

2 tsp. baking powder

½ tsp. baking soda

½ tsp. cinnamon

⅛ tsp. nutmeg

pinch of cloves

egg substitute equivalent to 2 eggs, or 4 egg whites

¼ cup canola oil

1 cup fat-free sour cream

1 large Granny Smith apple, peeled and shredded

½ cup fresh, or frozen, cranberries, cut in half

½ cup chopped walnuts, *optional*

1. Preheat oven to 400°F. Spray nonstick canola spray on bottom of 12 muffin cups.

2. In large bowl, whisk together flour, sugar, baking powder, baking soda, cinnamon, nutmeg, and cloves.

3. In medium bowl, whisk together egg substitute, oil, and sour cream until blended.

4. Stir apples and cranberries, and walnuts you wish, into wet ingredients. Mix well.

5. Add wet mixture to dry mixture, stirring just until blended.

6. Divide batter among muffin cups.

7. Bake 15 minutes, or until toothpick inserted in centers of muffins comes out clean.

8. Cool 5–10 minutes before serving.

Lemon Blueberry Muffins

Sally Holzem,
Schofield, WI

Makes 18 servings
Prep. Time: 15 minutes
Baking Time: 26 minutes

2½ cups all-purpose flour

¼ cup sugar

2 tsp. baking powder

½ tsp. baking soda

¼ tsp. salt

1½ cups low-fat buttermilk

⅓ cup olive oil

1 Tbsp. grated lemon rind

1 tsp. vanilla extract

egg substitute equivalent to 1 egg, or 2 egg
   whites, beaten

1½ cups frozen, unsweetened blueberries,
   thawed

2 Tbsp. sugar

1 Tbsp. lemon juice

1. Combine first 5 ingredients in a large bowl. Make a well in center of mixture.

2. In a separate bowl, combine buttermilk, oil, lemon rind, vanilla, and egg substitute.

3. Add wet ingredients to well in flour mixture, stirring just until dry ingredients are moistened.

4. Fold in blueberries.

5. Spoon batter into muffin pans coated lightly with cooking spray, or lined with paper baking cups, filling ⅓ full.

6. Bake muffins at 375°F for 20 minutes, or until tester inserted in centers of muffins comes out clean.

7. In a small bowl, combine 2 Tbsp. sugar and lemon juice.

8. Brush hot muffins with lemon-sugar mixture.

9. Bake an additional 6 minutes, or until golden brown.

Morning Glory Muffins

**Mary Jane Hoober,
Shipshewana, IN**

Makes about 36 muffins
Prep. Time: 25-30 minutes
Baking Time: 20 minutes

3 eggs

1 cup vegetable oil

2 tsp. vanilla extract

1¼ cups sugar

2 cups, plus 2 Tbsp., flour

2 tsp. baking soda

2 tsp. cinnamon

½ tsp. salt

2 cups grated carrots

1 cup raisins

½ cup chopped nuts

½ cup grated coconut

1 apple, peeled, cored, and grated, or
   chopped finely

1. In a large mixing bowl beat eggs. Then
add oil, vanilla, and sugar and combine well.

2. In a separate mixing bowl, stir together
flour, baking soda, cinnamon, and salt. When
well mixed, add remaining ingredients.

3. Pour dry ingredients into creamed
ingredients. Blend just until everything is
moistened.

4. Fill greased muffin tins ⅔ full. Bake at
350°F for 20 minutes, or until tester inserted
in center comes out clean.

Double Chocolate Muffins

**Janet Groff,
Stevens, PA**

Makes 12 muffins
Prep. Time: 15 minutes
Baking Time: 30 minutes

½ cup dry quick oats

1 cup plus ⅓ cup milk, *divided*

1 cup all-purpose flour

½ cup whole wheat flour

2 Tbsp. bran

½ cup sugar

¼ cup brown sugar

⅓ cup cocoa powder

¼ tsp. salt

1 rounded tsp. baking powder

1 egg

¼ cup vegetable oil

1 Tbsp. vanilla extract

¾ cup chocolate chips

Glaze:

1–2 Tbsp. peanut butter

1½ cups confectioners' sugar

water

1. In a microwavable container, combine quick oats and ⅓ cup milk. Microwave on High 1½ minutes. Set aside.

2. In a large bowl, combine flours, bran, sugars, cocoa powder, salt, and baking powder.

3. In a separate bowl, stir together oats mixture, egg, oil, 1 cup milk, vanilla, and chocolate chips.

4. Gently fold wet ingredients into dry ingredients, mixing just until moistened.

5. Spoon batter into 12 greased muffin cups, making each ¾ full.

6. Bake at 350°F for 30 minutes, or until toothpick inserted in muffin tops comes out clean. Allow muffins to cool for 10 minutes before removing from tins.

7. *To make glaze:* Combine peanut butter and confectioners' sugar in a small bowl. Add water to desired consistency and stir until smooth. Drizzle over warm muffins.

Soups, Stews, Chilis, and Chowders

Soups, Stews, Chilis, and Chowders

Soups

Chicken Spinach Soup

Carna Reitz,
Remington, VA

Makes 4-6 servings
Prep. Time: 5 minutes
Cooking Time: 20 minutes

6½ cups chicken broth, *divided*

2 cups cooked chicken

1-2 cups frozen chopped spinach

salt and pepper, to taste

½ cup flour

1. Put 6 cups broth, chicken, spinach, and salt and pepper in a large stockpot. Bring to a boil.

2. Meanwhile, mix flour and remaining ½ cup broth together in a jar. Put on lid and shake until smooth. When soup is boiling, slowly pour into soup to thicken, stirring constantly.

3. Continue stirring and cooking until soup thickens.

Soups

Chicken Barley Soup

**Ida H. Goering,
Dayton, VA**

Makes 6 servings
Prep. Time: 20 minutes
Cooking Time: 1 hour

6 cups low-sodium, fat-free chicken broth

1½ cups diced carrots

1 cup diced celery

½ cup chopped onion

¼ cup uncooked barley

2–3 cups (about 6 oz.) cooked and cut-up chicken

14½-oz. can diced tomatoes, no salt added, undrained

½ tsp. black pepper

1 bay leaf

2 Tbsp. chopped fresh parsley, or 2 tsp. dried parsley

1. Combine all ingredients except parsley in large kettle.

2. Cover and bring to boil.

3. Simmer, covered, for one hour. Stir occasionally.

4. Just before serving, remove bay leaf. Stir in parsley.

Chicken Noodle Soup

Mary Martins,
Fairbank, IA

Makes 12 servings
Prep. Time: 1 hour
Cooking Time: 3–3½ hours

4-lb. stewing chicken, skin removed and cut up

2 qts. water

2 14½-oz. cans low-fat, low-sodium chicken broth

5 celery ribs, coarsely chopped, *divided*

3 medium carrots, sliced, *divided*

2 medium onions, quartered, *divided*

⅔ cup coarsely chopped green bell pepper, *divided*

½ tsp. pepper

1 bay leaf

2 tsp. salt

8 oz. uncooked whole wheat noodles

1. In large stockpot, combine chicken, water, broth, half the celery, half the carrots, half the onions, half the green pepper, ½ tsp. pepper, and bay leaf. Bring to a boil.

2. Reduce heat. Cover and simmer 2½ hours, or until chicken is tender.

3. Remove chicken from broth. When cool enough to handle, remove meat from bones and cut into bite-sized pieces. Discard bones and skin. Set chicken aside. (This will equal about 3 lbs. cooked meat.)

4. Strain broth and skim fat.

5. Return broth to pot. Add salt and remaining celery, carrots, onions, and green pepper.

6. Bring to a boil. Reduce heat. Cover and simmer 10–12 minutes, or until vegetables are crisp-tender.

7. Remove bay leaf. Add noodles and chicken.

8. Cover and simmer 12–15 minutes, or until pasta is tender.

Chicken Tortellini Soup

**Mary Seielstad,
Sparks, NV**

Makes 4–6 servings
Prep. Time: 10–15 minutes
Cooking Time: 25 minutes

1 Tbsp. butter or margarine

4 cloves garlic, minced

5 cups chicken broth

9-oz. pkg. frozen cheese tortellini

1½ cups diced cooked chicken

14-oz. can stewed tomatoes

10-oz. pkg. frozen spinach

½ tsp. pepper

1 tsp. dried basil

¼ cup grated Parmesan cheese

1. In large saucepan, melt butter and sauté garlic for 2 minutes over medium heat.

2. Stir in broth and tortellini and bring to a boil. Cover, reduce heat, and simmer 5 minutes.

3. Add cooked chicken, tomatoes, frozen spinach, pepper, and basil and simmer 10–15 minutes. Stir every 3 minutes or so, breaking up frozen spinach and blending it into the soup.

4. Serve when soup is heated through, along with Parmesan cheese to spoon over individual servings.

Soups

Chicken Taco Soup

**Mary Puskar,
Forest Hill, MD**

Makes 4 servings
Prep. Time: 25 minutes
Cooking Time: 40 minutes

2 chicken breast halves

3 cups water

2 stalks celery

1 medium-sized onion

2 carrots

2 Tbsp. vegetable or canola oil

1 Tbsp. chili powder

1 Tbsp. cumin

4½-oz. can green chilies

14-oz. can chicken broth

14-oz. can beef broth

14½-oz. can diced tomatoes, undrained

1 Tbsp. Worcestershire sauce

tortilla chips, broken

Monterey Jack cheese, grated

1. In a large stockpot, cook chicken breasts in water until tender. Remove meat, reserving cooking water. When chicken is cool enough to handle, chop into bite-sized pieces. Set aside.

2. Chop celery and onion. Grate carrots.

3. In stockpot used for cooking chicken, sauté vegetables in oil.

4. Combine all ingredients in stockpot, except the cooked chicken, tortilla chips, and cheese. Cover and simmer 15 minutes.

5. Add diced chicken. Heat through.

6. Top each serving with broken tortilla chips and grated cheese.

Pasta Fagioli

Stacie Skelly,
Millersville, PA

Makes 8–10 servings
Prep. Time: 20 minutes
Cooking Time: 1½ hours

1 lb. ground beef

1 cup diced onions

1 cup julienned carrots

1 cup chopped celery

2 cloves garlic, minced

2 14½-oz. cans diced tomatoes, undrained

15-oz. can red kidney beans, undrained

15-oz. can great northern beans, undrained

15-oz. can tomato sauce

12-oz. can V8 juice

1 Tbsp. vinegar

1½ tsp. salt

1 tsp. dried oregano

1 tsp. dried basil

½ tsp. pepper

½ tsp. dried thyme

½ lb. ditali pasta

1. Brown ground beef in a large stockpot. Drain off drippings.

2. To browned beef, add onions, carrots, celery, and garlic. Sauté for 10 minutes.

3. Add remaining ingredients, except pasta, and stir well. Simmer, covered, for 1 hour.

4. About 50 minutes into cooking time, cook pasta in a separate saucepan, according to the directions on the package.

5. Add drained pasta to the large pot of soup. Simmer for 5–10 minutes and serve.

NOTE

If you can't find these short tubes, you can substitute elbow macaroni.

Minestrone Soup

**Lydia Konrad,
Edmonton, Alberta**

Makes 12 servings,
about ¾ cup per serving
Prep. Time: 15 minutes
Cooking Time: about 2 hours

1½ lbs. 90%-lean ground beef

1 cup diced onions

1 cup diced zucchini

1 cup cubed potatoes

1 cup sliced carrots

½ cup diced celery

1 cup shredded cabbage

15-oz. can tomatoes, chopped

1½ qts. water

1 bay leaf

½ tsp. dried thyme

2 tsp. salt

pepper, to taste

1 tsp. Worcestershire sauce

¼ cup uncooked brown rice

½ cup freshly grated Parmesan cheese

1. Brown ground beef in large soup kettle. Drain off grease.

2. Add vegetables, water, seasonings, and Worcestershire sauce and bring to a boil.

3. Sprinkle rice into mixture. Cover and simmer for at least 1 hour.

4. Remove bay leaf. Sprinkle with Parmesan cheese and serve with brown bread.

Hearty Beef Barley Soup

**Karen Gingrich,
New Holland, PA**

Makes 4–5 servings
Preparation Time: 5–10 minutes
Cooking Time: 35 minutes

1 lb. beef tips

2 cups sliced fresh mushrooms

¼ tsp. garlic powder

32-oz. can (3½ cups) beef broth

2 medium-sized carrots, sliced

¼ tsp. dried thyme

dash of pepper

½ cup quick-cooking barley

1. Cook beef in nonstick saucepan until browned and juices evaporate, about 10 minutes, stirring often.

2. Add mushrooms and garlic powder and cook until mushrooms begin to wilt, about 5 minutes.

3. Add broth, carrots, thyme, and pepper.

4. Heat to boiling. Stir in barley. Cover and cook over low heat for 20 minutes, or until barley is tender.

Soups

Cheeseburger Soup

Jean Hindal,
Grandin, IA
Beverly High,
Ephrata, PA
Sherlyn Hess,
Millersville, PA

Makes 8 servings
Prep. Time: 30 minutes
Cooking Time: 20-30 minutes

½ lb. ground beef

¾ cup chopped onions

¾ cup shredded carrots

¾ cup diced celery

¼ tsp. dried basil

1 tsp. dried parsley flakes

4 Tbsp. butter or margarine, *divided*

3 cups chicken broth

2 cups diced potatoes, peeled or unpeeled

¼ cup flour

1½ cups milk

¾ tsp. salt

¼–½ tsp. pepper

8 oz. cheddar cheese, grated

¼ cup sour cream

1. In saucepan, brown beef. Drain. Set aside.

2. In same saucepan, sauté onions, carrots, celery, basil, and parsley in 1 Tbsp. butter until vegetables are tender.

3. Add broth, potatoes, and beef. Bring to boil. Reduce heat, cover, and simmer for 10–12 minutes, or until potatoes are tender.

4. While meat and potatoes cook, in small skillet melt 3 Tbsp. butter. Stir in flour until smooth. Cook and stir 3–5 minutes.

5. Reduce heat to low. Add milk, salt, and pepper. Stir until mixture thickens and becomes smooth.

6. Slowly stir in grated cheese, about ½ cup at a time. Continue to stir until cheese is fully melted and blended into white sauce.

7. Blend in sour cream. Heat, but do not boil.

8. When vegetables are tender and cheesy white sauce is finished, pour the white sauce into the vegetable mixture and gently stir together.

9. When well mixed and heated through, serve.

Soups

Broccoli Rabe and Sausage Soup

Carlene Horne,
Bedford, NH

Makes 4 servings
Prep. Time: 15 minutes
Cooking Time: 15 minutes

2 Tbsp. olive oil

1 onion, chopped

1 lb. sweet or spicy sausage, casing removed, sliced

1 bunch broccoli rabe, approximately 5 cups chopped

32-oz. chicken broth

1 cup water

8 oz. frozen tortellini

1. Heat olive oil in a soup pot.

2. Add onion and sausage and sauté until tender.

3. Add broccoli rabe and sauté a few more minutes.

4. Pour broth and water into pan; bring to simmer.

5. Add tortellini and cook a few minutes until tender.

TIPS

1. Substitute any green such as Swiss chard, kale, or spinach for the broccoli rabe.
2. Serve with grated cheese and crusty bread.

Soups

Turkey Sausage and Cabbage Soup

**Bonita Stutzman,
Harrisonburg, VA**

Makes 8 servings
Prep. Time: 20 minutes
Cooking Time: 1 hour, or more

1½ cups chopped onions

2 cloves garlic, finely chopped

¾ lb. turkey sausage, chopped in small pieces

6 cups shredded green cabbage

3 lbs. canned tomatoes, no salt added, undrained

1½ qts. water

1 Tbsp. dried basil

2 tsp. dried oregano

¼ tsp. black pepper

1. Spray inside bottom of stockpot lightly with cooking spray. Sauté onions and garlic until tender.

2. Add chopped sausage. Cook until lightly browned.

3. Stir in remaining ingredients.

4. Cover. Simmer until cabbage is very tender, about an hour.

Soups

Tuscany Peasant Soup

Alice Valine,
Elma, NY

Makes 8 servings
Prep. Time: 20 minutes
Cooking Time: 25 minutes

½ lb. bulk turkey sausage

1 onion, chopped

2–3 cloves garlic, minced

2 15-oz. cans cannellini beans, or great northern beans, rinsed and drained

2 14½-oz. cans diced tomatoes, no salt added, undrained

2 14-oz. cans low-fat, low-sodium chicken broth

2 tsp. no-salt Italian seasoning

3 medium zucchini, sliced

4 cups fresh spinach leaves, chopped, or baby spinach, unchopped

shredded Parmesan, or Romano, cheese, *optional*

1. In Dutch oven or stockpot, cook sausage over medium heat until no longer pink. Drain off drippings.

2. Add onion and garlic. Sauté until tender.

3. Stir in beans, tomatoes, broth, seasoning, and zucchini. Cook uncovered 10 minutes.

4. Add spinach and heat until just wilted.

5. Serve with cheese, if you wish.

Soups

Italian Sausage Soup

Esther Porter,
Minneapolis, MN

Makes 6–8 servings
Prep. Time: 15–25 minutes
Cooking Time: 65–70 minutes

1 lb. Italian sausage, casings removed

1 cup chopped onions

2 large garlic cloves, sliced

5 cups beef stock, or 3 14½-oz. cans beef
  broth

2 cups chopped or canned tomatoes

8-oz. can tomato sauce

1½ cups sliced zucchini

1 carrot, thinly sliced

1 medium-sized green bell pepper, diced

1 cup green beans, frozen or fresh

2 Tbsp. dried basil

2 Tbsp. dried oregano

8-10-oz. pkg. cheese tortellini

salt, to taste

pepper, to taste

freshly grated Parmesan cheese for topping

1. Sauté sausage in heavy Dutch oven over medium heat until cooked through, about 10 minutes, breaking it up as it browns with a wooden spoon.

2. Using a slotted spoon, transfer sausage to a large bowl. Pour off all but 1 Tbsp. drippings from Dutch oven. Add onions and garlic to the 1 Tbsp. drippings and sauté until clear, about 5 minutes.

3. Return sausage to pan. Add beef stock, tomatoes, tomato sauce, zucchini, carrot, pepper, green beans, basil, and oregano. Simmer 30–40 minutes, or until vegetables are tender.

4. Add tortellini and cook 8–10 minutes. Season to taste with salt and pepper.

5. Ladle hot soup into bowls and sprinkle with Parmesan cheese.

Variations:

1. Use leftover meat and vegetables from your refrigerator, instead of the sausage and the vegetables listed above.

2. Substitute V8 juice for half of the beef stock or tomatoes.

3. When you're in a hurry, use Italian-style frozen vegetables instead of fresh beans, carrot, and zucchini.

4. Instead of tortellini, use ½-lb. pkg. small pasta shells, uncooked.
   —Michelle Scribano, Harrisonburg, VA

Soups

Mom's Soup

Chrissy Baldwin,
Mechanicsburg, PA

Makes 8–10 servings
Prep. Time: 20 minutes
Cooking Time: 35 minutes

3 cups diced potatoes

16-oz. frozen broccoli and cauliflower

1 cup chopped carrots

1 cup chopped onions

3 celery ribs, chopped

12-oz. ham cubes

4 chicken bouillon cubes

3 cups water

1 tsp. salt

¼ tsp. pepper

1 stick (8 Tbsp.) butter

½ cup flour

2 cups milk

1 cup shredded cheese

1. In soup pot, combine potatoes, broccoli and cauliflower, carrots, onions, celery, ham, bouillon, water, salt, and pepper. Simmer for 20 minutes or until vegetables are tender.

2. In separate saucepan, make a white sauce. Melt butter over low heat and stir in flour to make a thick paste. Whisk in milk. Bring to a boil and stir for 2–3 minutes.

3. Add white sauce to soup pot and simmer for 10 minutes.

4. Add shredded cheese and stir until melted.

TIP

Simply keep this on the stove or place in slow cooker to keep warm.

Meatball Tortellini Soup

**Lucille Amos,
Greensboro, NC**

Makes 4 servings
Prep. Time: 5 minutes
Cooking Time: 20–25 minutes

14-oz. can beef broth

12 frozen Italian meatballs

1 cup stewed tomatoes

11-oz. can Mexican style corn, drained

1 cup (20) frozen cheese tortellini

1. Bring broth to boil in a large stockpot.

2. Add meatballs. Cover and reduce heat. Simmer 5 minutes.

3. Add tomatoes and corn. Cover and simmer 5 minutes more.

4. Add tortellini. Cover and simmer 5 more minutes, or until tortellini is tender.

Potato-Cheese Soup

Mary Kathryn Yoder,
Harrisonville, MO

Makes 5 servings
Prep. Time: 20 minutes
Cooking Time: 20 minutes

4 medium-sized potatoes, peeled and cut into chunks

4 slices bacon

1 small onion, chopped, *optional*

4 cups milk

¾ tsp. salt

pepper, to taste

¾ cup shredded cheese, your choice of flavors

1. Place potato chunks in a saucepan. Add 1-inch water. Cover and cook over low heat until very tender.

2. Meanwhile, cut bacon into 1-inch lengths. Place in a large saucepan, along with the onion if you wish. Cook until tender.

3. When potatoes become tender, mash in their cooking water.

4. Add mashed potatoes and milk to bacon, and onion if using.

5. Stir in salt, pepper, and cheese. Cook over low heat, stirring occasionally to distribute cheese as it melts.

6. Soup is ready when cheese is melted and soup is hot.

TIPS

1. When you mash the potatoes, you can let them be a little lumpy. That adds interesting texture to the soup.
2. You can use leftover mashed potatoes to make this recipe if you have them.

Ham and Bean Soup

**Diane Eby,
Holtwood, PA**

Makes 6-8 servings
Prep. Time: 5 minutes
Cooking Time: 15-20 minutes

1 qt. water

2 cups fully cooked ham, diced

40½-oz. can great northern beans

½ lb. Velveeta cheese, cubed

1. Place water and ham in a large stockpot. Cook for 5 minutes.

2. Add beans. Heat through.

3. Add cheese. Stir until cheese melts.

Soups

Fresh Vegetable Soup

Sandra Chang,
Derwood, MD

Makes 4-6 servings
Prep. Time: 25-30 minutes
Cooking Time: 60-70 minutes
Standing Time: 1 hour

4 Tbsp. butter

½ cup of each:

    diced celery

    diced onions

    small chunks of peeled carrots

    chopped cabbage

    diced zucchini

    fresh or frozen whole kernel corn

    fresh or frozen cut-up green beans

2 cups canned whole tomatoes

4 cups beef stock

2 Tbsp. sugar

salt, to taste

pepper, to taste

½ cup fresh or frozen petite peas

1. In 4-qt. saucepan, melt butter. Sauté celery, onions, carrots, cabbage, and zucchini in butter until vegetables are soft but not brown.

2. Add rest of ingredients, except ½ cup peas.

3. Simmer gently for 30–45 minutes, or until vegetables are cooked but not mushy.

4. Take pan off heat and stir in peas. Allow soup to stand for 1 hour before serving.

5. Reheat just until heated through and serve.

Soups

Easy Cream of Vegetable Soup

Norma Grieser,
Sebring, FL

Makes 6 cups
Prep. Time: 20 minutes
Cooking Time: 20 minutes

¼ cup chopped celery

¼ cup chopped onion

1 Tbsp. canola oil

3 Tbsp. flour

½ tsp. salt

pepper, to taste

1 bay leaf, or herb of your choice

3 cups skim milk

2 cups fresh or frozen vegetables of your choice, cut up or sliced (spinach, asparagus, broccoli, cauliflower, peas, carrots, tomatoes, mushrooms); if using canned vegetables, use ones without added salt

1. In large stockpot, sauté celery and onion in oil.

2. Over low heat, stir in flour, salt, pepper, and herb.

3. Add milk, stirring constantly. Cook over medium heat until hot and bubbly.

4. Steam or microwave vegetables until crisp-tender.

5. Remove bay leaf, if using. Stir vegetables into thickened creamy sauce and heat through.

TIPS

1. If you want cream of chicken soup, add reduced-sodium chicken bouillon.
2. This recipe can be used as soup itself, or you can use it in any recipe calling for cream soup.

Soups

Roasted Vegetable Gazpacho

**J. B. Miller,
Indianapolis, IN**

Makes 6 servings
Prep. Time: 30 minutes
Baking Time: 20–25 minutes
Chilling Time: 4 hours

2 red bell peppers, left whole

2 yellow bell peppers, left whole

2 large red onions, quartered

2 Tbsp. extra-virgin olive oil

black pepper, to taste

1 lb. (about 4 cups) medium zucchini, cut in
½-inch-thick slices

2 lbs. (about 7 medium) vine-ripened
tomatoes, cored, quartered, and seeds
removed

3 cloves garlic

2 Tbsp. chopped fresh basil

1 Tbsp. chopped fresh oregano

1 cup cold water

2 Tbsp. lime juice, or more to taste

1. Preheat oven to 375°F.

2. Place peppers and onions in large
mixing bowl. Toss with olive oil and black
pepper.

3. Spoon peppers and onions into large
shallow baking dishes or onto cookie sheets
with sides. Allow seasoned olive oil to remain
in mixing bowl. Place peppers and onions in
oven.

4. Meanwhile, stir zucchini and tomatoes
into large mixing bowl with remaining
seasoned olive oil.

5. After peppers and onions have roasted
10–12 minutes, add zucchini and tomatoes to
baking dishes.

6. Roast 10–12 minutes, or until peppers
are soft and vegetables have browned along
the edges and wrinkled. Total roasting time
will be 20–25 minutes.

7. Remove baking dishes from oven. Lift
out peppers and place in bowl. Cover with
plastic wrap. Let cool 10 minutes. Then peel
and seed peppers over a bowl, saving the
juices.

8. Coarsely chop all vegetables.

9. Place chopped vegetables in food
processor together with garlic, basil, oregano,
and 1 cup cold water.

10. Blend at high speed until smooth.
Strain through a fine mesh sieve.

11. Place mixture in covered container.
Refrigerate 4 hours before serving.

12. Adjust seasoning with pepper to taste.

13. Mix in lime juice just before serving.

Wild-Rice Mushroom Soup

Kelly Amos,
Pittsboro, NC

Makes 4 servings

Prep. Time: 15–20 minutes
Cooking Time: 35 minutes

1 Tbsp. olive oil

half a white onion, chopped

¼ cup chopped celery

¼ cup chopped carrots

1½ cups sliced fresh white mushrooms

½ cup white wine, or ½ cup low-sodium, fat-free chicken broth

2½ cups low-sodium, fat-free chicken broth

1 cup fat-free half-and-half

2 Tbsp. flour

¼ tsp. dried thyme

black pepper, to taste

1 cup cooked wild rice

1. Put olive oil in stockpot and heat. Carefully add chopped onion, celery, and carrots. Cook until tender.

2. Add mushrooms, white wine, and chicken broth.

3. Cover and heat through.

4. In a bowl, blend half-and-half, flour, thyme, and pepper. Then stir in cooked wild rice.

5. Pour rice mixture into hot stockpot with vegetables.

6. Cook over medium heat. Stir continually until thickened and bubbly.

Soups

Stuffed Sweet Pepper Soup

**Moreen Weaver,
Bath, NY**

Makes 10 servings
Prep. Time: 20 minutes
Cooking Time: 1 hour

1 lb. 95%-lean ground beef

2 qts. low-sodium tomato juice

3 medium red, or green, bell peppers, diced

1½ cups chili sauce, no salt added

1 cup uncooked brown rice

2 celery ribs, diced

1 large onion, diced

3 low-sodium chicken bouillon cubes

2 garlic cloves, minced

1. In large kettle over medium heat, cook beef until no longer pink. Drain off drippings.

2. Add remaining ingredients. Bring to a boil.

3. Reduce heat. Simmer, uncovered, for 1 hour, or until rice is tender.

Lentil Soup

**Marcia S. Myer,
Manheim, PA**

Makes 6 servings
Prep. Time: 15 minutes
Cooking Time: 1 hour

2 large onions, chopped

1 carrot, chopped

½ tsp. dried thyme

½ tsp. dried marjoram

3 cups low-sodium, fat-free chicken, or
   vegetable, broth

1 cup uncooked lentils

¼ cup chopped fresh parsley

1 lb. canned tomatoes, no salt added,
   undrained

¼ cup sherry, *optional*

⅔ cup grated low-fat cheese, *optional*

1. Spray bottom of large stockpot with nonstick cooking spray. Sauté onions and carrot 3–5 minutes.

2. Add thyme and marjoram.

3. Add broth, lentils, parsley, and tomatoes.

4. Cover and simmer about 45 minutes, or until lentils are tender.

5. Stir in sherry if you wish.

6. Top each individual serving of soup with 1½ Tbsp. grated cheese if you wish.

Baked Potato Soup

Flo Quint,
Quinter, KS
Susan Nafziger,
Canton, KS

Makes 6-8 servings
Prep. Time: 30 minutes
Cooking Time: 15-20 minutes

sticks (12 Tbsp.) butter

up flour

ps milk

ps baked potatoes (about 5 large
otatoes), peeled and cubed

een onions, sliced thin

2 strips bacon (according to your taste
reference), cooked and crumbled

cups shredded cheese

. sour cream, *optional*

sp. salt, *optional*

sp. pepper, *optional*

Melt butter in large stockpot. Add flour
stir until smooth over medium heat.

2. Add milk, stirring often until thickened.
Be careful not to scorch.

3. Add potatoes and onions and bring to
a boil. Reduce heat and simmer 5 minutes,
stirring often.

4. Remove from heat and add bacon,
cheese, and sour cream if desired. Stir until
melted.

5. Add seasonings if desired and blend
thoroughly.

Variation:
Instead of 7 cups milk, you can use 4 cups
milk and 3 cups chicken broth.

Soups

Quickie French Onion Soup

Mary Puskar,
Forest Hill, MD

Makes 6–8 servings
Prep Time: 5–10 minutes
Cooking Time: 1 hour

½ stick (4 Tbsp.) butter

3–4 good-sized onions (enough to make 5 cups sliced onions)

¼ cup flour

6 cups beef broth, or 3 14½-oz. cans beef broth, or 6 cups water with 6 beef bouillon cubes

6–8 melba rounds, *optional*

2 cups grated mozzarella cheese, *optional*

1. Melt butter in a large saucepan.

2. Meanwhile, slice onions.

3. Sauté onions in butter. After they become tender, continue cooking over low heat so that they brown and deepen in flavor, up to 30 minutes.

4. Sprinkle with flour. Cook 2 minutes.

5. Stir in broth, or water and bouillon cubes. Cover.

6. Heat to boiling and simmer 20 minutes.

7. Ladle into individual serving bowls.

8. Top each with melba rounds and/or grated cheese if you wish. For extra beauty and flavor, broil until cheese melts, but first make sure that the soup bowls can withstand the broiler heat. They could crack.

TIP

This recipe doubles very easily.

Soups

Creamy Asparagus Soup

Mary E. Riha,
Antigo, WI

Makes 4 servings
Prep. Time: 30 minutes
Cooking Time: 15–20 minutes

¼ cup sesame seeds

2 Tbsp. olive oil

1 medium onion, chopped

2 medium potatoes, cubed

4 cups chicken stock, *divided*

1 lb. raw asparagus, broken in 1-inch pieces

1 tsp. salt

dash of pepper

dash of nutmeg

sour cream

salted sunflower seeds, *optional*

1. In stockpot, sauté sesame seeds in olive oil until brown. Add onion and potatoes. Cook and stir until potatoes begin to stick.

2. Add 2 cups stock, asparagus, salt, and pepper. Bring to boil. Reduce heat and simmer until potatoes are done.

3. Carefully pour one fourth of hot mixture into blender. Cover and blend until smooth. (Hold the lid on with a potholder to keep the heat from pushing it off.)

4. Put pureed soup back in stockpot. Continue blending cooked soup, one-fourth at a time. Continue to add pureed soup back into stockpot.

5. When all soup has been pureed, add 2 more cups chicken stock to soup in stockpot. Heat thoroughly.

6. Add a dash of nutmeg.

7. Top each serving with a dollop of sour cream, and a sprinkling of sunflower seeds if desired.

Soups

Creamy Broccoli Soup

SuAnne Burkholder,
Millersburg, OH

Makes 3-4 servings
Prep. Time: 10-15 minutes
Cooking Time: 15-20 minutes

4 cups milk, *divided*

1 Tbsp. chicken-flavored soup base

1½ cups cut-up broccoli

2 Tbsp. cornstarch

salt, to taste

1. Heat 3 cups milk and chicken base in a stockpot over low heat until hot.

2. Meanwhile, place cut-up broccoli in a microwave-safe dish. Add 1 Tbsp. water. Cover. Microwave on High for 1½ minutes. Stir. Repeat until broccoli becomes bright green and just-tender. Be careful not to overcook it! Drain broccoli of liquid.

3. In a small bowl, or in a jar with a tight-fitting lid, mix together 1 cup milk and cornstarch until smooth. Slowly add to hot milk mixture.

4. Simmer gently, stirring constantly. When slightly thickened, add broccoli and salt.

Cheesy Broccoli Cauliflower Soup

Marcia S. Myer,
Manheim, PA

Makes 5-6 servings
Prep. Time: 20 minutes
Cooking Time: 40-45 minutes

6 Tbsp. butter

¼ cup chopped onion

½ cup flour

2 cups milk

1 cup (4 oz.) cubed Velveeta or American
   cheese

2 14-oz. cans chicken broth

2 cups chopped broccoli, fresh or frozen

2 cups chopped cauliflower, fresh or frozen

¼ cup finely chopped or grated carrots

¼ cup chopped celery

salt, to taste

¼ tsp. pepper

1. Melt butter in large saucepan. Stir in onion and sauté until just tender.

2. Stir in flour until well blended. Slowly add milk over medium heat, stirring constantly until thickened and smooth.

3. Stir in cheese, continuing to stir until cheese melts. Set aside.

4. In a separate saucepan, simmer broccoli, cauliflower, carrots, and celery in chicken broth until almost tender.

5. Season with salt, if you wish, and pepper.

6. Pour cheesy sauce into vegetables and heat through.

Variations:
1. Instead of chicken broth, use 2 chicken bouillon cubes and 1¾ cups water in Step 4.

2. Instead of cauliflower, use 2 additional cups broccoli, fresh or frozen.
   —Mary Jane Musser, Manheim, PA

Flavorful Tomato Soup

Shari Ladd,
Hudson, MI

Makes 4 servings
Prep. Time: 10 minutes
Cooking Time: 20 minutes

2 Tbsp. chopped onions

1 Tbsp. extra-virgin olive oil

3 Tbsp. flour

2 tsp. sugar

½ tsp. pepper

¼ tsp. dried basil

½ tsp. dried oregano

¼ tsp. dried thyme

1 qt. stewed tomatoes, no salt added, undrained

2 cups skim milk

1. Sauté onions in oil in stockpot.

2. Stir in flour, sugar, and seasonings.

3. Stir in stewed tomatoes, stirring constantly. Bring to a boil and boil 1 minute.

4. Add 2 cups milk. If soup is too thick, add a little water. Stir well.

5. Simmer 10 minutes but do not boil.

Tomato Basil Soup

**Barbara Kuhns,
Millersburg, OH**

Makes 4–6 servings
Prep. Time: 15 minutes
Cooking Time: 25 minutes

1 stick (8 Tbsp.) butter

¼ cup finely chopped onion

2 10½-oz. cans condensed tomato soup

2 cups tomato sauce

6-oz. can tomato paste

2 14½-oz. cans chicken broth

3 tsp. basil

¼ cup brown sugar

garlic cloves, minced, *optional*

⅓ cup flour

1 cup heavy whipping cream

1. Melt butter in soup pot.

2. Add and sauté onion until softened.

3. Add condensed soup, sauce, paste, broth, basil, brown sugar, and garlic (if using).

4. Cook, covered, until hot.

5. Whisk together flour and cream.

6. Add and heat gently, stirring, until soup is steaming and thick. Do not boil.

Egg Drop Soup

**Susan Guarneri,
Three Lakes, WI**

Makes 6-7 servings
Prep. Time: 10 minutes
Cooking Time: 25 minutes

2 Tbsp. cornstarch

6 cups chicken stock

2 Tbsp. soy sauce

3 Tbsp. white vinegar

1 small onion, minced

3 eggs, beaten

salt and pepper, to taste

sweet pepper flakes, *optional*

1. In stockpot, mix cornstarch with ½ cup cold chicken stock. When smooth, gradually add remaining chicken stock over medium heat, stirring continuously to keep cornstarch suspended and mixture smooth. Turn heat to low.

2. Add soy sauce, vinegar, and onion. Bring to low simmer (barely boiling).

3. Quickly stir in beaten eggs, swirling the broth and eggs in a circular motion to create "egg threads" in the soup. When all eggs are in the broth, allow to cook without stirring for 1 minute.

4. Remove pan from heat. Add salt and pepper to taste. Add sweet pepper flakes, if desired, before serving.

Soups

Stews

Meatball Stew

Hope Comerford,
Clinton Township, MI

Makes 6–8 servings
Prep. Time: 30 minutes
Cooking Time: 2¼ hours

Meatballs:

2 lbs. lean ground beef

2 eggs

1–1½ cups bread crumbs

1 Tbsp. dried minced onion

1 Tbsp. garlic powder

1 tsp. salt

¼ tsp. pepper

Stew:

2–4 Tbsp. olive oil

2 potatoes, peeled and cubed

4 carrots, peeled and sliced

1 large onion, chopped

4 cups green beans, cut into ½-inch pieces

1 cup chopped tomatoes

10-oz. can tomato sauce

10 cups water

1. Mix together all of the meatball ingredients. Form the meatball mixture into 1-inch balls.

2. Heat up the olive oil and brown the meatballs in batches just until the sides are slightly browned.

3. Set the meatballs aside.

4. In a large stockpot, place all of the potatoes, carrots, onion, green beans, and chopped tomatoes. Add in the meatballs.

5. Pour in the can of tomato sauce, then the water. Stir gently.

6. Bring the soup to a boil, then reduce the heat to low and let it simmer for 2 hours.

TIP

While this takes a little bit of time to prepare, the effort is worth it! It is one of my most favorite "comfort meals!"

Stews

Hearty Beef Stew

Hope Comerford,
Clinton Township, MI

Makes 6–8 servings
Prep. Time: 30 minutes
Cooking Time: about 2 hours

1½ lbs. stew beef

1 Tbsp. olive oil

4–5 carrots, chopped

4 stalks celery, chopped

1 large onion, chopped

4 small- or medium-sized potatoes, diced

14½- oz. can diced tomatoes

6-oz. can tomato paste

7 cups beef stock

1 tsp. onion powder

1 tsp. salt

1 tsp. pepper

1 tsp. oregano

2 bay leaves

1. Lightly brown the stew beef in 1 Tbsp. olive oil in the bottom of a stew pot.

2. Add in the carrots, celery, and onion and cook until the onions are translucent.

3. Add in the potatoes, diced tomatoes, tomato paste, beef stock, onion powder, salt, pepper, oregano, and bay leaves. Stir well.

4. Bring to a boil.

5. Reduce to a simmer and cover. Cook for an additional 2 hours. Remove bay leaves before serving.

Chicken and Chili Stew

Susan Kasting,
Jenks, OK

Makes 4 servings
Prep. Time: 20 minutes
Cooking Time: 30 minutes

14½-oz. can low-sodium, fat-free chicken broth, *divided*

1 lb. boneless, skinless chicken breasts, cut into bite-sized pieces

4 cloves garlic, minced

1-2 jalapeño peppers, seeded and diced

1 Tbsp. cornstarch

1 medium red bell pepper, diced

1 medium carrot, sliced

15-oz. can corn, no salt added, drained

1 tsp. cumin

2 Tbsp. chopped cilantro

1. In good-sized stockpot, heat ¾ cup broth to boiling.

2. Add chicken to broth. Cook about 5 minutes, or until no longer pink.

3. Add garlic and jalapeño peppers. Cook 2 minutes.

4. In a bowl, stir cornstarch into remaining broth.

5. When smooth, add to chicken mixture. Cook, stirring, until thickened.

6. Stir in remaining ingredients.

7. Cover. Let simmer 20 minutes, stirring occasionally.

Stews

Lentil Barley Stew with Chicken

**Ilene Bontrager,
Arlington, KS**

Makes 4 servings
Prep. Time: 15 minutes
Cooking Time: 1–2 hours

$\frac{1}{3}$ cup uncooked lentils

$\frac{1}{3}$ cup uncooked green split peas

$\frac{1}{3}$ cup uncooked pearl barley

1 carrot, finely diced

half an onion, chopped

1 small rib celery, sliced thin

$\frac{1}{4}$ tsp. pepper

1 qt. low-sodium, fat-free chicken, or beef, broth

1 cup chicken, cooked and diced

1. Rinse lentils, peas, and barley.

2. Place in 4–6-qt. stockpot. Add all remaining ingredients, except chicken.

3. Simmer, covered, 1–2 hours, or until lentils, peas, and barley are soft.

4. Stir in chicken. Cover and heat through

Oyster Stew

**Dorothy Reise,
Severna Park, MD**

Makes 4 servings
Prep. Time: 10–15 minutes
Cooking Time: 15 minutes

2–3 dozen fresh oysters in liquid

2 Tbsp. butter

1 Tbsp. onion, chopped

3 Tbsp. flour

3 cups milk

1 tsp. salt

1/2 tsp. pepper

1/2 tsp. parsley, chopped

pinch of celery seed, *optional*

dash of paprika, *optional*

1. In a small skillet over medium heat, pre-cook oysters in their own liquid until edges curl and oysters become plump. Set aside.

2. In large stockpot, melt butter, add onion, and sauté until soft.

3. Over medium heat, add flour and stir until smooth.

4. Slowly add milk, stirring constantly until thickened.

5. Add the pre-cooked oysters and liquid, salt, pepper, parsley, and celery seed and paprika if you wish. Mix well.

6. Heat thoroughly and serve.

Mushroom Stew

**Lauren Bailey,
Mechanicsburg, PA**

Makes 10 servings
Prep. Time: 20 minutes
Cooking Time: 30–35 minutes

5 Tbsp. butter, *divided*

1 Tbsp. oil

2 bay leaves

1 large onion, chopped

2 cloves minced garlic (use more if you wish)

2 Tbsp. flour

1 cup chicken broth

1 cup tomato juice, or fresh tomato puree

2 cups cut-up tomatoes, fresh or canned

1½ lbs. fresh mushrooms, chopped

1 tsp. dried thyme

salt and pepper, to taste

1½ cups red wine

1. In medium-sized saucepan melt 2 Tbsp. butter and oil. Add bay leaves and onion. Sauté until onions are golden. Stir in garlic and sauté one more minute.

2. Stir in flour and lower the heat. Cook several minutes on low, stirring constantly.

3. Add broth and tomato juice. Stir with whisk to remove all lumps. Add cut-up tomatoes.

4. In larger pot, sauté mushrooms in 3 Tbsp. butter. Add thyme over high heat. Add tomato mixture, salt, and pepper. Lower heat and simmer for 20 minutes.

5. Remove bay leaves. Add wine and stir for one minute.

Stews

Speedy International Stew

**Mabel Shirk,
Mount Crawford, VA**

Makes 4 servings
Prep. Time: 5 minutes
Cooking Time: 5–10 minutes

2 14½-oz. cans stewed tomatoes (Italian, Mexican, or Cajun)

15-oz. can black beans, drained and rinsed

16-oz. can corn kernels, drained and rinsed

1. Place all ingredients in a medium saucepan.

2. Cover and cook over medium heat for 5–10 minutes, stirring occasionally.

Chilis

Quick and Easy Chili

Carolyn Spohn,
Shawnee, KS

Makes 3–4 servings
Prep. Time: 10 minutes
Cooking Time: 25 minutes

½ lb. ground beef, or turkey, browned and drained

1 medium-sized onion, chopped

2 cloves garlic, minced

2 15-oz. cans chili-style beans with liquid

8-oz. can tomato sauce

TIP

Leftovers make good chili dogs.

1. Brown ground beef in a large skillet.

2. Drain, leaving about 1 tsp. drippings in pan. Sauté onion and garlic until softened.

3. Add beans, with liquid, and the tomato sauce. Bring to a slow boil.

4. Reduce heat to simmer and cook for 15 minutes.

5. Return meat to skillet. Heat together for 5 minutes.

Chilis

Chunky Beef Chili

Ruth C. Hancock,
Earlsboro, OK

Makes 4 servings
Prep. Time: 30 minutes
Cooking Time: 1¾–2¼ hours

2 Tbsp. vegetable oil, *divided*

1 lb. beef stew, cut into 1½-inch thick pieces

1 medium onion, chopped

1 medium jalapeño pepper with seeds, minced, *optional*

½ tsp. salt

2 14½-oz. cans chili-seasoned diced tomatoes

1. Heat 1 Tbsp. oil in stockpot over medium heat until hot.

2. Brown half of beef in oil. Remove meat from pot and keep warm.

3. Repeat with remaining beef. Remove meat from pot and keep warm.

4. Add remaining 1 Tbsp. oil to stockpot, along with the onion, and the pepper if you wish.

5. Cook 5–8 minutes, or until vegetables are tender. Stir occasionally.

6. Return meat and juices to stockpot. Add salt and tomatoes.

7. Bring to a boil. Reduce heat. Cover tightly and simmer 1¾–2¼ hours, or until meat is tender but not dried out.

Beef and Black Bean Chili

Eileen B. Jarvis,
Saint Augustine, FL

Makes 8 servings
Prep. Time: 15 minutes
Cooking Time: 15–20 minutes

1 lb. 95%-lean ground beef

2 15-oz. cans no-salt-added black beans, rinsed and drained, *divided*

½ cup water

1 cup medium, or hot, chunky salsa

2 8-oz. cans no-salt-added tomato sauce

1 Tbsp. chili powder

low-fat sour cream, *optional*

reduced-fat cheddar cheese, grated, *optional*

1. Brown meat in large saucepan over medium-high heat. Drain off drippings.

2. While meat cooks, drain, rinse, and mash 1 can black beans.

3. Add mashed beans, second can of rinsed and drained beans, water, salsa, tomato sauce, and chili powder to saucepan. Stir well.

4. Cover. Cook over medium heat for 10 minutes. Stir occasionally.

5. If you wish, top individual servings with sour cream and/or reduced-fat cheese.

Adirondack Three Alarm Chili

**Joanne Kennedy,
Plattsburgh, NY**

Makes 8 servings
Prep. Time: 25 minutes
Cooking Time: 3 hours

¾ lbs. 90%-lean ground beef

medium onions, diced

garlic cloves, crushed

green pepper, chopped

8-oz. can crushed tomatoes

15½-oz. cans kidney beans, drained

6-oz. can no-added-salt tomato sauce

Tbsp. brown sugar

tsp. dried oregano

¼–1 tsp. crushed red pepper

Tbsp. chili powder

tsp. salt, *optional*

1. Brown ground beef in large soup pot.

2. Add and sauté onions, garlic, and green pepper.

3. Add the rest of ingredients. Simmer on low heat for 3 hours.

Variations:
Add a can of corn, or replace some of the meat with more beans. Simmer the chili in a slow cooker instead of on the stovetop.

Chilis

Scrumptious White Chili

**Gloria L. Lehman,
Singers Glen, VA
Lauren Bailey,
Mechanicsburg, PA**

Makes 6 servings
Prep. Time: 20–25 minutes
Cooking Time: 25 minutes

½ Tbsp. oil

large onion, chopped

cloves garlic, minced

cups chopped cooked chicken

-oz. can chopped mild green chilies

½–1 Tbsp. diced jalapeño pepper, *optional*

½ tsp. ground cumin

tsp. dried oregano

0½-oz. can condensed chicken broth

0½-oz. can refilled with water

5-oz. can great northern beans

½ tsp. cayenne, or to taste

alt, to taste

oz. shredded Monterey Jack cheese

½ cup low-fat sour cream

chopped green onions, *optional*

resh cilantro, *optional*

1. In large stockpot, sauté onion and garlic n oil over medium heat.

2. Add chicken, chilies, jalapeño pepper if you wish), cumin, oregano, chicken broth, water, and beans to stockpot and stir well. Bring to a boil, reduce heat, and simmer, overed, 10–15 minutes.

3. Just before serving, add cayenne, salt, cheese, and sour cream. Heat just until cheese is melted, being careful not to let the soup boil.

4. Serve at once, garnished with chopped green onions and fresh cilantro if desired.

TIP

If you don't have cooked chicken, cut up 1½ lbs. skinless chicken breasts (about 1½ breasts) into 1-inch chunks. Follow Step 2 and proceed with the directions as given, being sure to simmer until the chicken is no longer pink.

Chilis

Turkey Chili

**Julette Rush,
Harrisonburg, VA**

Makes 5 servings
Prep. Time: 15 minutes
Cooking Time: 30 minutes

½ lb. ground turkey breast

1 cup chopped onions

½ cup chopped green bell pepper

½ cup chopped red bell pepper

14½-oz. can diced tomatoes, no salt added, undrained

15-oz. can solid-pack pumpkin

15½-oz. can pinto beans, rinsed and drained

½ cup water

2 tsp. chili powder

½ tsp. garlic powder

¼ tsp. black pepper

¾ tsp. ground cumin

14½-oz. can low-sodium, fat-free chicken broth

1 cup low-fat shredded cheddar cheese

1. In large stockpot, sauté turkey, onions, and bell peppers until turkey is browned and vegetables are softened.

2. Mix in tomatoes, pumpkin, beans, water, seasonings, and broth. Reduce heat to low.

3. Cover and simmer 20 minutes. Stir occasionally.

4. Top individual servings with cheese.

Chilis

Turkey Chili

Jackie Stefl,
East Bethany, NY

Makes 10 servings
Prep. Time: 15 minutes
Cooking Time: 2 hours 10 minutes

medium onion

medium green bell pepper

½ lbs. extra-lean ground turkey breast

Tbsp. extra-virgin olive oil

5½-oz. can kidney beans, rinsed and drained

5¼-oz. can black beans, rinsed and drained

5¼-oz. can corn, no salt added, drained

8-oz. can crushed tomatoes, no salt added, undrained

Tbsp. chili powder

tsp. cinnamon

tsp. ground cumin

low-sodium beef bouillon cubes

cups water

½ cups grated low-fat cheddar cheese, *optional*

¼ cup low-fat sour cream, *optional*

1. Chop onion and green pepper. Place in large stockpot, along with ground turkey and olive oil.

2. Sauté until meat is no longer pink and vegetables are tender.

3. Stir kidney and black beans and corn into stockpot.

4. Stir tomatoes, seasonings, bouillon cubes, and water into pot.

5. Cover. Simmer 2 hours. Stir occasionally.

6. Garnish individual servings, if you wish, with 1 rounded Tbsp. low-fat cheese and sour cream.

TIP

For spicier chili, add more chili powder to taste.

Chilis

Sausage Chili

**Norma I. Gehman,
Ephrata, PA**

Makes 4-6 servings
Prep. Time: 15 minutes
Cooking Time: 15 minutes

lb. loose sausage

¼ cup diced onion

Tbsp. flour

5½-oz. can chili beans in chili sauce

4½-oz. can diced tomatoes, undrained

1. Brown sausage in a large stockpot.

2. Add diced onion. Cook over medium eat until tender.

3. When onion is cooked, sprinkle 2 Tbsp. flour over mixture. Stir until flour is absorbed.

4. Add chili beans and diced tomatoes with juice. Mix well.

5. Simmer, covered, for 15 minutes.

TIPS

1. For more zip, use hot Italian sausage.
2. Crumble corn chips into the bottom of each serving bowl. Spoon chili over top of chips. Or crumble corn chips over top of each individual serving.
3. Grate your favorite cheese over top of each individual serving.
4. This recipe tastes even better when warmed up a day later.

Chilis

Three Bean Chili

Deb Kepiro,
Strasburg, PA

Makes 6 servings
Prep. Time: 15 minutes
Cooking Time: 30–60 minutes

1 large onion, chopped

2 Tbsp. oil

2 cups diced cooked chicken

15½-oz. can kidney beans, rinsed and drained

15½-oz. can pinto beans, rinsed and drained

15½-oz. can black beans, rinsed and drained

2 14½-oz. cans diced tomatoes

1 cup chicken broth

¾ cup salsa

1 tsp. cumin

¼ tsp. salt

shredded cheese, *optional*

green onions, *optional*

sour cream, *optional*

1. In a soup pot, sauté onion in oil until tender.

2. Add chicken, beans, tomatoes, broth, salsa, cumin, and salt.

3. Bring to a boil. Cover. Reduce heat and let simmer for 30–60 minutes.

4. If desired, garnish with shredded cheese, green onions, and sour cream.

Variation:
Add 1 cup corn, 1 Tbsp. chili powder, and 15½-oz. can undrained chili beans. Use 1 lb ground beef, browned, instead of chicken.
—Moreen Weaver, Bath, N

Vegetarian Chili

**Lois Hess,
Lancaster, PA**

Makes 8 servings
Prep. Time: 30 minutes
Cooking Time: 30 minutes

cup tomato juice, no salt added

½ cup raw bulgur

Tbsp. olive, canola, or saffron oil

cloves garlic

½ cups chopped onion

cup chopped celery

cup chopped carrots

cup chopped tomatoes

tsp. cumin

tsp. dried basil

-1½ tsp. chili powder, depending on your
taste preference

cup chopped green bell peppers

16-oz. cans red kidney beans, rinsed and
drained

uice of half a lemon

Tbsp. tomato paste, no salt added

dash cayenne pepper, or 1 tsp. coarsely
ground black pepper

chopped fresh parsley, for garnish

1. Heat tomato juice to a boil. Pour over bulgur in a bowl. Cover and let stand 15 minutes.

2. Meanwhile, sauté garlic and onion in oil in large stockpot.

3. Add celery, carrots, tomatoes, and spices.

4. When vegetables are almost tender, add peppers. Cook until tender.

5. Stir in all remaining ingredients except parsley. Cover and heat gently.

6. Top individual servings with parsley.

Chilis

Chickpea Chili

**Thelma Wolgemuth,
Immokalee, FL**

Makes 8 servings, ½ cup chili plus ¼ cup
brown rice and 1 Tbsp. yogurt per serving
Prep. Time: 15 minutes
Cooking Time: 35–40 minutes

1 small onion, minced

2 cloves garlic, minced

15-oz. can garbanzo beans, drained

2 8-oz cans tomato sauce

1 Tbsp. chili powder

1 tsp. ground cumin

½ tsp. dried oregano

cayenne pepper, to taste

⅔ cup fat-free plain yogurt

2 cups hot cooked brown rice

1. Sauté onion and garlic over medium
heat in a large saucepan.

2. Stir in garbanzo beans, tomato sauce,
chili powder, cumin, oregano, and cayenne.

3. Simmer, uncovered, about 30 minutes,
stirring occasionally. (If mixture becomes too
thick, add water.)

4. Pour into serving dish and top with
yogurt.

5. Serve with hot, cooked rice on the side.

Chowders

Basic Chowder Recipe

**Janie Steele,
Moore, OK**

Makes 6–8 servings
Prep. Time: 20 minutes
Cooking Time: 45 minutes

1 Tbsp. olive oil or butter

1–2 cups chopped onion

2 carrots, sliced

2 ribs celery, sliced

3–4 large potatoes, cubed

2 cups chicken broth

13-oz. can evaporated milk

½ tsp. garlic salt

pepper, to taste

2 cups milk

1. In oil or butter, sauté onion, carrots, and celery until they begin to soften.

2. Add potatoes and broth.

3. Bring to a boil, lower heat, and cover. Cook until potatoes soften.

4. Mash some of potatoes against side of pan.

5. Stir in evaporated milk, garlic salt, and pepper.

6. Add 2 cups milk.

7. Continue to cook and mash more potatoes until desired consistency.

Variations:

1. New England Clam: add 2 cans clams to completed chowder.

2. Corn: add 2 cups frozen corn or 1 can corn.

3. Ham: add 1 cup chopped ham.

4. Bacon: add 2 chopped or crumbled pieces of cooked bacon.

5. Add a bay leaf, minced garlic, and dried thyme to taste. Remove bay leaf before serving.

Chowders

Sweet Potato Chowder

**Deborah Heatwole,
Waynesboro, GA**

Makes 6 servings
Prep. Time: 15 minutes
Cooking Time: 25–30 minutes

1 celery rib, chopped

½ cup cooked, finely chopped, lean ham

2 Tbsp. olive oil

2 14½-oz. cans low-fat, low-sodium chicken broth

3 medium white potatoes, peeled and cubed

2 large sweet potatoes, peeled and cubed

2 Tbsp. dried minced onion

½ tsp. garlic powder

½ tsp. dried oregano

½ tsp. dried parsley

¼ tsp. black pepper

¼ tsp. crushed red pepper flakes

¼ cup flour

2 cups skim milk

1. In large stockpot, sauté celery and ham in oil.

2. Stir in broth. Add white and sweet potatoes and seasonings.

3. Bring almost to a boil. Reduce heat, cover, and simmer for 12 minutes, or until potatoes are tender.

4. Combine flour and milk in a bowl until smooth. Stir into soup.

5. Bring to a boil. Cook, stirring continually, for 2 minutes, or until thickened and bubbly. Be careful not to scorch or curdle milk.

Harvest Corn Chowder

**Flossie Sultzaberger,
Mechanicsburg, PA**

Makes 10 servings
Prep. Time: 20 minutes
Cooking Time: 40 minutes

1 medium onion, chopped

1 Tbsp. trans-fat–free tub margarine

2 14½-oz. cans no-salt-added cream-style corn

4 cups no-salt-added whole kernel corn

4 cups peeled, diced potatoes

6-oz. jar sliced mushrooms, drained

½ medium green pepper, chopped

½–1 medium sweet red pepper, chopped

10¾-oz. can lower-sodium, lower-fat
   mushroom soup

3 cups fat-free milk

pepper, to taste

½ lb. bacon, cooked and crumbled

1. In a large saucepan, sauté onion in margarine until tender.

2. Add cream-style corn, kernel corn, potatoes, mushrooms, peppers, soup, and milk. Add pepper, to taste.

3. Simmer 30 minutes or until vegetables are tender.

4. To serve, garnish with bacon.

Chowders

White Chili

Ruth E. Martin,
Loysville, PA

Makes 6 servings
Prep. Time: 15–20 minutes
Cooking Time: 20 minutes

2 cups diced potatoes, peeled or unpeeled

/₂ cup water

2 cups chopped broccoli, fresh, or 10-oz. pkg. chopped broccoli, frozen

2 Tbsp. onion

1 cup corn

/₄–¹/₂ cup cooked, diced ham, *optional*

3 cups milk

/₂ tsp. salt, *optional*

/₈ tsp. pepper

1 tsp. powdered chicken bouillon, or 1 chicken bouillon cube

/₂ cup Velveeta cheese, cubed

1. In medium-sized saucepan, cook potatoes in water. When potatoes are almost soft, add broccoli and onion. Cook until tender.

2. Add corn, ham, if you wish, milk, seasonings, and bouillon. Heat, but do not boil.

3. Turn off and add cubed cheese. Let cheese melt for about 3–4 minutes. Stir and serve.

Italian Clam Chowder

Susan Guarneri,
Three Lakes, WI

Makes 8 servings
Prep. Time: 30 minutes
Cooking Time: 4–5 hours

lbs. sweet Italian sausage

onion, chopped

medium potatoes, unpeeled and cubed

12-oz. cans beer

cups water or chicken broth

pt. cream

½ cup nonfat dry milk

dozen large fresh clams, chopped, or 6½-oz. can clams

-oz. can minced clams

½ tsp. salt

¼ tsp. pepper

tsp. dried basil

1. Cut sausage into ½-inch slices. Place in large Dutch oven and brown until no longer pink. Set sausage aside.

2. Reserve 2 Tbsp. drippings in Dutch oven. Add onion, potatoes, beer, water or broth, cream, dry milk, clams, salt, pepper, and basil. Stir until well mixed.

3. Place Dutch oven in the oven. Bake at 275°F for 4–5 hours. (Do not increase the temperature or the chowder may boil and then the cream will curdle.)

4. One hour before the end of the baking time, stir in the reserved sausage.

NOTE

I got this recipe from my Italian neighbor when I lived in Baltimore, Maryland. Fresh clams were easy to get and this filled up the entire family with leftovers for lunch. The chowder is even better the next day.

Salmon Chowder

Millie Martin,
Mount Joy, PA
Betty K. Drescher,
Quakertown, PA

Makes 6 servings
Prep. Time: 15–20 minutes
Cooking Time: 35 minutes

3 potatoes, diced

2 Tbsp. minced onion

2 Tbsp. diced celery

1 lb. can salmon, no salt added

½ cup corn

1 tsp. sage

1 tsp. dried basil

pepper, to taste

1 qt. skim milk

2 Tbsp. chopped fresh parsley

lemon zest, *optional*

1. In stockpot, cook potatoes, onions, and celery in small amount of water until tender.

2. Empty salmon into bowl. Remove bones and skin from salmon. Pull fish apart into pieces.

3. Add salmon, corn, sage, basil, pepper, and milk to vegetables in stockpot.

4. Cover. Heat slowly until very hot.

5. Top with chopped parsley, and lemon zest if you wish.

Main Dishes

Beef

Hearty Pot Roast

**Colleen Heatwole,
Burton, MI**

Makes 12 servings, about 1 cup per serving
Prep. Time: 30 minutes
Roasting Time: 2–2½ hours
Standing Time: 10 minutes

-lb. beef roast, ideally rump roast

 medium red potatoes, cut in thirds

 medium carrots, quartered

 ribs celery, chopped

 medium onions, sliced

½ cup flour

-oz. can tomato paste

¼ cup water

 tsp. instant beef bouillon, or 1 beef bouillon cube

¼ tsp. pepper

1. Place roast in 9x13-inch baking pan or roaster.

2. Arrange vegetables around roast.

3. Combine flour, tomato paste, water, bouillon, and pepper in small bowl.

4. Pour over meat and vegetables.

5. Cover. Roast at 325°F for 2–2½ hours, or until meat thermometer registers 170°F.

6. Allow meat to stand for 10 minutes.

7. Slice and place on platter surrounded by vegetables.

8. Pour gravy over top. Place additional gravy in bowl and serve along with platter.

Variation:

You can make this in a large oven cooking bag. Combine flour, tomato paste, water, bouillon, and pepper in a bowl. Pour into cooking bag. Place in 9x13-inch baking pan. Add roast to bag in pan. Add vegetables around roast in bag. Close bag with its tie. Make six ½-inch slits on top of bag. Roast according to instructions in Step 5 and following.

Savory Sweet Roast

Marie Hostetler,
Nappanee, IN

Makes 6–8 servings
Prep. Time: 20 minutes
Roasting Time: 2 hours
Standing Time: 20 minutes

3–4-lb. beef roast

1–2 Tbsp. olive oil

1 medium-sized onion, chopped

10¾-oz. can cream of mushroom soup

½ cup water

1 tsp. prepared mustard

2 tsp. salt

¼ cup vinegar

¼ cup sugar

1 tsp. Worcestershire sauce

1. In a large skillet, brown roast on all sides in olive oil.

2. Meanwhile, in a mixing bowl, blend together all other ingredients.

3. When roast is browned, place in roasting pan. Pour sauce ingredients over meat.

4. Cover and roast at 350°F for 2 hours, or until tender.

5. Let meat stand for 20 minutes. Slice and serve with sauce.

TIPS

1. The sauce that the roast is cooked in makes a succulent gravy. Serve over the meat, and over potatoes, rice, or pasta, if you've made one of them as a go-along.
2. I like to cut potato wedges and place them on top of the meat before roasting it. I like to do the same with julienned carrot sticks. Either of those combinations gives you a good meal all in one pan.

Beef

Aunt Iris's Barbecue Brisket

Carolyn Spohn,
Shawnee, KS

Makes 10 servings, 2 oz. meat with a little sauce
Prep. Time: 20-30 minutes
Marinating Time: 8 hours, or overnight
Baking Time: 3-4 hours
Standing Time: 30 minutes

-lb. lean beef brisket
¼ tsp. garlic powder
¼ tsp. onion powder
¼ tsp. celery salt
 oz. liquid smoke
 tsp. Worcestershire sauce

Barbecue sauce:
⅓ cup honey
¼ cup light soy sauce
⅓ cup ketchup
½ tsp. Tabasco sauce
 tsp. dry mustard
 tsp. paprika
 cup apple cider vinegar
 cup orange juice
 tsp. salt

1. Sprinkle both sides of brisket with garlic powder, onion powder, and celery salt. Sprinkle liquid smoke on both sides.

2. Place in large bowl or roaster. Refrigerate overnight, tightly covered.

3. In morning, drain meat. Return meat to pan.

4. Sprinkle with Worcestershire sauce.

5. Bake covered at 225°F for 3–4 hours, or until meat thermometer registers 175°F.

6. While brisket is roasting, prepare barbecue sauce by combining all ingredients in saucepan.

7. Cook uncovered, stirring occasionally, until sauce comes to a boil.

8. Continue simmering for 30 minutes, or until sauce thickens and reduces down.

9. When time is up on roast, turn off oven, but keep meat in oven for 30 more minutes.

10. Slice brisket and serve with barbecue sauce alongside or spooned over meat.

Beef

Herb-Marinated Steak

Linda E. Wilcox,
Blythewood, SC

Makes 4 servings
Prep. Time: 10 minutes
Marinating Time: 6–8 hours
Broiling Time: 12–18 minutes
Standing Time: 10 minutes

¼ cup chopped onion

2 Tbsp. fresh parsley

2 Tbsp. balsamic vinegar

1 Tbsp. olive oil

2 tsp. Dijon-style mustard

1 clove garlic, minced

1-lb. London broil, or chuck steak

1. Combine onion, parsley, vinegar, oil, mustard, and garlic in a bowl.

2. Place London broil or chuck steak in a sturdy plastic bag. Add onion mixture, spreading it on both sides of the meat. Close bag securely.

3. Place filled bag in a long dish in case of any leaks. Marinate in refrigerator 6–8 hours, or overnight. Turn it over at least once while marinating.

4. Pour off marinade. Place steak on rack in broiler pan so meat is about 5 inches from heat source. Broil about 6–8 minutes on each side for rare; 9 minutes on each side for medium.

5. When finished broiling, allow meat to stand for 10 minutes.

6. Carve diagonally across the grain into thin slices.

TIP

You can grill the steak, rather than broiling it.

Beef

Marinated Flank Steak

Flo Mast,
Broadway, VA

Makes 4–6 servings
Prep. Time: 10–15 minutes
Marinating Time: 3 hours
Broiling Time: 12 minutes
Standing Time: 10 minutes

½ cup bottled teriyaki sauce

¼ cup soy sauce

4 cloves garlic, chopped

2-lb. flank steak

¼ cup spicy brown mustard

TIP

Broil 1–2 minutes longer on each side for a medium-well-done steak.

1. In a shallow baking dish, combine the teriyaki sauce, soy sauce, and garlic.

2. Make ¼-inch-deep cuts about ½ inch apart on both sides of the steak, cutting diagonally across the grain.

3. Rub both sides with mustard. Place steak in marinade.

4. Cover and refrigerate for up to 3 hours, turning occasionally.

5. Preheat the broiler and line a shallow pan with foil. Broil for 6 minutes on each side for medium rare, basting once on each side with remaining marinade. Let rest before slicing across grain.

Beef

Wonderfully Tender Round Steak

Dorothy VanDeest,
Memphis, TN

Makes 6–8 servings
Prep. Time: 10 minutes
Cooking Time: 1½ hours

10¾-oz. can cream of mushroom soup

1 Tbsp. Worcestershire sauce

1 Tbsp. dried minced onion, or 2–3 Tbsp. chopped onion

3- to 4-lb. boneless round steak

1. Mix soup, Worcestershire sauce, and onion together in a small bowl.

2. Pour into large electric frying pan.

3. Place round steak on top of mixture.

4. Cover and cook on low for 45 minutes.

5. Turn meat over and cook on low for 45 minutes more.

6. Cut into serving-size pieces. Top with delicious gravy to serve.

Veggie and Beef Stir-Fry

Margaret H. Moffitt,
Middleton, TN

Makes 4 servings
Prep. Time: 15–20 minutes
Cooking Time: 30–35 minutes

/₄ lb. beef tenderloin

2 tsp. olive oil

1 onion, chopped coarsely

1 small zucchini, chopped coarsely

3 cups coarsely chopped broccoli florets

half a small yellow squash, chopped coarsely

½ cup uncooked brown rice

1 cup water

1 tsp. low-sodium teriyaki sauce

1. Cut beef into ¼-inch-wide strips.

2. In a good-sized skillet, stir-fry beef in 2 tsp. olive oil just until no longer pink, about 2 minutes.

3. Add onion and other vegetables. Stir-fry until tender-crisp, about 5–7 minutes.

4. To cook rice, place rice and water in a saucepan. Cover, and bring to a boil. Adjust heat so that mixture simmers, covered. Cook rice until tender, about 20–25 minutes.

5. Just before serving over rice, add teriyaki sauce to beef and vegetables.

Flavorful Beef Stroganoff

Susan Guarneri,
Three Lakes, WI

Makes 6 servings
Prep. Time: 25 minutes
Cooking Time: 1 hour 20 minutes

2 lbs. boneless chuck

¼ cup flour

1 tsp. salt

2 Tbsp. butter

1 medium-sized onion, chopped

1 clove garlic, crushed

10¾-oz. can cream of mushroom soup

½ tsp. cinnamon

¼ tsp. allspice

1 cup water

4-oz. can sliced mushrooms, undrained

1 pt. sour cream

1. Cut chuck in strips ½-inch thick.

2. Mix flour and salt. Dredge meat in flour/salt mixture.

3. Melt butter in large skillet. Brown flour-coated meat in butter over high heat. Stir often so that meat browns on all sides.

4. When meat is browned, turn down heat and add onion, garlic, soup, cinnamon, allspice, and water.

5. Cover and simmer 1 hour.

6. Reduce heat and stir in mushrooms and sour cream. Do not allow to boil, but simmer, covered, until heated through. Serve over egg noodles.

Beef

Grandma's Best Meatloaf

**Nanci Keatley,
Salem, OR**

Makes 10 servings, 1 slice per serving
Prep. Time: 15–25 minutes
Baking Time: 1 hour 5 minutes
Standing Time: 10 minutes

2 lbs. 90%-lean ground beef

2 Tbsp. chopped fresh Italian parsley

1 tsp. dried oregano

1 small onion, chopped fine

4 cloves garlic, minced

/₄ cup plus 2 Tbsp. Romano cheese, *optional*

/₂ cup dried bread crumbs

½ cup ketchup

½ cup egg substitute

1 tsp. black pepper

1 tsp. kosher salt

TIP

This is great for meatloaf sandwiches the next day—if you have any left!

1. In a large mixing bowl, mix together ground beef, parsley, oregano, onion, garlic, optional cheese, bread crumbs, ketchup, egg substitute, pepper, and salt.

2. Roll mixture into a large ball.

3. Place in well-greased 9x13-inch baking dish or roaster, flattening slightly.

4. Bake at 375°F for 1 hour. Keep in oven 5 more minutes with oven off and door closed.

5. Remove meatloaf from oven. Let stand 10 minutes before slicing to allow meatloaf to gather its juices and firm up.

Beef

Homemade Hamburgers

Janet Derstine,
Telford, PA

Makes 6 servings
Prep. Time: 30–35 minutes
Baking Time: 60 minutes

1 cup bread crumbs

½ cup milk

1 lb. ground beef

¼ cup chopped onion

1 tsp. salt

¼ tsp. pepper

Sauce:

3 Tbsp. brown sugar

1 Tbsp. vinegar

¼ cup ketchup

1 Tbsp. Worcestershire sauce

¼ cup barbecue sauce

½ cup water

1. In good-sized mixing bowl, moisten bread crumbs with milk.

2. Add ground beef, onion, salt, and pepper. Mix well. Set aside.

3. In a mixing bowl, mix sauce ingredients together.

4. Shape hamburger mixture into 6 patties.

5. Place in single layer in baking dish.

6. Pour sauce over patties.

7. Cover and bake at 375°F for 30 minutes.

8. Remove cover and bake another 30 minutes, basting occasionally with sauce.

TIP

You can double or triple the patties and freeze them for a later meal. (I make the sauce while I bake them.)

Beef

Baked Rice Moussaka

Rhoda Atzeff,
Harrisburg, PA

Makes 12 servings, ½ cup per serving
Prep. Time: 30 minutes
Baking/Cooking Time: 1 hour 20 minutes

1½ lbs. round steak, minced

1 Tbsp. canola oil

/₄ cup chopped green pepper

/₂ cup chopped onion

1 clove garlic, minced

/₂ cup uncooked rice

1 cup stewed tomatoes

1 tsp. salt

/₂ tsp. pepper

/₂ tsp. paprika

/₂ tsp. dried mint

2 cups hot water

3 eggs

Juice of ½ lemon

1. In a saucepan brown meat with canola oil. Add green pepper, onion, garlic, rice, tomatoes and seasonings. Sauté for 5 minutes.

2. Add water and mix well. Pour into baking dish.

3. Beat eggs well and stir in lemon juice. Pour over meat mixture.

4. Bake at 350°F for 1 hour.

Shepherd's Pie

Judi Manos,
West Islip, NY

Makes 6 servings
Prep. Time: 15 minutes
Cooking/Baking Time: 50 minutes

¼ lbs. red potatoes, unpeeled and cut in chunks

3 garlic cloves

lb. 95%-lean ground beef

2 Tbsp. flour

cups fresh vegetables of your choice (for example, carrots, corn, green beans, peas)

¼ cup beef broth, canned, or boxed, or your own homemade

Tbsp. ketchup

¼ cup fat-free sour cream

½ cup shredded reduced-fat sharp cheddar cheese, *divided*

1. In saucepan, cook potatoes and garlic in 1½ inches boiling water for 20 minutes, or until potatoes are tender.

2. Meanwhile, brown beef in large nonstick skillet.

3. Stir in flour. Cook 1 minute.

4. Stir in vegetables, broth, and ketchup. Cover. Cook 10 minutes, stirring frequently.

5. Drain cooked potatoes and garlic. Return to their pan.

6. Stir in sour cream. Mash until potatoes are smooth and mixture is well blended.

7. Stir ¼ cup cheddar cheese into mashed potatoes.

8. Spoon meat mixture into well-greased 8x8-inch baking dish.

9. Cover with mashed potatoes.

10. Bake at 375°F for 18 minutes.

11. Top with remaining cheddar cheese. Bake 2 minutes more, or until cheese is melted.

Variation:
If you don't have access to fresh vegetables, use leftovers from your fridge or frozen ones.

Beef

Italian Stuffed Cabbage

**Maxine "Meme" Phaneuf,
Washington Township, MI
Hope Comerford,
Clinton Township, MI**

Makes 6–8 servings
Prep. Time: 40 minutes
Cooking Time: 50 minutes

1 whole head of green cabbage

1 lb. ground beef, browned and drained

1 cup uncooked white rice

1 large onion, chopped

½ cup finely chopped Italian parsley

2 large tomatoes, chopped

3 cloves garlic, finely chopped

1 tsp. salt

¼ tsp. pepper

¼ cup olive oil

½ cup lemon juice

1. Place the whole head of cabbage in the microwave and cook on high for 15 minutes.

2. In a bowl, mix together the browned ground beef, rice, onion, parsley, tomatoes, garlic, salt, pepper, olive oil, and lemon juice.

3. When the time is up on the microwave, let the cabbage cool slightly, then peel the leaves off of the core.

4. Thin the vein on each leaf.

5. Stuff each leaf with about 2–3 Tbsp. of the stuffing mixture; tuck the leaves and roll them.

6. Place each cabbage roll into the bottom of a stockpot. Make sure they're packed in very tightly. When all the leaves are stuffed and stuffed into the pot, place a lid inside the pot to weigh them down.

7. Pour water into the pot, just enough to cover the leaves.

8. Cover and cook on medium heat for 25 minutes.

9. Simmer on low for an additional 25 minutes.

Un-Stuffed Peppers

Pat Bechtel,
Dillsburg, PA
Sharon Miller,
Holmesville, OH

Makes 6 servings
Prep. Time: 10–12 minutes
Cooking Time: 25 minutes

lb. ground beef

0-oz. jar spaghetti sauce

Tbsp. barbecue sauce, *optional*

large green peppers (3–4 cups), coarsely
    chopped

¼ cups water

cup instant rice

1. In a 12-inch nonstick skillet, brown
ground beef. Drain off drippings.

2. Stir in all remaining ingredients. Bring
to a boil over high heat.

3. Reduce heat to medium-low and cook,
covered, for 20 minutes, or until liquid is
absorbed and rice is tender.

Variation:
Instead of spaghetti sauce and water,
substitute 4 cups tomato juice or V8 juice.
—Sharon Miller,
Holmesville, OH

Upside-Down Pizza

Julia Rohrer,
Aaronsburg, PA
Janet L. Roggie,
Lowville, NY

Makes 10 servings, 2½x4½-inch rectangle
Prep. Time: 20–30 minutes
Baking Time: 25–30 minutes

14 oz. 95%-lean ground beef

1 chopped onion

1 medium red, or green, bell pepper, chopped

1 tsp. dried basil

1 tsp. dried oregano

2 cups pizza, or spaghetti, sauce

¼ lb. fresh mushrooms, chopped, or 4-oz. can chopped mushrooms, drained

1 cup grated part-skim mozzarella cheese

Batter:

¾ cup egg substitute

1½ cups fat-free milk

1½ Tbsp. oil

½ tsp. salt

1 tsp. baking soda

1¾ cups flour

sprinkle of dried oregano

sprinkle of grated Parmesan cheese

1. Brown meat with onion and pepper in large nonstick skillet.

2. Stir in seasonings, sauce, and mushrooms. Simmer 5–8 minutes.

3. Place in well-greased 9x13-inch baking pan.

4. Cover with grated cheese.

5. Prepare batter by beating egg substitute, milk, and oil together in good-sized mixing bowl.

6. Add salt, baking soda, and flour. Stir just until mixed.

7. Pour over cheese-meat mixture. Do not stir.

8. Sprinkle with oregano and Parmesan cheese.

9. Bake at 400°F for 25–30 minutes or until toothpick inserted in center of dough comes out clean.

Beef

Pizza Cups

**Barbara Smith,
Bedford, PA**

Makes 6 servings
Prep. Time: 20 minutes
Baking Time: 12–15 minutes

¾ lb. ground beef

6-oz. can tomato paste

1 Tbsp. minced onion

½ tsp. salt

1 tsp. Italian seasoning

1 tube refrigerated biscuits

½–¾ cup shredded mozzarella cheese

1. In skillet, brown beef. Drain.

2. Stir in tomato paste, onion, and seasonings.

3. Cook over low heat for 5 minutes, stirring frequently. Mixture will thicken.

4. Meanwhile, place biscuits in greased muffin tins. Press them in so they cover the bottom and sides of each cup.

5. Spoon about ¼ cup meat mixture into each biscuit-lined cup. Sprinkle with cheese.

6. Bake at 400°F for 12–15 minutes, or until brown.

Beef

Reuben Casserole

Joleen Albrecht,
Gladstone, MI

Makes 8–10 servings
Prep. Time: 25 minutes
Baking Time: 25 minutes

1½ cups Thousand Island salad dressing

1 cup sour cream

1 Tbsp. minced onions

12 slices dark rye bread, cubed, *divided*

1 lb. sauerkraut, drained

1½ lbs. corned beef, sliced and cut into bite-sized pieces

2 cups shredded Swiss cheese

¼ cup butter or margarine, melted

1. In a mixing bowl, stir together dressing, sour cream, and onions. Set aside.

2. Arrange bread cubes in a greased 9x13-inch baking dish, setting aside approximately 1 cup cubes for the top.

3. Top the bread with a layer of sauerkraut followed by a layer of corned beef.

4. Spread dressing mixture over corned beef. Sprinkle with Swiss cheese.

5. Top with remaining bread cubes. Drizzle with melted butter.

6. Cover and bake at 350°F for 15 minutes. Uncover and continue baking for about 10 minutes or until bubbly.

Pork and Lamb

Cranberry-Glazed Pork Roast

Cova Rexroad,
Kingsville, MD

Makes 6 servings
Prep. Time: 15 minutes
Roasting Time: 2 hours
Standing Time: 25–30 minutes

2½–3-lb. pork roast

1 tsp. salt

¼–½ tsp. pepper

16-oz. can whole berry cranberry sauce

½ cup orange juice

¼ cup brown sugar

Variation:
For the glaze, use ¼ cup honey, 1 tsp. grated
orange peel, ⅛ tsp. cloves, and ⅛ tsp.
nutmeg, instead of orange juice and brown
sugar.

—Chris Peterson
Green Bay, W

1. Rub the pork roast with salt and pepper.
Bake uncovered at 350°F for 1½ hours.

2. Meanwhile, combine cranberry sauce,
orange juice, and brown sugar in a small
saucepan. Cook over low heat until mixture
comes to a boil, making a thin sauce.

3. After the meat has roasted, brush ¼ of
the sauce over the roast and bake uncovered
another 30 minutes.

4. Remove the roast from the pan and
place it on a serving platter. Cover with foil
and allow to stand for 25–30 minutes. Slice
thinly and serve with the remaining sauce.

Pork and Lamb

Brown Sugar and Dijon-Marinated Pork Tenderloin

J. B. Miller,
Indianapolis, IN

Makes 4-6 servings
Prep. Time: 5 minutes
Marinating Time: 2-3 hours
Grilling Time: 15 minutes

½ cup soy sauce

¼ cup sherry vinegar

½ tsp. Dijon mustard

¼ cup brown sugar

2-lb. pork tenderloin

1. Combine the first four ingredients in a large ziplock plastic bag to make the marinade.

2. Place tenderloin in marinade and close bag. Surround meat with marinade, and then place in refrigerator for 2–3 hours.

3. Heat grill to medium-high. Remove tenderloin from bag, patting dry.

4. Grill tenderloin until desired doneness, 160°F for medium. Thinly slice into medallions and serve.

TIPS

1. Be sure grill is hot before placing tenderloin on grill. Tenderloin should have a thin, crisp crust.
2. This is especially good served with garlic mashed potatoes or polenta.
3. You can also prepare the tenderloin in your broiler.
4. Use a meat thermometer to be sure the meat is cooked sufficiently.

Pork and Lamb

Barbecued Spareribs

Jane Geigley,
Lancaster, PA

Makes 3-4 servings
Prep. Time: 15 minutes
Baking Time: 3-4 hours
Grilling or Roasting Time: 30 minutes

3 lbs. spareribs

Sauce:
½ cup chopped onions

2 Tbsp. butter

2 10½-oz. cans tomato soup

1 tsp. hot sauce

1 Tbsp. vinegar

1 cup brown sugar

⅓ cup Worcestershire sauce

¼ tsp. ground cloves

1. Lay ribs in a single layer in a roaster or on a baking sheet with sides. Cover.

2. Bake at 300°F for 3–3½ hours, or until meat is fall-off-the-bones tender.

3. Meanwhile, in medium-sized saucepan, cook onion in butter until tender.

4. Stir in soup, hot sauce, vinegar, brown sugar, Worcestershire sauce, and cloves.

5. Simmer, uncovered, 5 minutes, stirring often.

6. Continue roasting ribs, uncovered, in oven. Or move to grill.

7. Brush with sauce and roast or grill 5 minutes.

8. Turn ribs over and brush with sauce. Roast or grill 5 more minutes.

9. Turn and brush with sauce for a total of 20 more minutes.

Finger-Lickin' Spareribs

Susan Guarneri,
Three Lakes, WI

Makes 4 servings
Prep. Time: 25 minutes
Cooking Time: 1 hour 25 minutes

2 lbs. spareribs, cut in pieces

¼ cup oil

¼ cup chopped onions

¼ cup chopped green pepper

1 cup pineapple juice

¼ cup vinegar

¾ cup water

2 Tbsp. ketchup

1 Tbsp. soy sauce

¼ tsp. Worcestershire sauce

1 medium clove garlic, minced

½ cup brown sugar

2 Tbsp. cornstarch

1. Brown spareribs in oil in large skillet. Remove meat and pour off all but 2 Tbsp. drippings.

2. Add onions and green pepper to drippings and cook until tender. Stir in juice, vinegar, water, ketchup, soy sauce, Worcestershire sauce, and garlic. Bring to boil.

3. Blend brown sugar and cornstarch together and quickly stir into boiling mixture until thickened (a minute or two).

4. Reduce heat to low simmer and add meat. Cook uncovered for 1 hour, or until

tender. Stir occasionally so the sauce and meat do not burn. Check meat from time to time—it may take less than an hour to cook to fork-tender.

Variation:
Add 1 cup pineapple chunks plus 1 cup juice for a heartier dish. These were favorite "finger-lickin'" favorites of my kids when they were growing up. They fought for the last morsels of the sauce.

Tuscan-Style Pork Ribs with Balsamic Glaze

J. B. Miller,
Indianapolis, IN

Makes 6-8 servings
Prep. Time: 30 minutes
Standing (or Chilling) Time: 2-8 hours
Roasting/Broiling Time: 2 hours

2 Tbsp. olive oil

2 Tbsp. chopped fresh rosemary leaves, or
   1 tsp. dried rosemary

1½ Tbsp. kosher salt

1½ Tbsp. fennel seeds, or 1½ tsp. ground
   fennel

2 tsp. pepper

2 tsp. fresh chopped sage, or 1 tsp. dried sage

2 tsp. fresh chopped thyme, or ½ tsp. dried
   thyme

2 tsp. paprika

1 tsp. crushed red pepper, *optional,*
   depending on how much heat you like

1 tsp. ground coriander

½ tsp. ground allspice

5 lbs. pork ribs

3 Tbsp. balsamic vinegar

1. In a small bowl, combine olive oil, rosemary, salt, fennel seeds, pepper, sage, thyme, paprika, red pepper, coriander, and allspice.

2. Rub spice paste all over ribs and let stand at room temperature for 2 hours, or refrigerate overnight.

3. Preheat oven to 325°F.

4. Arrange ribs on a large, rimmed baking sheet or roasting pan, meaty side up.

5. Roast ribs uncovered for 2 hours, or until tender.

6. Preheat broiler. Brush meaty side of ribs with balsamic vinegar and broil 6 inches from heat until browned, about 2 minutes.

7. Let stand for 5 minutes, then cut between ribs, or serve in slabs.

TIP

You can use this glaze on pork chops, lamb chops, and cuts of chicken.

Gourmet Pork Chops

Elsie R. Russett,
Fairbank, IA

Makes 6 servings, 1 pork chop per serving
Prep. Time: 15–20 minutes
Baking Time: 60–75 minutes

2 Tbsp. vegetable oil

2 Tbsp. flour

1/4 tsp. salt

dash of pepper

6 loin pork chops, 1/2-inch thick

10 1/2-oz. can lower-sodium, lower-fat cream of chicken soup

3/4 cup water

1 tsp. ground ginger

1 tsp. dried rosemary, crushed

1/2 cup whole wheat panko bread crumbs

1. Place oil in good-sized skillet.

2. Combine flour, salt, and pepper in shallow but wide dish.

3. Dredge chops in mixture one at a time.

4. Place 2 or 3 chops in oil in skillet at a time, being careful not to crowd skillet. Brown chops over medium to high heat, 3–4 minutes on each side, until a browned crust forms.

5. As chops brown, place in well-greased 7x11-inch baking dish.

6. In bowl, combine soup, water, ginger, and rosemary.

7. Pour over chops.

8. Sprinkle with half the panko bread crumbs.

9. Cover. Bake at 350°F for 50–60 minutes or until chops are tender but not dry.

10. Uncover. Sprinkle with remaining panko bread crumbs.

11. Bake uncovered 10–15 minutes. Remove from oven and serve.

Zingy Pork Chops

**Jean H. Robinson,
Cinnaminson, NJ**

Makes 4 servings
Prep. Time: 10 minutes
Cooking Time: 20–25 minutes

4 boneless pork loin chops (about 1 lb.)

2 Tbsp. olive oil

½ cup apricot preserves, or orange marmalade

juice and zest of 1 lemon

¼ tsp. salt

½ tsp. white pepper

1 Tbsp. ground ginger, *optional*

1. Brown chops 3 minutes per side in a heavy skillet in about 2 Tbsp. olive oil over high heat. Do not crowd the skillet or the chops will steam in their juices rather than brown. It's better to brown them in batches.

2. Remove chops from skillet and keep warm. Reduce heat to low.

3. Add apricot preserves, lemon juice and zest, salt, pepper, and ginger if you wish, to pan drippings, as well as any juice from the pork chop plate.

4. When sauce ingredients are thoroughly blended and hot, return chops to skillet. Spoon sauce over chops. Continue heating until chops are hot but not overcooked.

Pork and Lamb

Pork Chops with Apple Stuffing

**Arlene Yoder,
Hartville, OH**

Makes 6 servings, 1 pork chop per serving
Prep. Time: 20 minutes
Cooking Time: 45–60 minutes

 bone-in pork chops, at least 1-inch thick,
  about 2 lbs. total

 Tbsp. canola oil

/₄ cup chopped celery

/₄ cup chopped onion

 apples, peeled, cored, and diced

/₄ cup sugar

/₂ cup bread crumbs, or cracker crumbs

/₄ tsp. salt

/₄ tsp. pepper

 tsp. chopped parsley

1. Cut a pocket about 1½-inch deep into
he side of each chop for stuffing.

2. Heat oil in skillet.

3. Stir celery and onion into oil in skillet.
Cook over medium heat until tender, stirring
frequently.

4. Stir in diced apples. Sprinkle with sugar.

5. Cover skillet. Cook apples over low heat
until tender and glazed.

6. Stir in bread crumbs.

7. Stir in salt, pepper, and parsley.

8. Spreading open the pocket in each chop
with your fingers, stuff with mixture.

9. Return half of stuffed chops to skillet.
Brown on both sides over medium to high
heat.

10. Remove browned chops to platter.
Cover to keep warm.

11. Repeat Step 9 with remaining chops.

12. Return other chops to skillet.

13. Reduce heat. Add a few tablespoons of
water.

14. Cover. Cook slowly over low heat until
done, about 20–25 minutes.

Pork and Lamb

Healthy Joes

**Gladys M. High,
Ephrata, PA**

Makes 4 servings
Prep. Time: 20 minutes
Cooking Time: 20 minutes

¾ lb. 90%-lean ground pork loin

1 cup chopped onion

1 medium bell pepper, chopped

1½ cups diced tomatoes, no salt added, undrained

1 medium zucchini, shredded, *optional*

1 Tbsp. chili powder

1 tsp. paprika

½ tsp. minced garlic

pepper, to taste

3 Tbsp. tomato paste

4 whole wheat hamburger buns

1. In large skillet, cook ground pork, onion, and bell pepper until meat is brown and onion is tender. Drain off drippings.

2. Stir in diced tomatoes, zucchini if you wish, chili powder, paprika, garlic, and pepper. Cover and bring to a boil. Reduce heat.

3. Add tomato paste to thicken. Simmer, uncovered, for 5 minutes.

4. Spoon mixture into buns and enjoy.

Italian Barbecue

Pat Bishop,
Bedminster, PA

Makes 8–10 servings
Prep. Time: 10 minutes
Cooking Time: 80 minutes

lb. bulk sausage, uncooked

lb. chipped steak, uncooked

large onions, cut in rings

medium-sized green peppers, sliced

-oz. can sliced mushrooms, drained

28-oz. jar spaghetti sauce

Tbsp. dried oregano

alt, to taste

3–10 hoagie rolls

1. In a large skillet, brown the sausage. Remove from pan and set aside.

2. Brown chipped steak in the sausage drippings in the same skillet. Pull steak apart with 2 forks. Remove from pan and set aside.

3. Brown onions and peppers in skillet drippings. Stir meats back in and add remaining ingredients. Cover and simmer 1 hour.

4. Serve on hoagie rolls.

Pork and Lamb

Smoked Sausage and Sauerkraut

**Joan Terwilliger,
Lebanon, PA**

Makes 6-8 servings
Prep. Time: 20 minutes
Baking Time: 1¾-2 hours

2 Tbsp. butter

3 apples, peeled, halved, sliced thickly

1 large sweet onion, halved, sliced thickly

4 Yukon Gold potatoes, peeled, cut in ½-inch cubes

½ cup light brown sugar, packed

¼ cup Dijon mustard

½–1 lb. kielbasa, sliced ½ inch thick, depending on amount of meat you like

1 cup apple cider, or Riesling

2 lbs. sauerkraut, rinsed and drained

1. Melt butter in large ovenproof Dutch oven over medium-high heat.

2. Sauté apples and onion 10 minutes in butter, stirring occasionally.

3. Add potatoes.

4. In small bowl, mix together sugar and mustard. Add to onion-potato mixture.

5. Place sausage slices on top of onion-potato mixture.

6. Pour in cider or wine.

7. Place sauerkraut on top of sausage.

8. Bake, covered, at 350°F for 1¾–2 hours, or until potatoes are tender.

Papa's Kielbasa Bake

Elaine Patton,
West Middletown, PA

Makes 12 servings
Prep. Time: 20 minutes
Baking Time: 60 minutes

3 lbs. kielbasa, or Polish sausage

12-oz. bottle chili sauce

20-oz. can crushed pineapple, including juice

1/2 cup brown sugar

1. Cut kielbasa or sausage into 3/4-inch-thick slices. Place in roasting pan.

2. Mix in sauce, pineapple and juice, and brown sugar until well blended.

3. Cover. Bake at 350°F for 40 minutes.

4. Stir. Continue baking, uncovered, for another 20 minutes.

TIP

Any leftovers make great sandwiches.

Pork and Lamb

Cumberland Stockpot

Esther Porter,
Minneapolis, MN

Makes 4 servings
Prep. Time: 10 minutes
Cooking Time: 60–75 minutes

4 bratwurst

1 small head of red cabbage

1 cup apple juice

3 Tbsp. currant jelly

1 Tbsp. cider vinegar

1 tsp. juniper berries, *optional*

1. Place bratwurst in good-sized saucepan.

2. Shred or chop cabbage coarsely. Add to saucepan with bratwurst.

3. In a small bowl, mix together apple juice, currant jelly, and vinegar. Add juniper berries, if using. Pour into saucepan containing cabbage and bratwurst.

4. Cover and simmer for 60–75 minutes, or until cabbage is tender.

Mother's Baked Ham

Dawn Ranck,
Lansdale, PA

Makes 6-8 servings
Prep. Time: 10 minutes
Baking Time: 60–75 minutes

2 1-lb. slices ham steaks, each 1¼-inch thick

1 tsp. dried mustard

4 Tbsp. brown sugar

milk to cover ham

1. Place ham in large baking pan.

2. Rub with mustard.

3. Sprinkle with sugar.

4. Add enough milk to barely cover ham. (Pour milk in along the side of the meat slices so as not to wash off the mustard and sugar.)

5. Cover with foil.

6. Bake at 325°F for 60–75 minutes, or until milk is absorbed.

Scalloped Potatoes and Ham

Sandra Chang,
Derwood, MD

4 servings
Prep. Time: 15 minutes
Cooking Time: 30 minutes
Standing Time: 5 minutes

4 medium-sized potatoes, peeled and sliced

¼ cup chopped onions

1 Tbsp. flour, *divided*

1 tsp. salt, *divided*

⅛ tsp. pepper, *divided*

1 cup diced cooked ham

1⅔ cups milk

1 Tbsp. butter or margarine

½ cup (2 oz.) shredded cheddar cheese

sprinkle of paprika

1. Arrange half of potatoes in greased 2-qt. microwavable casserole dish.

2. Sprinkle with onions, 1½ tsp. flour, ½ tsp. salt, and a pinch of pepper.

3. Layer remaining potatoes into dish. Add a layer of ham. Sprinkle with remaining flour, salt, and pepper.

4. Pour milk over top. Dot with butter.

5. Cover and microwave at 50% power for 30 minutes, or until potatoes are tender. Rotate dish one-quarter turn every 8 minutes.

6. Sprinkle with cheese and paprika.

7. Microwave, uncovered, at 50% power for 2 minutes, or until cheese is melted.

8. Cover and let stand for 5 minutes before serving.

Ham Loaf

Inez Rutt,
Bangor, PA

Makes 6–8 servings
Prep. Time: 20-30 minutes
Baking Time: 1–1¼ hours

¾ lb. ground ham
¾ lb. ground pork
1 egg
¼ cup minced onions
½ cup cracker crumbs
½ cup milk
pepper, to taste

Glaze:
½ cup brown sugar
1 Tbsp. dry mustard
¼ cup vinegar

1. In a large mixing bowl, mix ham, pork, egg, onions, cracker crumbs, milk, and pepper together until well blended. Form into a loaf, and then place in greased loaf pan.

2. Make glaze by mixing brown sugar, dry mustard, and vinegar together until smooth.

3. Pour glaze over top of ham loaf.

4. Bake at 350°F for 1–1¼ hours, or until well browned. Baste occasionally with glaze during baking.

Variation:
Add 8-oz. can crushed pineapple and juice to the glaze.
—Mary E. Wheatley, Mashpee, MA
—Janice Yoskovich, Carmichaels, PA

Pork and Lamb

Stromboli

Monica Leaman Kehr,
Portland, MI

Makes 6 servings
Prep. Time: 20 minutes
Rising Time: 30–40 minutes
Baking Time: 20 minutes
Standing Time: 10 minutes

1 loaf frozen bread dough, thawed

Italian seasoning

2 cups grated mozzarella cheese

3 oz. sliced pepperoni

4 oz. chipped cooked ham

½ cup sliced black olives

⅓ cup sliced mushrooms, *optional*

2 Tbsp. chopped onions, *optional*

2 Tbsp. chopped green or red bell pepper,
  optional

1. Thaw bread dough and roll to 10x15-inch rectangle on lightly floured surface.

2. Sprinkle dough with Italian seasoning. Cover entire rectangle with cheese, pepperoni, ham, black olives, and any of the other ingredients you want. Press toppings down gently into dough.

3. Starting with the long side of the rectangle, roll dough up into a log shape. Seal ends by pinching dough together.

4. Carefully lift onto a lightly greased baking sheet. Cover and allow to rise 30–40 minutes.

5. Bake on sheet for 20 minutes at 400°F, or until lightly browned.

6. Allow to stand for 10 minutes before slicing.

TIP

Microwave pepperoni slices between paper towels before putting in stromboli to eliminate some calories.

Pork and Lamb

Italian Subs

Susan Kasting,
Jenks, OK

Makes 6 servings
Prep. Time: 15 minutes
Cooking Time: 15 minutes

6 Italian sausages

1 green bell pepper, sliced in ¼-inch strips

1 red bell pepper, sliced in ¼-inch strips

1 medium-sized onion, sliced in ¼-inch rounds

6 hoagie rolls, split

1. Pan-fry sausages, or grill, until browned on all sides.

2. In a separate pan sprayed with nonstick cooking spray, heat to medium-high heat and sauté the peppers and onions until tender-crisp.

3. Place one sausage and a generous amount of the pepper-onion mix in each hoagie roll. Serve immediately.

Hoosier Lamb Chops

Willard E. Roth,
Elkhart, IN

Makes 6 servings
Prep. Time: 10 minutes
Cooking Time: 20 minutes

1 Tbsp. oil

6 lamb chops

1 onion, finely chopped

1 Tbsp. balsamic vinegar

1 tsp. coarsely ground black pepper

¼ cup black currant or black raspberry jam

¼ cup red wine

1 Tbsp. chopped fresh mint

1. Heat oil in skillet over medium heat. Cook chops, 2 or 3 at a time, for 2 minutes per side until browned. Set aside. Reserve drippings.

2. Sauté onion for 1 minute in same skillet. Add vinegar, pepper, jam, and wine to skillet. Cook until thickened. Stir in fresh mint.

3. Return chops to skillet. Cook 2–3 minutes per side, or until just done. Adjust seasoning. Serve.

TIP

This sauce makes a good gravy for couscous. If you want to do that, double the amounts of the sauce ingredients and proceed according to the recipe.

Chicken

Chicken Baked with Red Onions, Potatoes, and Rosemary

Kristine Stalter,
Iowa City, IA

Makes 8 servings
Prep. Time: 10–15 minutes
Baking Time: 45–60 minutes

2 red onions, each cut into 10 wedges

1¼ lbs. new potatoes, unpeeled and cut into chunks

2 garlic bulbs, separated into cloves, unpeeled

salt and pepper, to taste

3 tsp. extra-virgin olive oil

2 Tbsp. balsamic vinegar

approximately 5 sprigs rosemary

8 chicken thighs, skin removed

1. Spread onions, potatoes, and garlic in single layer over bottom of large roasting pan so that they will crisp and brown.

2. Season with salt and pepper.

3. Pour over the oil and balsamic vinegar and add rosemary, leaving some sprigs whole and stripping the leaves off the rest.

4. Toss vegetables and seasonings together.

5. Tuck chicken pieces among vegetables.

6. Bake at 400°F for 45–60 minutes, or until chicken and vegetables are cooked through.

7. Transfer to a big platter, or take to the table in the roasting pan.

Chicken

Lemon-Chicken Oven Bake

Judi Manos,
West Islip, NY

Makes 4 servings
Prep. Time: 10-15 minutes
Baking Time: 45-50 minutes

/₄ cup zesty Italian dressing

½ cup chicken broth

1 Tbsp. honey

1½ lbs. bone-in chicken legs and thighs

1 lb. new potatoes, quartered

5 cloves garlic, peeled

1 lemon, cut in 8 wedges

1 tsp. dried rosemary, *optional*

1. In a mixing bowl, blend together dressing, broth, and honey.

2. Arrange chicken, potatoes, and garlic in well-greased 9x13-inch baking dish.

3. Drizzle with dressing mixture.

4. Situate lemons and rosemary, if using, among the chicken and potatoes.

5. Bake at 400°F for 45–50 minutes, or until chicken is done and potatoes are tender. (Temperature probe inserted into center of chicken should register 165°F.)

6. Serve lemons as garnish if you wish.

Chicken

Cranberry Chicken

Judi Manos,
West Islip, NY

Makes 8 servings
Prep. Time: 10 minutes
Baking Time: 50 minutes

4 lbs. skinless, bone-in chicken pieces; your choice of breast halves or thighs

16-oz. can whole berry cranberry sauce

8-oz. bottle Catalina dressing

1 envelope onion soup mix

1. Place chicken in single layer in two well-greased 9x13-inch baking dishes.

2. In mixing bowl, blend together cranberry sauce, Catalina dressing, and onion soup mix.

3. Pour over chicken pieces.

4. Bake 50 minutes, or until chicken is done. Thermometer inserted in center of meat should register 165°F.

Orange Chicken

Jan Mast,
Lancaster, PA

Makes 6 servings
Prep. Time: 5 minutes
Cooking/Baking Time: 40 minutes

6 boneless, skinless chicken breast halves

6-oz. can orange juice concentrate, undiluted

1 tsp. paprika

1 tsp. dried rosemary

1 tsp. dried basil

1. Place chicken on a baking sheet.

2. Broil 3–5 minutes on each side until golden brown.

3. Remove from oven and place meat in a 9x13-inch baking pan. Reduce heat to 350°F.

4. Pour orange juice concentrate over chicken. Sprinkle with paprika and then with herbs.

5. Bake uncovered 30 minutes, or until done and juices run clear when pierced with a fork.

Chicken

Almond Lemon Chicken

**Judi Janzen,
Salem, OR**

Makes 6 servings
Prep. Time: 35–40 minutes
Marinating Time: 1 hour
Cooking Time: 25–30 minutes

5 Tbsp. lemon juice

3 Tbsp. prepared mustard

2 cloves garlic, finely chopped

6 Tbsp. olive oil, *divided*

6 boneless, skinless chicken breast halves

1 cup sliced almonds

2 cups chicken broth

1 tsp. cornstarch dissolved in 1 Tbsp. water

2 Tbsp. orange or lemon marmalade

2 Tbsp. chopped fresh parsley

¼ tsp. red pepper flakes

1. In a large bowl, combine first three ingredients. Stir in 5 Tbsp. oil. Add chicken and marinate 1 hour at room temperature.

2. Meanwhile, in large skillet, sauté almonds in ½ Tbsp. oil until golden. Remove almonds from pan and set aside. Reserve drippings. Add remaining ½ Tbsp. oil.

3. Drain chicken, reserving marinade. Cook chicken over medium-high heat in skillet until brown on each side, about 6–10 minutes total, or until tender. Remove and keep warm.

4. Pour marinade into pan. Add chicken broth and cornstarch mixture. Cook over high heat, until it boils and is reduced by slightly more than half, about 5 minutes. Stir occasionally to loosen browned bits from skillet and to keep sauce smooth.

5. Add marmalade and stir over medium heat until melted. Stir in parsley and red pepper flakes.

6. Return chicken to pan and heat through.

7. Place chicken on serving platter. Spoon sauce over. Sprinkle with toasted almonds.

Oven Barbecued Chicken

Carol Eberly,
Harrisonburg, VA

Makes 8–12 servings
Prep. Time: 10 minutes
Baking Time: 1¼ hours

3 Tbsp. ketchup

2 Tbsp. Worcestershire sauce

2 Tbsp. vinegar

2 Tbsp. soy sauce

3 Tbsp. brown sugar

1 tsp. spicy brown mustard

1 tsp. salt

1 tsp. pepper

8–12 boneless, skinless chicken thighs

TIP

You can use chicken legs or chicken breasts, too. Check the legs after they've baked for a total of 50 minutes to be sure they're not drying out. Check breasts after they've baked for a total of 30 minutes to be sure they're not becoming dry.

1. In a mixing bowl, combine ketchup, Worcestershire sauce, vinegar, soy sauce, brown sugar, mustard, salt, and pepper. Blend well.

2. Lay chicken pieces in one layer in well-greased baking dish.

3. Pour sauce over top.

4. Bake at 350°F for 40 minutes.

5. Turn pieces over. Bake 35 more minutes.

Jalapeño Chicken

Hope Comerford,
Clinton Township, MI

Makes 4-6 servings
Prep. Time: 5 minutes
Cooking Time: 40-45 minutes

6-8 chicken thighs or legs, or a combination of the two

5 Tbsp. butter or coconut oil

10½ oz. jalapeño jelly (hot or mild depending on the spiciness you like)

2 Tbsp. minced onion

½ tsp. ginger

1 tsp. garlic powder

1 Tbsp. soy sauce, or liquid aminos

1. In a frying pan, melt the butter and sear the chicken on both sides over medium-high heat.

2. In a small bowl, mix together the jalepeño jelly, minced onion, ginger, garlic powder, and soy sauce. Pour this mixture over the chicken. Cover and cook on medium-low heat for 35 minutes, flipping occasionally.

3. Uncover and turn the heat up to medium-high. Baste the chicken and flip it frequently for 5–10 minutes more.

Honey-Glazed Chicken

**Laura R. Showalter,
Dayton, VA**

Makes 6-8 servings
Prep. Time: 10-20 minutes
Baking Time: 1½ hours

3 lbs. chicken pieces

5⅓ Tbsp. (⅓ cup) butter, melted

⅓ cup honey

2 Tbsp. prepared mustard

1 tsp. salt

1 tsp. curry powder, *optional*

1. Place chicken skin side up in a 9x13-inch baking dish. (The dish is just as tasty if you remove skin from chicken!)

2. Combine remaining ingredients in a small bowl. Pour over chicken.

3. Bake uncovered at 350°F for 1 hour. Baste every 15–20 minutes. Cover and continue baking 30 minutes, or until chicken is tender and juices run clear when pierced with a sharp fork.

TIP

If you are unable to baste the chicken while baking, double the sauce so that it almost covers the chicken.

Chicken

Barbecued Chicken Thighs

**Ida H. Goering,
Dayton, VA**

Makes 6 servings
Prep. Time: 10 minutes
Marinating Time: 2–4 hours
Grilling Time: 15–22 minutes

6 Tbsp. apple cider vinegar

3 Tbsp. canola oil

3 Tbsp. ketchup

¼ tsp. black pepper

¼ tsp. poultry seasoning

12 boneless, skinless chicken thighs

1. Combine all ingredients except chicken thighs in a large bowl.

2. Submerge thighs in sauce in bowl.

3. Marinate 2–4 hours, stirring several times to be sure meat is well covered.

4. Grill over medium heat, turning after 10–15 minutes.

5. Grill another 5–7 minutes. Watch carefully so meat doesn't dry out. Remove from grill earlier if finished.

Chicken Cacciatore

**Linda Thomas,
Sayner, WI**

Makes 4–5 servings
Prep. Time: 10 minutes
Cooking/Baking Time: 1 hour 10 minutes

/2 cup oil

❚ whole chicken, cut up

/4 cup water

❚0½-oz. can tomato soup

❚ Tbsp. cider vinegar

2 tsp. dried oregano

/2 tsp. salt

/4 tsp. pepper

❚ green pepper, sliced, *optional*

1. Heat oil in large skillet. Brown chicken pieces in batches, placing them in a greased ❚x13-inch baking dish as they finish browning.

2. In a small mixing bowl, combine water, soup, vinegar, oregano, salt, and pepper. Mix well; then spoon one-third of sauce over chicken pieces. Bake uncovered at 350°F for ❚5 minutes.

3. Remove from oven and spoon another one-third of the sauce over the chicken. Bake uncovered for another 20 minutes.

4. Remove from oven and spoon the remaining third of the sauce over the meat. Top with green pepper slices if you wish. Bake uncovered for 20–25 minutes more.

Salsa Chicken

**Barbara Smith,
Bedford, PA**

Makes 4 servings
Prep. Time: 10-15 minutes
Baking Time: 35-45 minutes

4 boneless, skinless chicken breast halves

4 tsp. dry taco seasoning mix

1 cup salsa

1 cup shredded cheddar cheese

2 Tbsp. sour cream, *optional*

1. Place chicken in a lightly greased 9x13-inch baking dish.

2. Sprinkle top and bottom of each breast with taco seasoning.

3. Spoon salsa over chicken.

4. Bake covered at 375°F for 25–30 minutes, or until chicken is tender and juicy. Sprinkle with cheese.

5. Return to oven and continue baking uncovered for 10 minutes, or until cheese is melted and bubbly.

6. Top with sour cream as you serve the chicken, if you wish.

Yogurt Chicken Curry

Laverne Nafziger,
Goshen, IN

Makes 12 servings
Prep. Time: 20 minutes
Marinating Time: 8 hours, or overnight
Cooking Time: 2 hours

2½ lbs. boneless, skinless chicken breasts, cut into 1-inch cubes

2 lbs. plain nonfat yogurt

4 heaping tsp. curry powder

2 heaping tsp. turmeric

1 heaping tsp. ground coriander

2 Tbsp. vegetable oil

1 large onion, chopped

5 garlic cloves, chopped

1-inch gingerroot, grated or finely chopped

½ tsp. salt

1 cup sour cream

1 medium potato, grated

1 cup chopped cilantro, *optional*

1. Mix chicken, yogurt, curry powder, turmeric, and coriander in large nonmetallic bowl. Marinate in refrigerator 8 hours or overnight.

2. Sauté onion, garlic, and ginger in oil in large stockpot 2–5 minutes until lightly brown.

3. Add chicken-yogurt mixture, salt, sour cream, and grated raw potato.

4. Cover. Simmer gently for 2 hours.

5. Just before serving, stir in cilantro if you wish.

6. Serve over cooked rice.

Chicken

Easy Chicken Enchiladas

**Lois Peterson,
Huron, SD**

Makes 4 servings
Prep. Time: 35–45 minutes
Baking Time: 40 minutes

10¾-oz. can cream of chicken soup

½ cup sour cream

1 cup picante sauce

2 tsp. chili powder

2 cups chopped cooked chicken

1 cup grated pepper jack cheese

6 6-inch flour tortillas

1 medium tomato, chopped

1 green onion, sliced

1. Stir soup, sour cream, picante sauce, and chili powder in a medium bowl.

2. In a large bowl, combine 1 cup sauce mixture, chicken, and cheese.

3. Grease 9x13-inch baking dish.

4. Divide mixture among tortillas.

5. Roll up each tortilla. Place in baking dish, seam side down.

6. Pour remaining sauce mixture over filled tortillas.

7. Cover. Bake at 350°F for 40 minutes or until enchiladas are hot and bubbling.

8. Top with chopped tomato and onion and serve.

Easy Chicken Fajitas

**Jessica Hontz,
Coatesville, PA**

Makes 4–6 servings
Prep. Time: 20 minutes
Marinating Time: 4–8 hours, or overnight
Cooking Time: 10 minutes

1 lb. boneless, skinless chicken breasts

1 pkg. dry Italian salad dressing mix

8-oz. bottle Italian salad dressing

1 cup salsa

1 green pepper, sliced

half a medium-sized onion, sliced

10 10-inch flour tortillas

Optional toppings:
shredded Monterey Jack cheese

shredded lettuce

sour cream

chopped tomatoes

salsa

hot pepper sauce

1. Cut chicken into thin strips. Place in large mixing bowl.

2. Add dry salad dressing mix and salad dressing. Mix well. Cover and marinade 4–8 hours in the fridge.

3. In a large skillet, combine drained chicken strips, salsa, and pepper and onion slices. Stir-fry until chicken is cooked and peppers and onions are soft.

4. Place chicken mix in tortillas with your choice of toppings.

Variation:
The cooked chicken can also be used on salads.

Skinny Chicken Stroganoff

Carol Sherwood,
Batavia, NY

Makes 6 servings
Prep. Time: 10–15 minutes
Cooking Time: 20–25 minutes

4 slices turkey bacon, cooked and broken

5 oz. uncooked whole wheat noodles

¾ cup reduced-fat sour cream

¼ cup all-purpose flour

14½-oz. can low-fat, low-sodium chicken broth

⅛ tsp. black pepper

1 lb. boneless, skinless chicken breasts, cut into ¼-inch strips

3 oz. sliced fresh mushrooms

1 cup chopped onion

1 clove garlic, pressed

2 Tbsp. snipped fresh parsley

1. Cook bacon until crisp in a large skillet. Remove from pan, break, and set aside.

2. Cook noodles according to package instructions. Drain and keep warm.

3. Meanwhile, in a good-sized bowl, whisk together sour cream and flour until smooth.

4. Gradually whisk in chicken broth until smooth. Stir in pepper. Set aside.

5. Heat skillet that you used for bacon over high heat until hot. Add chicken. Cook, stirring continually for 3 minutes, or until meat is no longer pink. Remove from pan and set aside. Keep warm.

6. Reduce heat to medium. Add mushrooms, onion, and garlic. Cook and stir 3 minutes.

7. Stir in chicken and bacon.

8. Stir in sour cream mixture. Bring to a boil.

9. Reduce heat. Simmer 2 minutes, stirring constantly.

10. Remove from heat. Stir in parsley.

11. Serve over prepared noodles.

Chicken in Alfredo Sauce

Joyce Clark,
East Amherst, NY

Makes 4-6 servings
Prep. Time: 20-30 minutes
Cooking/Baking Time: 30-35 minutes

½ cup cooked spinach, stems removed, or frozen chopped spinach, thawed

4 boneless, skinless chicken breast halves, slightly flattened

2 thin slices ham, each cut in half

¼ red bell pepper, cut in thin strips

1 Tbsp. butter

2 Tbsp. flour

1 clove garlic, minced

¾ cup whipping cream

1¼ cups milk

1 tsp. grated lemon peel

pinch of ground nutmeg

¼ tsp. salt

¼ cup grated Parmesan cheese

1 Tbsp. chopped fresh parsley

cooked rice or pasta

1. Squeeze spinach until dry. Divide evenly over chicken breasts. Top each breast with a half slice of ham and a few red pepper strips.

2. Roll breasts up firmly, beginning at thinnest end of breast. Secure each with a toothpick and place, seam side down, in a single layer in a greased baking pan. Set aside.

3. In a small saucepan, melt butter. Add flour, garlic, cream, milk, lemon peel, nutmeg, salt, Parmesan cheese, and parsley. Stir and blend well. Cook over low heat, stirring occasionally until sauce begins to gently boil. Then stir continuously until smooth and thickened. Pour over chicken rolls.

4. Cover and bake at 350°F for 20 minutes turning after 10 minutes. Baste rolls with sauce.

5. Uncover and stir sauce as well as you can. Spoon up over chicken. Bake 5–7 minutes more.

6. To serve, cut meat rolls in half and serve over rice or pasta. Whisk sauce smooth and ladle over top.

Chicken and Broccoli Bake

Jan Rankin,
Millersville, PA

Makes 12–16 servings
Prep. Time: 15 minutes
Baking Time: 30 minutes

2 10¾-oz. cans cream of chicken soup

2½ cups milk, *divided*

16-oz. bag frozen chopped broccoli, thawed and drained

3 cups cooked, chopped chicken breast

2 cups buttermilk baking mix

1. Mix soup and 1 cup milk together in large mixing bowl until smooth.

2. Stir in broccoli and chicken.

3. Pour into well-greased 9x13-inch baking dish.

4. Mix together 1½ cups milk and baking mix in mixing bowl.

5. Spoon evenly over top of chicken-broccoli mixture.

6. Bake at 450°F for 30 minutes.

Simmering Chicken Dinner

Trish Dick,
Ladysmith, WI

Makes 4 servings
Prep. Time: 10 minutes
Cooking Time: 40 minutes

2½ cups chicken broth

½ cup apple juice

1 bay leaf

½ tsp. garlic powder

½ tsp. paprika

¼ tsp. salt

1½ lbs. boneless, skinless chicken breasts, or thighs, cut into chunks

1 cup uncooked whole-grain rice

3 cups fresh, or frozen, vegetables (your choice of one, or a mix)

½ tsp. paprika, *optional*

parsley as garnish, *optional*

1. Heat chicken broth, apple juice, bay leaf, garlic powder, paprika, and salt in large skillet until boiling, stirring occasionally.

2. Add chicken. Cover. Reduce heat and simmer 10 minutes on low.

3. Turn chicken.

4. Add 1 cup rice around chicken.

5. Top with the vegetables.

6. Cover. Simmer 25 minutes, or until rice is cooked, vegetables are as soft as you like, and chicken is done.

7. Remove bay leaf.

8. Sprinkle with paprika and parsley before serving if you wish.

TIP

If you like a bit of zip, add curry powder in place of paprika.

Chicken

Chicken and Dumplings

Barbara Nolan,
Pleasant Valley, NY

Makes 4 servings
Prep. Time: 15 minutes
Cooking Time: 30 minutes

4 carrots, cut into ½-inch-thick slices

2 medium onions, cut into eighths

1 clove garlic, sliced thin

3 celery ribs, cut into ½-inch-thick slices

2 Tbsp. butter

3 Tbsp. flour

2 14-oz. cans chicken broth

1 lb. uncooked chicken cutlets, cut into 1-inch cubes

2 Tbsp. grated carrots

½ tsp. poultry seasoning

¼ tsp. garlic powder

⅛ tsp. black pepper

¼ cup half-and-half

fresh parsley

Dumplings:
1½ cups flour

2 tsp. baking powder

¾ tsp. salt

1 cup milk

1 egg

2 Tbsp. vegetable oil

1. Sauté carrot pieces, onions, garlic, and celery in butter in medium sauce pan for 3 minutes, or until vegetables soften.

2. Sprinkle with flour.

3. Stir to combine. Cook 1–2 minutes.

4. Stir in chicken broth, chicken, grated carrots, poultry seasoning, garlic powder, and pepper until smooth.

5. Bring to boil. Simmer 5 minutes, or until thickened, stirring constantly.

6. To prepare dumplings, mix together flour, baking powder, and salt in mixing bowl.

7. In a separate bowl, combine milk, egg, and oil.

8. Add egg-milk mixture to dry ingredients, barely mixing.

9. Drop dumpling batter by tablespoonfuls onto simmering chicken.

10. Cook 10 minutes uncovered.

11. Cover and cook an additional 10 minutes.

12. Pour half-and-half between dumplings into broth.

13. Scatter fresh parsley over top. Serve immediately.

TIP

Chop all veggies and chicken beforehand and refrigerate until you're ready to make the dish. Doing so makes it very fast to prepare this dish.

Chicken Divan

Linda Sluiter,
Schererville, PA

Makes 4 servings
Prep. Time: 20 minutes
Baking Time: 1 hour

2 cups cooked and cubed chicken

2 10¾-oz. cans cream of chicken soup

1 lb. frozen broccoli, thawed and drained

1 cup Minute Rice

2 Tbsp. butter, melted

1 cup milk

8 oz. shredded cheddar cheese

1. In large mixing bowl, stir together chicken, soup, broccoli, rice, butter, milk, and cheese.

2. Pour into greased 9x13-inch baking pan.

3. Bake, covered, at 350°F for 30 minutes.

4. Remove cover. Bake 30 more minutes.

Chicken Parmesan

Jessalyn Wantland,
Napoleon, OH

Makes 4 servings
Prep. Time: 10 minutes
Baking Time: 45 minutes

4 boneless, skinless chicken breast halves,
   about 6 oz. each

1 egg, beaten

¾ cup Italian-seasoned bread crumbs

25-oz. jar pasta sauce

1 cup shredded Parmesan cheese

1. Grease 7x11-inch baking dish.

2. Place egg in shallow bowl.

3. Place bread crumbs in another shallow bowl.

4. Dip each piece of chicken in egg, and then in bread crumbs.

5. Place coated chicken in baking dish.

6. Bake at 400°F for 30 minutes.

7. Spoon pasta sauce over chicken.

8. Top evenly with cheese.

9. Bake another 15 minutes, or until heated through and cheese is melted.

Chicken

Oven-Fried Chicken

Eleanor Larson,
Glen Lyon, PA

Makes 8 servings
Prep. Time: 5–10 minutes
Baking Time: 1 hour

½ cup flour

¼ tsp. paprika

½ tsp. salt

8 boneless, skinless chicken thighs, each about 6 oz.

1 stick (8 Tbsp.) butter, melted, *divided*

TIP

You can double this for a larger group.

1. Grease a 9x13-inch baking dish well.

2. Combine flour, paprika, and salt in plastic bag.

3. Drop chicken into bag, one piece at a time. Shake to coat well.

4. Place coated pieces of chicken in baking dish.

5. Pour half of melted butter evenly over chicken.

6. Bake at 375°F for 30 minutes.

7. Turn each piece over.

8. Pour remaining butter evenly over chicken.

9. Return to oven. Bake an additional 30 minutes.

Chicken

Corn Bread Chicken

Kaye Taylor,
Florissant, MO

Makes 6 servings
Prep. Time: 10 minutes
Cooking/Baking Time: 30 minutes

3½-oz. pkg. corn bread mix

1 envelope dry ranch salad dressing mix

1 cup milk

6 4-oz. boneless, skinless chicken breast
   halves

2 Tbsp. oil

1. In large resealable plastic bag, combine corn bread mix and salad dressing mix.

2. Pour milk into shallow bowl.

3. Dip chicken in milk, then place in bag with dry mixes and shake to coat.

4. In large skillet, heat oil over medium-high heat. Brown half the chicken on both sides. Remove and keep warm. Repeat with second batch. (Doing the chicken in two batches allows each piece to brown rather than steam, which happens when the skillet is crowded.)

5. Place browned chicken in 9x13-inch baking pan and bake uncovered for about 15 minutes, or until juices run clear.

Crispy Ranch Chicken

Barb Shirk, Hawkins, WI
Arlene Snyder, Millerstown, PA
Doyle Rounds, Bridgewater, VA
Pat Chase, Fairbank, IA

Makes 6-8 servings
Prep. Time: 10 minutes
Baking Time: 20-25 minutes

¾-2 cups crispy rice cereal

¾ cup grated Parmesan cheese

1 envelope dry ranch dressing mix

2 egg whites, beaten

8 boneless, skinless chicken thighs, about
   5 oz. each

1. Preheat oven to 350°F.

2. Spray a large baking sheet with nonstick cooking spray.

3. Combine rice cereal, Parmesan cheese, and dry dressing mix in a large bowl.

4. Place beaten egg whites in a medium-sized bowl.

5. Dip each chicken thigh in the egg whites, and then in the cereal.

6. Arrange the coated chicken on the prepared baking sheet.

7. Bake for about 20–25 minutes, or until chicken is golden and juices run clear when meat is pierced with a knife.

Variations:

1. Substitute crushed cornflakes for the rice cereal.

2. Substitute 1 stick (8 Tbsp.) melted butter for the 2 beaten egg whites.

3. Substitute 8 boneless, skinless chicken breast halves, or 1 cut-up fryer, for the thighs.

Baked Chicken Fingers

Lori Rohrer,
Washington Boro, PA

Makes 6 servings
Prep. Time: 20 minutes
Baking Time: 20 minutes

1½ cups fine, dry bread crumbs

½ cup grated Parmesan cheese

1½ tsp. salt

1 Tbsp. dried thyme

1 Tbsp. dried basil

7 boneless, skinless chicken breast halves, cut into 1½-inch slices

½ cup butter, melted

1. Combine bread crumbs, cheese, salt, and herbs in a shallow bowl. Mix well.

2. Dip chicken pieces in butter, and then into crumb mixture, coating well.

3. Place coated chicken on greased baking sheet in a single layer.

4. Bake at 400°F for 20 minutes.

Variations:

1. In Step 1 use 1 Tbsp. garlic powder, 1 Tbsp. chives, 2 tsp. Italian seasoning, 2 tsp. parsley, ½ tsp. onion salt, ½ tsp. pepper, and ¼ tsp. salt (instead of 1½ tsp. salt, 1 Tbsp. thyme, and 1 Tbsp. basil).
   —Ruth Miller,
   Wooster, OH

2. Use boneless, skinless chicken thighs, and do not cut them into slices. Bake at 350°F for 20 minutes. Turn chicken. Bake an additional 20 minutes.
   —Eleanor Larson,
   Glen Lyon, PA

Chicken

Honey-Baked Chicken Strips

**Jan Rankin,
Millersville, PA**

Makes 3-4 servings
Prep. Time: 20-30 minutes
Baking Time: 15 minutes

2 egg whites

1 Tbsp. honey

2 cups cornflake crumbs

¼–½ tsp. salt or garlic powder

1 lb. chicken tenders, cut into strips

1. Mix egg whites and honey together in a shallow bowl.

2. Place cornflake crumbs and seasoning in another shallow bowl.

3. Dip chicken strips into egg white–honey mixture.

4. Coat each strip with cornflake crumbs.

5. Place each strip on ungreased cookie sheet and bake at 400°F for 15 minutes.

Turkey

Orange-Glazed Turkey Cutlets

Rosemarie Fitzgerald,
Gibsonia, PA

Makes 4 servings
Prep. Time: 10 minutes
Cooking Time: 10 minutes

1 lb. turkey breast cutlets or slices

salt and pepper, to taste

ground cinnamon, to taste

2 tsp. oil

⅓ cup orange marmalade

⅛ tsp. ground cinnamon

⅛ tsp. ground nutmeg

⅛ tsp. ground ginger

1. Lightly sprinkle one side of cutlets with salt, pepper, and cinnamon, to taste.

2. In large nonstick skillet, over medium-high heat, sauté turkey cutlets in oil for 1–2 minutes per side, or until turkey is no longer pink in the center. Do in batches if your skillet isn't large enough to hold the cutlets all at once with space around each one.

3. Remove turkey as it finishes browning to platter and keep warm.

4. In small saucepan, over medium heat, combine marmalade, cinnamon, nutmeg, and ginger. Cook 1–2 minutes or until marmalade melts and mixture is heated through.

5. To serve, spoon marmalade sauce over cutlets.

Turkey Steaks Dijon

Christie Detamore-Hunsberger,
Harrisonburg, VA

Makes 4 servings
Prep. Time: 5 minutes
Cooking Time: 15 minutes

1 lb. turkey steaks

¼ tsp. black pepper, *optional*

1½ Tbsp. butter

1 cup beef broth

1 Tbsp. cornstarch dissolved in 3 Tbsp. water

1½ Tbsp. Dijon-style mustard

⅓ cup chopped onion, *optional*

1. Sprinkle turkey steaks with pepper if you wish.

2. Heat butter in skillet.

3. Brown steaks 3 minutes per side. Remove steaks and keep warm. Drain off drippings from skillet.

4. Slowly add broth to hot pan, stirring to dissolve brown particles from bottom of pan. Stir in cornstarch dissolved in water, stirring until thickened. Stir in mustard, and onion if you wish.

5. Reduce heat to medium. Return steaks to skillet and settle into sauce. Tilt pan and spoon sauce over top of steaks.

6. Cover and simmer 2–3 minutes, or just until turkey is done.

7. Place steaks on serving platter, and spoon sauce over before serving.

Turkey

Turkey Loaf

**Phyllis Good,
Lancaster, PA**

Makes 10 servings
Prep. Time: 15 minutes
Baking Time: 1½ hours
Standing Time: 10 minutes

2 lbs. ground turkey

16-oz. can whole berry cranberry sauce,
   divided

1 pkg. dry chicken-flavored stuffing

2 eggs

1. Mix all ingredients in a large bowl,
reserving ¼ cup cranberry sauce.

2. When thoroughly mixed, shape into
loaf. Place in lightly greased loaf pan.

3. Bake uncovered at 350°F for 1 hour.

4. Spread top of loaf with ¼ cup reserved
sauce. Return to oven and bake another
30 minutes.

5. Allow to stand for 10 minutes before
slicing to serve.

Turkey Supreme

Janet Suderman,
Indianapolis, IN

Makes 6 servings, about 1 cup per serving
Prep. Time: 15 minutes
Cooking Time: about 20 minutes

2 cups sliced fresh mushrooms

1 small onion, chopped

1 cup thinly sliced celery

10¾-oz. can lower-sodium, lower-fat cream of
   chicken soup

1 cup fat-free milk

2 cups cubed, cooked turkey

2 cups herb-flavored stuffing

½ cup fat-free sour cream

¼–½ tsp. pepper

¼ cup sliced almonds

1. Combine mushrooms, onion, and celery in 2-qt. microwave-safe casserole dish.

2. Microwave on High, uncovered, 5–6 minutes or until vegetables are tender, stirring once.

3. Remove from microwave and add soup, milk, turkey, stuffing, sour cream, and pepper. Top with sliced almonds.

4. Cover and microwave on High 10–12 minutes or until heated through. Let stand about 5 minutes before serving.

Turkey Meatloaf

**Delores A. Gnagey,
Saginaw, MI**

Makes 10 servings
Prep. Time: 20 minutes
Baking Time: 1½ hours
Standing Time: 10 minutes

2 lbs. skinless, dark and white turkey meat, ground

half a medium onion, minced (½ cup)

3 Tbsp. minced fresh parsley

2 egg whites, or egg substitute equivalent to 1 egg

¼ cup skim milk

1 tsp. dry mustard

¼ tsp. salt

¼ tsp. ground white pepper

⅛ tsp. nutmeg

2 slices whole wheat bread, lightly toasted, made into coarse crumbs

2 Tbsp. ketchup

2 Tbsp. water

1. Preheat oven to 350°F.

2. Mix together ground turkey, onion, and parsley in a large bowl. Set aside.

3. In a medium bowl, whisk egg whites, or egg substitute, until frothy.

4. Add milk, mustard, salt, pepper, and nutmeg to egg. Whisk to blend.

5. Add bread crumbs to egg mixture. Let rest 10 minutes.

6. Add egg mixture to meat mixture and blend well.

7. Shape into loaf. Place in 5x9-inch loaf pan.

8. Blend together ketchup and water in a small bowl. Spread mixture on top of meat.

9. Bake until meat is no longer pink, about 90 minutes.

10. Allow meat to stand 10 minutes before slicing to serve.

Turkey

Spinach Meatloaf

Ellie Oberholtzer,
Ronks, PA

Makes 6 servings, 1 slice per serving
Prep. Time: 25 minutes
Baking Time: 1 hour
Standing Time: 10 minutes

1 lb. 93%-lean ground turkey

10-oz. box frozen chopped spinach, thawed
     and squeezed dry

¼ cup chopped fresh cilantro, or fresh parsley

2 oz. crumbled fat-free feta cheese

2 Tbsp. molasses

¼ cup egg substitute

3 pieces millet, or other whole-grain, bread,
     toasted and crumbled

1–2 tsp. poultry seasoning

¼ tsp. salt

¼ tsp. pepper

1. In a large bowl, mix together turkey, spinach, cilantro, cheese, molasses, egg substitute, bread crumbs, poultry seasoning, salt, and pepper.

2. Form mixture into a loaf.

3. Place in greased loaf pan.

4. Bake at 350°F for 60 minutes.

5. Allow to stand 10 minutes before slicing and serving.

TIP

Instead of mixing the spinach into the loaf, sometimes I pat the meat mixture into a rectangular shape, about ½-inch thick, onto a piece of waxed paper. I spread the spinach on top, about ½ inch from all the edges. I press the spinach down to make it adhere. Then, using the waxed paper to lift the meat, I roll it into a loaf, taking care to keep the spinach from falling out. Remove waxed paper. Then bake as directed above.

Turkey

Turkey and Green Bean Casserole

Melva Baumer,
Mifflintown, PA

Makes 6 servings, about 10 oz. per serving
Prep. Time: 35–40 minutes
Baking Time: 30–40 minutes

2 lbs. frozen French-style green beans

2 Tbsp. trans-fat-free tub margarine

3 Tbsp. flour

¼ tsp. salt

dash of pepper

½ tsp. prepared mustard

1½ cups fat-free milk

½ cup low-fat mayonnaise

1½–2 Tbsp. lemon juice

4 cups cubed cooked turkey

½ cup freshly grated Parmesan cheese

1. Cook beans according to package directions. Drain.

2. Melt margarine in saucepan. Blend in flour, salt, pepper, and mustard.

3. Over low heat, add milk, stirring constantly until mixture is smooth and thickened.

4. Remove from heat. Fold in mayonnaise and lemon juice.

5. Stir in turkey.

6. Spread beans in greased shallow baking dish.

7. Spoon turkey sauce over top of beans.

8. Sprinkle with Parmesan cheese.

9. Bake at 350°F for 30–40 minutes, or until bubbly and heated through.

Turkey Barbecue Wonder

Erma Martin,
East Earl, PA
Janet Derstine,
Telford, PA

Makes 8 servings, about 3-4 oz. per serving
Prep. Time: 10 minutes
Cooking Time: 15 minutes

1 celery rib, chopped

1 medium onion, chopped

¼ cup chopped green bell pepper

1 Tbsp. oil

¼ cup brown sugar

¼ cup ketchup

¼ cup picante sauce

2 Tbsp. Worcestershire sauce

1½ tsp. chili powder

½ tsp. salt

⅓ tsp. pepper

dash of cayenne pepper

4 cups shredded, or cubed, cooked turkey

1. In a large skillet, sauté celery, onion, and green pepper in oil until tender.

2. Stir in brown sugar, ketchup, picante sauce, Worcestershire sauce, chili powder, salt, pepper, and cayenne pepper.

3. Bring to a boil. Reduce heat and simmer uncovered 3–4 minutes.

4. Add turkey. Simmer 10 minutes longer, or until heated through.

5. Serve on buns.

Turkey

Turkey Stir-Fry

Arianne Hochstetler,
Goshen, IN

Makes 6 servings
Prep. Time: 15–20 minutes
Cooking Time: 20 minutes

1½ lbs. boneless turkey, cut into strips

1 Tbsp. cooking oil

1 large onion, chopped

1 carrot, julienned

half a green pepper, sliced

2 cups fresh, sliced mushrooms

1 cup chicken broth

3 Tbsp. cornstarch

3 Tbsp. soy sauce

½ tsp. ginger

1 tsp. curry powder

2 cups pea pods, trimmed, or 2 cups frozen
   stir-fry vegetables

⅓ cup cashews, *optional*

cooked rice

1. In a large skillet or wok, stir-fry turkey in oil over medium-high heat until no longer pink, about 5–6 minutes. Remove turkey from pan and keep warm.

2. Stir-fry the onion, carrot, green pepper, and mushrooms until crisp-tender, about 5 minutes.

3. In a small bowl, combine chicken broth, cornstarch, soy sauce, ginger, and curry powder until smooth.

4. Add to the skillet. Cook and stir until thickened and bubbly.

5. Return turkey to skillet with pea pods. Cook and stir until heated through.

6. Serve over cooked rice. Top with cashews, if desired.

Variation:
You can use sliced beef, pork, or chicken instead of turkey.

TIPS

1. Chop all the vegetables before you cut the turkey into strips. Then all ingredients are ready to go as you need them.
2. Cook the rice at the same time as you are preparing and cooking the stir-fry.

Turkey

Wild-Rice Turkey-Sausage Bake

Carla Elliott,
Phoenix, AZ

Makes 10 servings
Prep. Time: 1 hour
Baking Time: 1½ hours

1 lb. lean sweet Italian turkey sausage

¾ cup uncooked wild rice, cooked according to package directions

¾ cup uncooked long-grain rice, cooked according to package directions

1 medium onion, chopped

1 cup diced celery

10¾-oz. lower-sodium, lower-fat cream of mushroom soup

¼ tsp. salt

¼ tsp. pepper

14½-oz. can chicken broth

4-oz. can sliced mushrooms, drained, *optional*

4 boneless, skinless chicken breast halves, cut into large bite-sized pieces

1. Brown sausage in skillet, stirring frequently to break up clumps, until no longer pink.

2. Drain off drippings.

3. In large bowl, mix together sausage, both cooked rices, onion, celery, soup, salt, pepper, broth, and mushrooms if you wish.

4. Spoon into greased 9x13-inch baking pan.

5. Push chicken pieces down into rice mixture.

6. Cover. Bake at 350°F for 1 hour.

7. Remove cover and check if mixture is soupy. If so, remove cover. If not, put cover back on. Continue baking 30 more minutes.

Seafood

Tilapia with Mango

Sherry Goss Lapp,
Lancaster, PA

Makes 4 servings
Prep. Time: 10 minutes
Baking Time: 30 minutes

4 6-oz. tilapia fillets

2 Tbsp. soy sauce

⅛ tsp. salt

⅛ tsp. pepper, or lemon pepper seasoning

1 Tbsp. butter, cut into chunks

1 mango, or slices of dried mango

1. Place tilapia fillets in baking pan.

2. Pour soy sauce over top of fish.

3. Sprinkle salt and pepper over fish. Lay butter on top.

4. Peel the mango and cut into lengthwise pieces. Lay around fish.

5. Bake covered at 400°F for 30 minutes. Turn mango slices after 15 minutes of baking.

Parsley Buttered Fish

Shirley Sears,
Tiskilwa, IL

Makes 2 servings
Prep. Time: 3 minutes
Cooking Time: 5-6 minutes

2 Tbsp. butter

2 Tbsp. lemon juice

1 lb. white fish fillets

1 Tbsp. chopped fresh parsley, or 1 tsp. dried

salt, to taste, *optional*

1. Place butter and lemon juice together in microwave-safe, 8x12-inch glass dish. Microwave on High 30–60 seconds, or until butter is melted. Stir.

2. Coat both sides of fillets with butter sauce.

3. Arrange fish in baking dish.

4. Cover with waxed paper.

5. Microwave on High until fish flakes easily, 5–6 minutes in 1000-watt oven.

6. Sprinkle with parsley, and salt if you wish, before serving.

Seasoned Salmon

Charmaine Caesar,
Lancaster, PA

Makes 3 servings
Prep. Time: 10 minutes
Baking Time: 15–20 minutes

1 lb. salmon filet

3 Tbsp. lemon juice

2 Tbsp. fresh dill, or 2 tsp. dried dill weed

2 Tbsp. minced garlic, or powdered garlic to taste

3 slices onion

1. Line a 9x13-inch baking pan with foil. Spray foil with nonstick spray.

2. Place fish on foil. Sprinkle with lemon juice.

3. Sprinkle with dill and garlic. Place onion slices on top.

4. Cover with second sheet of foil.

5. Bake at 450°F for 15–20 minutes, or until fish flakes easily. (Salmon is still pink after being fully cooked.)

Salmon Loaf

Clara Yoder Byler,
Hartville, OH

Makes 3–4 servings
Prep. Time: 15 minutes
Cooking Time: 1 hour
Standing Time: 10 minutes

14¾-oz. can salmon, drained and flaked

½ cup mayonnaise

10¾-oz. can cream of celery soup

1 egg, beaten

1 cup dry bread crumbs

½ cup chopped onion

1 Tbsp. lemon juice

1. Combine salmon, mayonnaise, soup, egg, bread crumbs, onion, and lemon juice in a bowl.

2. Shape into loaf. Place in greased 8½ x 4½ loaf pan.

3. Bake at 350°F for 1 hour.

4. Allow to stand 10 minutes before slicing.

Seafood

Oven-Fried Catfish

Karen Waggoner,
Joplin, MO

Makes 4 servings
Prep. Time: 15 minutes
Baking Time: 25–30 minutes

4 catfish fillets (6 oz. each)

1 cup cornflake crumbs

¼ tsp. celery salt

½ tsp. onion powder

¼ tsp. paprika

⅛ tsp. pepper

1 egg white

2 Tbsp. milk

1. Pat fish dry with paper towels. Set aside.

2. In glass pie plate, combine crumbs, celery salt, onion powder, paprika, and pepper.

3. In a shallow bowl, beat egg white. Add milk.

4. Dip fillets in egg white mixture, then dip into crumb mixture, coating well.

5. Place in greased 9x13-inch baking dish.

6. Bake, uncovered, at 350°F for 25–30 minutes, or until fish flakes easily with a fork.

Seafood

Cajun Shrimp

**Mary Ann Potenta,
Bridgewater, NJ**

Makes 4–5 servings
Prep. Time: just minutes!
Cooking Time: 10–12 minutes

1½ sticks (12 Tbsp.) butter, *divided*

½ cup chopped green onions

1 tsp. minced garlic

1 tsp. cayenne pepper

½ tsp. white pepper

½ tsp. black pepper

¼ tsp. dry mustard

½ tsp. salt

1 tsp. Tabasco sauce

2 lbs. shrimp, peeled and cleaned

cooked rice

NOTE

This is hot! You can tone things down by reducing the amounts of the cayenne, white, and black pepper and the Tabasco sauce.

1. Melt 1 stick of butter in large skillet. Add onions and garlic and sauté until clear, but not brown, about 1 minute.

2. Add peppers, mustard, and salt. Cook and stir for 3 minutes.

3. Mix in half-stick of butter and Tabasco sauce until blended.

4. Add shrimp. Cook just until pink. Do not overcook.

5. Serve over cooked rice.

Scallops in Wine Sauce

**Doris M. Zipp,
Germantown, NY**

Makes 2-4 servings
Prep. Time: 10 minutes
Cooking Time: 10 minutes

1 stick (8 Tbsp.) butter

1 lb. scallops

2 Tbsp. flour

½ cup dry white wine

fresh parsley

1. Melt butter in skillet.

2. Add scallops and sauté until barely cooked.

3. Sprinkle flour over scallops. Stir until flour is moistened. Add wine. Stir and simmer just until a creamy sauce appears. Be careful not to overcook the scallops.

4. Garnish with parsley.

TIP

This makes a great sauce and works well served with spaghetti.

Scalloped Scallops

**Flossie Sultzaberger,
Mechanicsburg, PA**

Makes 4-6 servings
Prep. Time: 15 minutes
Baking Time: 25 minutes

1 stick (8 Tbsp.) butter

1 cup snack-cracker crumbs

½ cup soft bread crumbs

1 lb. scallops (if large, cut in half)

dash of salt

dash of pepper

1. Melt butter in saucepan.

2. Stir in cracker crumbs and bread crumbs.

3. Butter a 1½–2-qt. casserole.

4. Place half the scallops in bottom of baking dish.

5. Sprinkle with salt and pepper.

6. Cover with half buttered crumbs.

7. Repeat layers.

8. Bake at 400°F for 25 minutes.

TIP

Add a few shrimp to the scallops for a very special dish.

Jamaica's Seafood Medley

Mary Ann Lefever,
Lancaster, PA

Makes 4 servings
Prep. Time: 15–20 minutes
Marinating Time: 2 hours
Cooking Time: 15–20 minutes

2 Tbsp. packed brown sugar

1½ Tbsp. orange juice

1½ Tbsp. lime juice

2 cloves garlic, minced

½ tsp. minced ginger

1 tsp. grated orange peel

1 tsp. grated lime peel

1 tsp. salt

½ tsp. black pepper

⅛ tsp. ground cinnamon

dash ground cloves

½ tsp. Tabasco sauce

½ lb. orange roughy, cut into bite-sized pieces

½ lb. sea scallops, cut in half, or quarters if very large

½ lb. shrimp, shelled and deveined

¾ cup baby corn ears, snapped in fourths, or ¾ cup corn kernels

1 Tbsp. green onions, sliced

half a green bell pepper, julienne-sliced

1 Tbsp. olive oil

1. Combine sugar, juices, and seasonings in a bowl or jar with a tight-fitting lid.

2. Place seafood in a good-sized bowl. Pour seasoned juices over seafood. Mix well.

3. Cover and refrigerate at least 2 hours.

4. Drain seafood and discard marinade.

5. In a large skillet or saucepan, sauté seafood and vegetables in olive oil over medium heat for 15 minutes, or until fish is just tender and vegetables are crisp-tender.

Crab Imperial

Cheryl A. Lapp,
Parkesburg, PA

Makes 4–6 servings
Prep. Time: 5 minutes
Cooking Time: 20 minutes

1 lb. crabmeat

3 Tbsp. butter

2 whole garlic cloves, chopped fine

¼ tsp. onion powder

16-oz. jar Alfredo sauce

1. Cut crabmeat into small pieces.

2. Melt butter in a large skillet. Sauté crab with garlic and onion powder for 10 minutes, or until meat is hot and garlic is softened.

3. Add Alfredo sauce. Simmer over low heat another 10 minutes, stirring frequently. (Thin with ½ cup milk if the sauce seems too thick.)

4. Serve over hot cooked noodles.

Crab Pizza

Sharon Easter,
Yuba City, CA

Makes 6–8 servings
Prep. Time: 10 minutes
Baking Time: 13-15 minutes

½ stick (4 Tbsp.) butter

6 green onions, sliced thin

8-oz. pkg. cream cheese, cubed

½ lb. flaked crabmeat

prepared pizza crust

1. Melt butter in a large skillet. Add onions and cook until onions soften.

2. Toss cubed cream cheese into skillet. Heat until bubbly and melted, stirring frequently to prevent scorching.

3. Break up crab with a fork. Stir into creamy sauce in skillet. Continue heating over low heat until crab is also hot.

4. Meanwhile, heat a large pizza crust on a baking sheet in a 400°F oven for 5 minutes. Remove crust from oven.

5. Turn oven to 450°F. Spoon crab mixture onto crust. Place pizza in oven and bake 8 minutes.

Tuna Noodle Casserole

Carol Lenz,
Little Chute, WI
Rosemarie Fitzgerald,
Gibsonia, PA

Makes 6–8 servings
Prep. Time: 15 minutes
Baking Time: 30–45 minutes

2 cups dry elbow macaroni

2 6-oz. cans tuna, packed in water

2 10¾-oz. cans mushroom soup

2 cups shredded cheddar cheese

salt and pepper, to taste

1 cup frozen peas, *optional*

¾ cup cornflake crumbs, *optional*

1. Cook macaroni according to package directions. Drain. Place cooked pasta in a large mixing bowl.

2. Stir in tuna, soup, cheese, salt and pepper, and peas if you wish. Stir together gently until well mixed.

3. Place in lightly greased 2-qt. casserole. Top with cornflake crumbs if you wish.

4. Bake uncovered at 350°F for 30–45 minutes, or until heated through and bubbly.

Seafood

Tuna Bake with Cheese Swirls

**Mary Ann Lefever,
Lancaster, PA**

Makes 4–6 servings
Prep. Time: 30 minutes
Baking Time: 25 minutes

½ cup diced green bell peppers

½ cup chopped onions

3 Tbsp. butter

6 Tbsp. flour

2 cups milk

6½- or 7-oz. can tuna

Cheese Swirls:

1½ cups buttermilk biscuit mix, or refrigerated
  biscuits

½ cup milk, if using biscuit mix

¾ cup grated cheddar cheese

2 Tbsp. chopped pimentos

1. In saucepan, sauté green pepper and onions in butter until soft but not brown.

2. Blend in flour and cook over low heat a few minutes to get rid of raw flour taste.

3. Gradually stir in milk. Cook over low heat, stirring continually until smooth.

4. Add tuna.

5. Spoon into greased 9x13-inch baking pan. Set aside.

6. To make cheese swirls, prepare biscuits with milk according to package directions. Or open refrigerated biscuits.

7. On lightly floured board, roll out to 8x13-inch rectangle.

8. Sprinkle with cheese and chopped pimentos. Press into dough to help adhere.

9. Roll up jelly-roll fashion.

10. Cut roll into 8 slices.

11. Flatten slightly and place on top of tuna mixture.

12. Bake at 450°F for 25 minutes, or until tuna mix is bubbly and biscuits are browned.

Meatless

Zucchini Supper

**Susan Kasting,
Jenks, OK**

Makes 8 servings, 3¼x4½-inch rectangle
per serving
Prep. Time: 15 minutes
Baking Time: 25–30 minutes

4 cups thinly sliced zucchini

1 cup reduced-fat buttermilk baking mix

½ cup chopped green onions

½ cup freshly grated Parmesan cheese

2 Tbsp. chopped parsley, fresh or dried

½ tsp. dried oregano

½ tsp. pepper

½ tsp. garlic powder

½ tsp. seasoned salt

¼ cup canola oil

½ cup fat-free milk

1 cup egg substitute

1. In a large mixing bowl, mix together zucchini, baking mix, green onions, cheese, parsley, oregano, pepper, garlic powder, seasoned salt, oil, milk, and egg substitute.

2. Pour into well-greased 9x13-inch baking pan.

3. Bake at 350°F for 25–30 minutes, or until firm.

4. Serve warm or at room temperature.

Stuffed Zucchini

Janet Batdorf,
Harrisburg, PA

Makes 6–8 servings
Prep. Time: 25 minutes
Baking Time: 25 minutes

1 large, or 2 medium, zucchini

3 Tbsp. butter, at room temperature

1 cup dry bread crumbs

2 Tbsp. chopped onion

½ cup spaghetti sauce, your favorite kind

1-2 good shakes of salt

1-2 full grinds of pepper

1-2 pinches dried oregano

¾ cup Italian cheese, or your favorite variety, grated

1. Parboil zucchini by submerging it in boiling salted water in large stockpot for 15 minutes (10 minutes for smaller size). Or cut in half lengthwise and cook in microwave until soft in center.

2. When cool enough to handle, scoop out pulp in the center and reserve, leaving a ½-inch "shell" all around.

3. In a good-sized mixing bowl, mix pulp with butter, bread crumbs, onion, sauce, salt, pepper, and oregano.

4. Fill zucchini shells with mixture. Sprinkle with cheese.

5. Place zucchini "boats," stuffed side up, next to each other in a lightly greased baking dish. Bake at 350°F until heated through, about 25 minutes.

TIP

I always use this recipe when I have oversized zucchini, especially at the end of summer.

Meatless

Exceptional Eggplant Casserole

Lisa Good,
Harrisonburg, VA

Makes 6-8 servings
Prep. Time: 15-20 minutes
Baking Time: 45-50 minutes

½ cup chopped onions

½ cup chopped green peppers

½ cup chopped celery

1 tsp. oil

2 8-oz. cans tomato sauce

⅓ cup brown sugar

1½ tsp. dried oregano

½ tsp. minced garlic

1 medium-sized eggplant, peeled or unpeeled,
    sliced in ⅛-inch-thick slices

1½ cups mozzarella cheese

1. In a large skillet or saucepan, sauté the onions, green peppers, and celery in the oil.

2. Add the tomato sauce, brown sugar, oregano, and garlic to the sautéed vegetables. Mix well.

3. Layer ⅓ of the sauce mixture, ⅓ of the eggplant, and ⅓ of the cheese into a greased 2-qt. baking dish. Repeat the layers twice.

4. Bake uncovered at 350°F for 45–50 minutes.

Meatless

Crustless Spinach Quiche

Elaine Vigoda,
Rochester, NY

Makes 16 servings, 1 slice of an 8-slice pie
per serving
Prep. Time: 10 minutes
Baking Time: 30–35 minutes
Standing Time: 10 minutes

1 cup flour

1 tsp. salt

1 tsp. baking powder

¾ cup egg substitute

1 cup fat-free milk

2 Tbsp. trans-fat-free tub margarine, melted

½ medium onion, chopped

10-oz. pkg. frozen spinach, thawed and
squeezed dry

12 oz. 75%-less-fat shredded cheddar cheese

¼ tsp. nutmeg

1. In a large mixing bowl, blend together
flour, salt, baking powder, egg substitute,
milk, and margarine.

2. Stir in onion, spinach, and cheese.

3. Pour into 2 greased pie pans. Sprinkle
with nutmeg.

4. Bake at 350°F until set and light golden
brown, about 30–35 minutes. To test if the
quiche is done, put the blade of a knife into
the center of the baking dish. If the knife
comes out clean, the quiche is finished.
If it doesn't, continue baking for another
5 minutes. Test again. Repeat if necessary.

5. Allow quiche to stand 10 minutes before
cutting and serving. The standing time will
allow the filling to firm up.

TIPS

1. You'll need to defrost the package of spinach before making this recipe. If you have
time (8 hours or so), you can let it thaw in a bowl in the fridge. If you decided to
make this quiche on short notice, and the spinach is frozen solid, lay the spinach
in a shallow, microwave-safe dish, and defrost it in the microwave until thawed.
(You can remove the box either before or after thawing the spinach.) When thawed,
place the spinach in a strainer and press a spoon against it to remove as much of
the water as possible. Or squeeze the spinach in your hand to remove the water.
Then mix the spinach in with the rest of the ingredients and proceed with Step 3.
2. You can freeze the quiche after you've baked it. When ready to serve, allow to thaw.
Then bake for 10 minutes, or until heated through.

Meatless

Eggplant Parmesan

Mary Ann Bowman,
East Earl, PA

Makes 6 main-dish servings
Prep. Time: 15 minutes
Broiling/Baking Time: 40–45 minutes

1 medium eggplant, unpeeled

2 Tbsp. olive oil, *divided*

1 cup bread crumbs

½ tsp. dried basil

¾ cup grated Parmesan cheese, *divided*

2 Tbsp. chopped parsley

⅛ tsp. pepper

1 tsp. dried oregano

6 tomatoes, chopped

2 green bell peppers, chopped

2 onions, chopped

1 clove garlic, chopped

2 Tbsp. tomato paste

1 cup grated Swiss cheese

1. Preheat oven to broil.

2. Cut eggplant into 6 slices, each ½-inch thick.

3. Place slices on cookie sheet. Brush with half the olive oil.

4. Broil 5 minutes, or until golden.

5. Turn slices. Brush other sides with remaining oil.

6. Return to broiler and brown second sides.

7. Place browned eggplant in lightly greased 9x13-inch baking pan, sprayed generously with nonstick cooking spray.

8. Mix together bread crumbs, basil, ½ cup Parmesan cheese, parsley, pepper, and oregano in a small bowl. Sprinkle over eggplant.

9. Combine in saucepan tomatoes, peppers, onions, garlic, and tomato paste. Simmer uncovered about 20 minutes.

10. Spread on top of crumb mixture.

11. Top with Swiss cheese and ¼ cup Parmesan cheese.

12. Bake uncovered at 375°F for 10–15 minutes.

TIP

You can make this ahead and refrigerate it until you're ready to heat and serve it.

Meatless

Stuffed Eggplant

**Jean Harris Robinson,
Pemberton, NJ**

Makes 4 servings
Prep. Time: 30 minutes
Baking Time: 30-45 minutes

2 large eggplants

1 medium onion, chopped

4 tomatoes, chopped

3 medium green bell peppers, chopped

1 rib celery, chopped

¼ cup olive oil

2 eggs, beaten

1 tsp. salt

1 tsp. pepper

1 cup grated Parmesan cheese

¼ tsp. cayenne pepper, *optional*

½ tsp. grated garlic, *optional*

1. Cut eggplants in half and scrape out seeds. Parboil* 15 minutes.

2. After eggplant halves have drained, remove pulp within ½-inch of outer "shell." Chop pulp. Set aside.

3. Place eggplant shells, cut side up, in 12x24-inch baking dish.

4. Empty stockpot of water. Place onion, tomatoes, peppers, celery, and olive oil in stockpot. Cook until soft and almost a puree. Remove from heat.

5. Stir in eggplant pulp, beaten eggs, salt, and pepper.

6. Fill eggplant halves with the mixture. Sprinkle with cheese, and cayenne pepper and garlic if you wish.

7. Distribute any leftover stuffing in baking dish around eggplant halves.

8. Bake at 350°F for 30–45 minutes, or until eggplant is tender and cheese is brown.

*To parboil eggplants, submerge unpeeled halves in a stockpot of boiling water with a shake of salt added. Cook in boiling water for 15 minutes. Remove and drain.

TIP

I have used 4-5 whole canned tomatoes when I haven't been able to find fresh tomatoes. Before adding them to the mixture (Step 4), I've chopped them, and drained off as much of their liquid as I could.

Meatless

Sun-Dried Tomato Casserole

Barbara Jean Fabel,
Wausau, WI

Makes 12 servings
Prep. Time: 15–20 minutes
Standing Time: 8 hours or overnight, plus 10 minutes
Baking Time: 40 minutes

2 9-oz. pkgs. cheese ravioli (look for them in the dairy case)

half an 8-oz. jar sun-dried tomatoes in oil, drained and chopped

1½ cups shredded cheddar cheese

1½ cups shredded Monterey Jack cheese

8 eggs, beaten

2½ cups milk

1–2 Tbsp. fresh basil, snipped, or 1–2 tsp. dried basil

1. Grease a 3-qt. baking dish. Place uncooked ravioli evenly in bottom.

2. Sprinkle ravioli with tomatoes. Top evenly with cheeses. Set aside.

3. In a mixing bowl, whisk eggs and milk until well combined. Pour over layers in casserole dish.

4. Cover and chill for 8 hours or overnight.

5. Bake, uncovered, at 350°F for 40 minutes, until center is set and knife inserted in center comes out clean.

6. Let stand 10 minutes before serving. Just before serving, sprinkle with basil.

TIP

If you don't like sun-dried tomatoes, replace them with something you do like, such as sliced black olives or artichokes.

Chile Rellenos Casserole

Elena Yoder,
Albuquerque, NM

Makes 12 servings
Prep. Time: 30 minutes
Baking Time: 35-40 minutes

1 can of 18-20 whole green chilies

1 lb. Monterey Jack cheese

sprinkle of garlic salt

4 eggs

1 Tbsp. flour

1 cup milk

3/4 tsp. salt

1/4-1/2 tsp. pepper

1/2 lb. cheddar, or longhorn, cheese, grated

1. Spray 9x13-inch baking pan with nonstick cooking spray.

2. Wearing gloves, cut chilies in half and remove seeds and membranes.

3. Cut Monterey Jack cheese into strips. Place strips in chili halves. Place stuffed chilies in pan side by side, cut side up.

4. Sprinkle with garlic salt.

5. In a mixing bowl, beat eggs. Stir in flour, milk, salt, and pepper.

6. Pour over chilies.

7. Sprinkle with grated cheese.

8. Bake at 350°F for 35–40 minutes, or until set and beginning to brown.

TIP

You can put this together the day before you want to serve it. Or stuff the chilies and freeze them until you need a quick meal. Then proceed with Step 5.

Meatless

Corn Casserole

**Beth Nafziger,
Lowville, NY**

Makes 10 servings, about 5-6 oz. per
serving
Prep. Time: 25-30 minutes
Baking Time: 45 minutes

1 large onion, chopped

2 medium green bell peppers, chopped

2 Tbsp. canola oil

¼ cup flour

2 cups frozen or canned corn

2 cups cooked long-grain rice

14½-oz. can diced tomatoes

4 hard-cooked eggs, yolks removed, chopped

2 cups extra-sharp 75%-less-fat shredded
   cheddar cheese, *divided*

2 Tbsp. Worcestershire sauce

2-3 tsp. hot pepper sauce

¾ tsp. salt

1 tsp. pepper

1. In a large skillet, sauté chopped onion
and green peppers in oil until tender.

2. Stir in flour. Remove from heat.

3. Add remaining ingredients except for
½ cup of the cheese. Pour into greased 2¼-qt.
baking dish.

4. Bake, uncovered, at 350°F for 45
minutes. Top with remaining cheese.

Moroccan-Spiced Sweet Potato Medley

Pat Bishop,
Bedminster, PA

Makes 6 main-dish servings
Prep. Time: 20 minutes
Cooking Time: 35–40 minutes

1 medium onion, sliced

2 tsp. olive oil

2 garlic cloves, crushed

1½ tsp. ground coriander

1½ tsp. ground cumin

¼ tsp. ground red pepper

2 medium (about 1½ lbs.) sweet potatoes, peeled and cut into ½-inch-thick slices

14-oz. can stewed tomatoes, no salt added, undrained

¾ cup uncooked bulgur

2¼ cups water

15-oz. can garbanzo beans, rinsed and drained

½ cup dark raisins

1 cup loosely packed fresh cilantro leaves, chopped

1. In a large stockpot, sauté onion in oil until tender and golden.

2. Add garlic, coriander, cumin, and red pepper. Cook 1 minute.

3. Add sweet potato slices, tomatoes, bulgur, and water. Heat to boiling.

4. Reduce heat, cover, and simmer 20 minutes, or until potatoes are fork-tender.

5. Stir in beans, raisins, and cilantro. Heat through.

Meatless

Veggie Burgers

Esther Becker,
Gordonville, PA

Makes 12–14 servings
Prep. Time: 20 minutes (after soaking and cooking)
Cooking Time: 8–10 minutes

1 cup dry oat bran

1 cup dry oats

1 cup cooked brown rice

½ cup dry lentils, soaked and cooked

½ cup dry black beans, soaked and cooked

½ cup dry black-eyed peas, soaked and cooked

½ cup salsa

½ cup chopped onions

half a green pepper, chopped

6 oz. firm tofu, at room temperature

4-oz. pkg. cream cheese, softened

cooking oil

1. Mix all ingredients except cooking oil together and shape into 12–14 patties.

2. Brown on both sides in a skillet in enough oil to cover the bottom of the pan.

Spicy Mexican Bean Burgers

Lois Hess,
Lancaster, PA

Makes 4 burgers
Prep. Time: 30 minutes
Baking Time: 15–20 minutes

16-oz. can red kidney beans, rinsed, drained, and mashed

½ cup chopped onion

half a green bell pepper, chopped

1 carrot, steamed and mashed

⅛ cup salsa, your choice of flavors

1 cup whole wheat bread crumbs

½ cup whole wheat flour

½ tsp. black pepper, *optional*

dash of chili powder

1. Preheat oven to 400°F.

2. Combine all ingredients in a good-sized bowl. Add more flour to create a firmer mixture or more salsa if mixture is too stiff.

3. Form into 4 balls and then flatten into patties.

4. Place on a baking sheet, lightly sprayed with cooking spray.

5. Bake 15–20 minutes, or until firm and brown.

6. Serve on a whole wheat bun with lettuce, tomato, and salsa.

Meatless

Vegetarian Black Bean Burritos

**Maricarol Magill,
Freehold, NJ**

Makes 8 burritos
Prep. Time: 10 minutes
Cooking/Baking Time: 40 minutes

1¼ cup water

1 Tbsp. butter

½ cup long-grain rice

½ tsp. salt

8 10-inch flour tortillas

10-oz. pkg. frozen corn

15-oz. can spicy black-bean chili

8-oz. can tomato sauce

shredded cheddar, Monterey Jack, or pepper
jack cheese

1. In a medium-sized saucepan, bring water and butter to a boil.

2. Stir in rice and salt. Cover. Simmer over low heat until rice is cooked, about 20 minutes.

3. Meanwhile, wrap tortillas in foil. Heat oven to 350°F and then heat tortillas until warm, about 15 minutes.

4. When rice is done, stir in corn, black-bean chili, and tomato sauce. Heat to boiling over medium-high heat. Boil one minute.

5. Assemble burritos by spooning rice mixture onto tortillas. Top with cheese of your choice. Fold in tops of tortillas and roll up.

Mjadra (Lentils and Rice)

Hope Comerford,
Clinton Township, MI

Makes 4-6 servings
Prep. Time: 1 hour 20 minutes
Cooking Time: 20-25 minutes

½ cup olive oil

2 large sweet onions, chopped

1 cup dried lentils

4 cups water

¼ cup lemon juice

⅛ tsp. pepper

1 tsp. salt

1 cup uncooked white rice

1. Heat the olive oil over medium-high heat. Add the onions and let brown lightly. Reduce the heat to low and cover. Let the onions caramelize for at least 1 hour.

2. Rinse the lentils then add them to the water. Bring to a boil and cook for 15 minutes.

3. When the onions are done, mix them with the cooked lentils, lemon juice, pepper, salt, and uncooked white rice.

4. Cover and cook for 20–25 minutes, or until the rice and lentils are fluffy.

Serving Suggestion:
Serve with pita bread or on a bed of lettuce.

Meatless

TIPS ✓

1. As the vegetables cook in Step 6, keep checking that they are not getting too dry. Add water or tomato juice to vegetables if needed.
2. If you are not cooking for vegetarians or vegans, you can use broth or stock in place of water.

Lentil, Rice, and Veggie Bake

**Andrea Zuercher,
Lawrence, KS**

Makes 12 servings, 3-inch-square per
serving
Prep. Time: 20 minutes
Cooking/Baking Time: 65–70 minutes

1 cup uncooked long-grain rice

5 cups water, *divided*

2 cups red lentils

2 tsp. vegetable oil

2 small onions, chopped

6 cloves garlic, minced

2 fresh tomatoes, chopped

²/₃ cup chopped celery

²/₃ cup chopped carrots

²/₃ cup chopped summer squash

16-oz. can tomato sauce, *divided*

2 tsp. dried, or 2 Tbsp. fresh basil, *divided*

2 tsp. dried, or 2 Tbsp. fresh oregano, *divided*

2 tsp. ground cumin, *divided*

³/₄ tsp. salt, *divided*

¹/₂ tsp. pepper, *divided*

1. Cook rice according to package
directions, using 2 cups water and cooking
about 20 minutes. Set aside.

2. Cook lentils with remaining 3 cups
water until tender, about 15 minutes. Set
aside.

3. Heat oil in good-sized skillet over
medium heat. Being careful not to splash
yourself with hot oil, stir in onions and
garlic. Sauté 5 minutes, or until just tender.

4. Stir in tomatoes, celery, carrots, squash,
and half the tomato sauce.

5. Season with half the herbs and
seasonings.

6. Cook until vegetables are tender. Add
water if too dry.

7. Place cooked rice, lentils, and vegetables
in well-greased 9x13-inch baking pan, or
equivalent-size casserole dish. Layer, or mix
together, whichever you prefer.

8. Top with remaining tomato sauce, herbs,
and seasonings.

9. Bake at 350°F for 30 minutes, or until
bubbly.

Meatless

Pasta and Pizza

Pasta and Pizza

Pasta

Mostaccioli

**Sally Holzem,
Schofield, WI**

Makes 8 servings
Prep. Time: 45 minutes
Baking Time: 30-45 minutes

½ lb. bulk Italian sausage

½ cup chopped onion

16-oz. can tomato paste

½ cup water

½ tsp. oregano

¼ tsp. pepper

4-oz. can sliced mushrooms, drained

14½-oz. can diced tomatoes, undrained

¾ cup tomato juice

8-oz. pkg. mostaccioli noodles, *divided*

1½ cups cottage cheese

½ tsp. marjoram

12 oz. shredded mozzarella cheese, *divided*

¼ cup grated Parmesan cheese

1. Brown sausage and onions in saucepan, stirring often to break up clumps. When pink no longer remains, drain off drippings.

2. Stir in tomato paste, water, oregano, pepper, mushrooms, tomatoes, and tomato juice.

3. Cover. Simmer 30 minutes over medium heat.

4. Meanwhile, prepare noodles according to package directions. Drain well.

5. In mixing bowl, combine cottage cheese and marjoram.

6. In greased 7x13-inch baking pan, layer in half of noodles.

7. Top with half of meat sauce.

8. Sprinkle with half of mozzarella.

9. Spoon cottage cheese mixture over top and spread as well as you can.

10. Layer on remaining noodles.

11. Top with remaining meat sauce.

12. Sprinkle with remaining mozzarella cheese.

13. Sprinkle with Parmesan cheese.

14. Bake at 350°F for 30–45 minutes, or until bubbly, heated through, and lightly browned.

Super Creamy Macaroni and Cheese

**Jean Butzer, Batavia, NY
Arlene Leaman Kliewer, Lakewood, CO
Esther Burkholder, Millerstown, PA
Hazel Lightcap Propst, Oxford, PA
Karla Baer, North Lima, OH**

Makes 8–10 servings
Prep. Time: 5–10 minutes
Baking Time: 1 hour 20 minutes

1-lb. uncooked elbow macaroni

4 cups shredded cheddar cheese, or ½ lb. cubed Velveeta cheese

2 10¾-oz. cans cheddar cheese, or cream of celery, soup

3½ cups milk

1½ cups cooked ham, chopped, *optional*

1 tsp. salt, *optional*

¼ tsp. pepper, *optional*

1. Combine all ingredients in a buttered 3-qt. casserole or baking dish.

2. Cover and bake at 350°F for 1 hour.

3. Stir up from bottom.

4. Bake uncovered an additional 20 minutes.

Lasagna

**Colleen Heatwole,
Burton, MI**

Makes 8–12 servings
Prep. Time: 45 minutes
Baking Time: 30 minutes

1 lb. ground beef

1 clove garlic, minced

1 scant Tbsp. basil

¾ tsp. salt

28- to 32-oz. can stewed tomatoes, or 28-oz. jar pasta sauce

6-oz. can tomato paste

½ tsp. oregano

10 oz. lasagna noodles, *divided*

3 cups cottage cheese

½ cup grated Parmesan cheese

1 lb. mozzarella cheese, grated

2 Tbsp. parsley flakes

2 eggs, beaten

½ tsp. pepper

1. Brown beef slowly in stockpot. Stir frequently to break up clumps. Pour off drippings.

2. Stir in garlic, basil, salt, tomatoes or pasta sauce, tomato paste, and oregano. Mix well.

3. Simmer, uncovered, 30 minutes.

4. Meanwhile, cook pasta al dente, according to package directions. Drain well.

5. In large bowl, combine cottage cheese, Parmesan cheese, mozzarella cheese, parsley flakes, beaten eggs, and pepper.

6. Place half the noodles in greased 9x13-inch baking dish.

7. Cover with half the meat sauce.

8. Top with half the cheese mixture.

9. Repeat layers, ending with cheese mixture.

10. Bake at 375°F for 30 minutes, or until bubbly and heated through.

Variation:

Instead of ground beef, use ½ lb. bulk hot Italian sausage. Brown it as instructed for ground beef and drain off drippings.
—Monica Leaman Kehr, Portland, MI

TIP

You can assemble this lasagna ahead of time through Step 9. Cover and refrigerate. When ready to bake, allow 15 minutes longer in oven, or bake at 200°F for 2 hours if baking during church for a noon potluck. Cover during baking if baking 2 hours.

Vegetarian Lasagna Roll-Ups

Judy Buller,
Bluffton, OH

Makes 12 servings
Prep. Time: 30 minutes
Baking Time: 25–30 minutes

12 uncooked whole-grain lasagna noodles

2 eggs, slightly beaten

2½ cups ricotta cheese

2½ cups (10 oz.) shredded mozzarella cheese, *divided*

½ cup Parmesan cheese

1 pkg. frozen, chopped spinach, thawed and squeezed dry, or 4 cups chopped fresh spinach that has been microwaved on High 1-2 minutes and squeezed dry

¼ tsp. salt

¼ tsp. pepper

1-2 cups black beans, rinsed

23½-oz. jar spaghetti sauce, your favorite variety, *divided*

1. Cook lasagna noodles according to box directions. Drain and rinse well. Lay flat.

2. In a good-sized mixing bowl, mix together eggs, ricotta cheese, 1½ cups mozzarella cheese, Parmesan cheese, spinach, salt, and pepper.

3. Spread about ⅓ cup mixture on each noodle.

4. Sprinkle each noodle with black beans. Press down to make beans adhere.

5. Spread 1 cup spaghetti sauce in bottom of well-greased 9x13-inch baking pan.

6. Roll up noodles and place seam-side down in baking pan.

7. Top rolls with remaining sauce. Sprinkle with 1 cup mozzarella cheese.

8. Bake uncovered at 350°F for 25–30 minutes, or until heated through.

TIP

You can assemble this dish ahead of time through Step 7, and then freeze or refrigerate it until you're ready to use it. Allow more time to bake if the dish is cold, probably 45-50 minutes total. But check while baking so as not to have it dry out or be overbaked.

Household-Size Ziti Bake

Joy Reiff,
Mount Joy, PA

Makes 6-8 servings
Prep. Time: 30 minutes
Baking Time: 45-60 minutes

1 lb. ziti, or rigatoni

1¼ lbs. ground beef

1 lb. ricotta, or cottage, cheese

½ cup grated Parmesan cheese

3 Tbsp. chopped fresh parsley

1 egg, beaten

½ tsp. salt

¼–½ tsp. pepper, according to your taste
 preference

6 cups spaghetti sauce

½ lb. mozzarella sauce, shredded

1. Prepare ziti according to package directions. Drain and set aside.

2. Brown ground beef. Stir frequently to break up clumps. Cook until pink no longer remains. Drain off drippings.

3. Stir in ricotta cheese, Parmesan cheese, parsley, egg, salt, and pepper.

4. Add spaghetti sauce. Stir until well mixed.

5. Add ziti. Toss gently to coat well.

6. Spoon into greased 9x13-inch baking pan.

7. Pour remaining spaghetti sauce over ziti mixture. Sprinkle with cheese.

8. Bake at 350°F for 45–60 minutes, or until bubbly and heated through.

Spinach Cheese Manicotti

**Kimberly Richard,
Mars, PA**

Makes 6 servings
Prep. Time: 35 minutes
Baking Time: 45–60 minutes

15-oz. container ricotta cheese

10-oz. pkg. frozen chopped spinach, thawed
    and squeezed dry

½ cup minced onion

1 egg

2 tsp. parsley

2 tsp. basil

½ tsp. black pepper

½ tsp. garlic powder

1½ cups shredded mozzarella, *divided*

½ cup grated Parmesan, *divided*

26-oz. jar spaghetti sauce

1½ cups water

1 cup diced fresh tomatoes

8-oz. pkg. uncooked manicotti shells

1. In large bowl combine ricotta, spinach, onion, and egg.

2. Stir in parsley, basil, black pepper, and garlic powder.

3. Mix in 1 cup mozzarella and ¼ cup Parmesan cheese.

4. In separate bowl, mix together sauce, water, and tomatoes.

5. Grease 9x13-inch baking pan. Spread 1 cup spaghetti sauce in bottom of pan.

6. Stuff uncooked manicotti with ricotta mixture. Arrange in single layer in baking pan.

7. Cover stuffed manicotti with remaining sauce.

8. Sprinkle with remaining cheeses.

9. Cover. Bake 45–60 minutes, or until noodles are soft.

Pasta Primavera

**Marcia S. Myer,
Manheim, PA**

Makes 6 main-dish servings
Prep. Time: 20–30 minutes
Cooking Time: 25 minutes

3 cups broccoli florets, cut bite-sized

½ lb. fresh mushrooms, quartered

2 small zucchini, sliced into ¼-inch-thick rounds

1 Tbsp. olive oil

1–3 cloves garlic, minced, according to your taste preference

1 pt. cherry tomatoes, halved

8-oz. pkg. whole-grain fettuccine

black pepper, to taste

3 Tbsp. grated reduced-fat Parmesan cheese

Sauce:

¾ cup skim milk

1 Tbsp. olive oil

⅔ cup part-skim ricotta cheese

¼ cup grated reduced-fat Parmesan cheese

2 Tbsp. chopped fresh basil, or 1 Tbsp. dried basil

2 tsp. dry sherry

1. In large microwave-safe bowl, layer in broccoli, mushrooms, and zucchini. Cover bowl and microwave on High for 2 minutes.

2. Stir. Cover and cook another 2 minutes on High, or until tender-crisp.

3. In nonstick skillet, heat olive oil. Add garlic and sauté for 1 minute. Add tomatoes and sauté for 2 minutes, or until tomatoes are slightly cooked but not wilted.

4. Cook fettuccine as directed with no salt. Drain. Keep warm.

5. Prepare sauce by combining milk, oil, ricotta cheese, Parmesan cheese, basil, and sherry in a blender.

6. Process until smooth. Heat sauce until warm, on stove or in microwave.

7. In large serving bowl, toss drained pasta, vegetables, and sauce.

8. Garnish with black pepper and 3 Tbsp. grated Parmesan cheese.

Creamy Beef and Pasta Casserole

**Virginia Graybill,
Hershey, PA**

Makes 6 servings, 4-inch square per serving
Prep. Time: 25 minutes
Baking Time: 30 minutes

1 lb. 90%-lean ground beef

8-oz. pkg. noodles, or macaroni

8-oz. pkg. fat-free cream cheese, softened

10¾-oz. can lower-fat, lower-sodium cream of mushroom soup

1 cup fat-free milk

½ cup no-salt ketchup

1. Cook ground beef in nonstick skillet until no longer pink, stirring frequently to break up clumps. Drain off any drippings.

2. Cook noodles or macaroni al dente as directed on package. Drain.

3. Mix pasta and beef in large mixing bowl.

4. In another mixing bowl, blend together cream cheese, soup, milk, and ketchup.

5. Stir sauce into pasta and beef.

6. Pour into greased 9x13-inch baking pan.

7. Bake at 350°F for 30 minutes, or until bubbly and heated through.

Pasta Pizza Pronto

Shari Jensen,
Fountain, CO

Makes 6 servings
Prep. Time: 20 minutes
Baking Time: 37–40 minutes

Crust:

2 cups uncooked elbow macaroni

3 eggs

⅓ cup finely chopped onions

1 cup shredded cheddar cheese

Topping:

1½ cups prepared pizza or pasta sauce

3-oz. pkg. sliced pepperoni

2¼-oz. can sliced olives, drained

1 cup toppings: mix or match sliced
mushrooms, diced cooked ham or chicken,
diced bell peppers

1½ cups shredded mozzarella cheese

1. In a saucepan, cook macaroni according
to package directions. Drain well.

2. In a large bowl, beat eggs. Stir in onions,
cheddar cheese, and cooked macaroni.

3. Spread pasta mixture evenly on
generously greased 14–16-inch pizza pan.

4. Bake at 375°F for 25 minutes on lower
oven rack. Remove from oven.

5. Top with your favorite pizza or pasta
sauce. Spread to within ½-inch of edge, using
the back of a spoon.

6. Top evenly with pepperoni, olives, and
1 cup of the other toppings.

7. Finish by sprinkling with mozzarella
cheese.

8. Return to oven and bake 12–15 minutes
longer, until cheese is bubbly.

9. Remove from oven and slice with pizza
cutter into 6–8 slices. Serve warm.

TIPS

1. Don't overload with toppings.
   Stay within the 1-cup
   suggestion.
2. Using the lower shelf of oven
   will crisp the crust. If not
   available in your oven, the
   middle shelf is okay.
3. Keep pasta pieces touching
   each other; no gaps.

Classic Pesto

**Leona Yoder,
Hartville, OH**

Makes about 1½ cups
Prep. Time: 10 minutes

2 cups lightly packed fresh basil

1 cup (about 5 oz.) grated Parmesan cheese

½–⅔ cup extra-virgin olive oil

1–2 cloves garlic, *optional*

1. Whirl basil, Parmesan, half the oil, and, if desired, garlic in a blender or food processor until smooth. Add more oil, if needed.

2. If you're not ready to use the pesto immediately, cover and refrigerate it for up to 5 days. Or freeze it if you want to store it longer.

3. Serve over your favorite cooked pasta, or on bruschetta.

Alfredo Sauce

Barbara Kuhns,
Millersburg, OH

Makes 2½–3 cups
Prep. Time: 3–5 minutes
Cooking Time: 20 minutes

1 stick (8 Tbsp.) butter

1 pt. heavy cream

1 tsp. garlic powder

pepper, *optional*

½ cup Parmesan cheese

2 Tbsp. cream cheese, softened

1. Lightly brown butter in a small saucepan.

2. Add rest of ingredients and simmer over low heat for 15 minutes, or until all ingredients are well blended.

3. Stir occasionally to prevent sticking and scorching.

Pizza

Crazy Crust Pizza

**Pamela Metzler,
Gilman, WI**

Makes 8 servings
Prep. Time: 20 minutes
Baking Time: 20 minutes
Standing Time: 5 minutes

2 cups flour

4 eggs

2½ tsp. salt, *divided*

1½ cups milk

1 lb. ground beef, or sausage

½–1 cup chopped onions, according to your
   taste preference

2 tsp. dried oregano

pepper, to taste

26-oz. can tomato sauce

½–1 cup shredded mozzarella cheese

½–1 cup shredded cheddar cheese

1. In a mixing bowl, mix together flour, eggs, 2 tsp. salt, and milk until smooth. Pour into a greased and floured jelly-roll pan.

2. In a large skillet, brown ground beef and onions. Season with oregano, ½ tsp. salt, and pepper. Stir in tomato sauce. Pour over crust.

3. Sprinkle cheeses evenly over top.

4. Bake at 475°F for 20 minutes. Let stand 5 minutes before cutting.

Personal Pizza

**Ruth Shank,
Gridley, IL**

Makes 6 servings
Prep. Time: 10–20 minutes
Resting Time: 10 minutes
Baking Time: 9–12 minutes, per baking
sheet

3 cups flour

1½ cups whole wheat flour

2 Tbsp., or 2 envelopes, rapid-rise yeast

1½ tsp. salt

1½ tsp. sugar

1½ cups hot (120–130°F) water

cornmeal

pizza or spaghetti sauce, toppings, and cheese

1. Stir flours, yeast, salt, and sugar together in a large bowl.

2. Stir in hot water until dough pulls away from sides of the bowl.

3. Turn out onto floured surface and knead 5 minutes, until smooth.

4. Place dough on a floured surface, cover with plastic wrap, and let rest 10 minutes. (Dough will just start to rise.)

5. Divide dough into 6 pieces. Shape each piece into a disk.

6. Put oven rack in lowest position. Preheat oven to 500°F.

7. Sprinkle a cookie sheet with cornmeal and place individual dough crusts on the sheet. (You'll be able to fit more than one dough crust on a sheet.)

8. Top each dough crust with pizza sauce, your favorite toppings, and cheese.

9. Bake on the oven's lowest rack position for 9–12 minutes.

NOTE

With individual-sized pizzas, each person may choose the toppings he or she likes best.

Mexican Pizza

Erma Martin,
East Earl, PA
Ruth Ann Bender,
Cochranville, PA

Makes 12–16 servings
Preparation Time: 30 minutes
Baking Time: 8–10 minutes

2 8-oz. tubes refrigerated crescent rolls

8-oz. pkg. cream cheese, softened

1 cup sour cream

1 lb. ground beef

1 envelope dry taco seasoning mix

2¼-oz. can sliced ripe olives, drained

1 medium tomato, chopped

¾ cup shredded cheddar cheese

¾ cup shredded mozzarella cheese

1 cup shredded lettuce

Variations:

1. Add ¼ cup chopped onions and ½ cup chopped green pepper to the toppings in Step 6.

2. Replace taco seasoning and water in Step 4 with 1 minced garlic clove, ¼ cup chopped green chilies, ¼ tsp. dried oregano, ½ tsp. salt, and a scant ½ tsp. cumin powder. Simmer for 5 minutes; then proceed with rest of the recipe.
   —Bonita Ensenberger, Albuquerque, NM

1. Flatten crescent rolls onto an ungreased 10x15-inch baking pan. Seal the seams.

2. Bake at 375°F for 8–10 minutes. Cool.

3. Meanwhile, combine cream cheese and sour cream. Spread on cooled crust.

4. Brown beef in a skillet. Drain off drippings. Stir in taco seasoning. Add water according to seasoning package directions. Simmer for 5 minutes.

5. Spread meat over cream cheese layer.

6. Layer olives, tomato, cheeses, and lettuce over top.

7. Cut into serving size pieces. Refrigerate or serve immediately.

Chicken Fajita Pizza

Ann Henderson,
Cincinnati, OH

Makes 6–8 servings
Prep. Time: 20–30 minutes
Baking Time: 15–20 minutes

1 Tbsp. oil

1 small boneless, skinless chicken breast, about ¾ lb., cut into 2x½-inch strips

1 clove garlic, pressed, or ½ tsp. garlic powder

1-2 tsp. chili powder, according to your taste preference

½ tsp. salt

1 cup onions, thinly sliced

1 cup combination of green, red, and orange pepper slices

10-oz. pkg. refrigerated pizza crust

cornmeal

½ cup salsa or picante sauce

2 cups shredded Monterey Jack cheese

1. Heat oil in skillet. Add chicken strips and stir-fry just until lightly browned.

2. Stir in garlic, chili powder, and salt. Add onions and peppers and cook for 1 minute until tender-crisp.

3. Unroll dough and roll onto cornmeal-covered pizza stone. Par-bake dough at 425°F for 8–10 minutes.

4. Spoon chicken and vegetable mixture onto crust. Cover with salsa and cheese.

5. Bake at 425°F for about 5 more minutes, or until crust is browning.

Vegetable Pizza

Deborah Heatwole,
Waynesboro, GA

Makes 6 main-dish servings
Prep. Time: 20 minutes
Rising Time: 20–30 minutes
Baking Time: 15–20 minutes

1 Tbsp. yeast

1 tsp. sugar

3/4 cup warm water

1 Tbsp. oil

1 tsp. salt

1½ cups whole wheat flour

1½ cups all-purpose flour

1 large tomato, peeled and thinly sliced

1 tsp. olive oil

1 tsp. Italian herb seasoning, no salt added,
    divided

pepper, to taste

1 large onion, sliced

1 large green bell pepper, sliced

¼ cup black olives, sliced

1½ cups sliced fresh mushrooms

3/4 cup grated low-sodium, low-fat mozzarella
    cheese

1. In a large bowl, dissolve yeast and sugar in water.

2. Stir in oil, salt, and whole wheat flour.

3. Add all-purpose flour gradually until dough is soft but not too sticky.

4. Knead on a lightly floured board for 5 minutes.

5. Cover with a towel. Let rise in a warm place 20–30 minutes.

6. Pat dough out onto a 12–15-inch pizza stone or pizza pan.

7. Bake at 400°F for 5 minutes. Remove from oven.

8. Layer with thinly sliced tomatoes.

9. Brush with oil. Sprinkle with ½ tsp. Italian seasoning and pepper.

10. Layer with remaining vegetables.

11. Top with cheese.

12. Sprinkle with ½ tsp. Italian seasoning.

13. Bake at 400°F for 10–15 minutes, or until crust is done and vegetables are tender.

14. Cut pizza into 6 pieces. Serve 1 piece to each person.

Caramelized Pear, Onion, and Gorgonzola Cheese Pizza

**Kathy Hertzler,
Lancaster, PA**

Makes 8 servings
Prep. Time: 25 minutes
Baking Time: 20 minutes

2 firm but ripe pears

2 Tbsp. butter

1 large yellow onion

1 fresh or frozen (pre-baked) whole wheat
   pizza crust

¼ lb. Gorgonzola cheese

½ cup chopped hazelnuts, *optional*

1. Thinly slice (¼-inch thick) pears and
sauté over medium heat in 2 Tbsp. butter for
5 minutes.

2. Thinly slice onion and add to pears.
Turn heat to low. Sauté slowly for 10 minutes,
or until onion is soft but the pears still hold
their shape. The onions should be caramel-
colored, but not browned.

3. Scatter mixture evenly over pizza crust.

4. Crumble Gorgonzola cheese and scatter
evenly over pears and onions.

5. Add hazelnuts if you wish.

6. Bake following the packaged pizza crust
instructions.

7. Cut into 16 appetizer or snack-sized
wedges.

Pizza Roll-Ups

**Vonnie Oyer,
Hubbard, OR**

Makes 10 servings
Prep. Time: 30 minutes
Standing and Rising Time: 1½ hours
Baking Time: 20-25 minutes

1½ Tbsp. yeast

⅜ cup warm (110-115°F) water

1½ Tbsp. sugar, *divided*

1½ Tbsp plus ½ tsp. shortening

1⅓ tsp. salt

1½ cups hot (120-130°F) water

5-6 cups flour

2 cups shredded mozzarella cheese

½ tsp. salt

½ tsp. parsley

1 tsp. Italian seasoning

¼ tsp. pepper

Sauce:

2 cups tomato sauce

1½ tsp. sugar

1½ tsp. Italian seasoning

1½ tsp. parsley

1½ tsp. dried basil

½ tsp. garlic powder

¼ tsp. pepper

1. In a small bowl dissolve yeast and ½ tsp. sugar in ⅜ cup warm water.

2. In a large bowl, combine 1½ Tbsp. sugar, shortening, salt, and hot water. Add yeast mixture.

3. Stir in flour. Knead for 10 minutes, or until smooth and elastic. Place in greased bowl, turning once.

4. Let rise to double. Punch down and let rest 10 minutes.

5. Roll dough into a 14-inch-wide strip, ¼-inch thick.

6. In a small bowl, mix cheese with ½ tsp. salt, ½ tsp. parsley, 1 tsp. Italian seasoning, and ¼ tsp. pepper. Sprinkle over dough. Press slightly into dough.

7. Roll up dough beginning with a narrow end, like a jelly roll. Cut roll into 1-inch-thick slices.

8. Grease 2 baking sheets, or line with parchment paper. Place roll-ups on baking sheets, cut side up, and let stand 10–20 minutes.

9. Bake at 400°F for 20–25 minutes.

10. Mix tomato sauce and the seasonings and herbs in a saucepan. Heat. Serve roll-ups with small bowls of sauce for dunking.

Quick Pizza Dough

Becky Frey,
Lebanon, PA

Makes 2 10-inch pizza crusts
Prep. Time: 10 minutes
Rising Time: 5 minutes
Baking Time: 20 minutes

1 Tbsp. yeast

1 cup warm water

1 Tbsp. sugar

½ tsp. salt

2 Tbsp. canola oil

1¼ cups all-purpose flour

1¼ cups whole wheat flour

1. In a good-sized bowl, dissolve yeast in water.

2. Stir in sugar, salt, and oil.

3. Add enough of each flour to make a fairly stiff dough.

4. Cover bowl and set in warm place. Let dough rise 5 minutes.

5. Turn dough onto countertop. Knead until smooth and elastic, using whatever you need of remaining flour.

6. Spray 2 10-inch pizza pans with nonstick cooking spray. Press dough onto pans, stretching as needed.

7. Spread with your favorite low-calorie toppings.

8. Bake at 400–425°F for about 20 minutes, or until lightly browned.

TIP

We like to top our pizzas with caramelized onions and bell pepper. Slice 2 large onions and chop 1 large red or green pepper. Put 1 Tbsp. or less olive oil in a large nonstick skillet. Stir in onion and pepper. Cook on low heat, covered, for 45-60 minutes. Stir occasionally. When onions are golden and as tender as you like them, remove from heat and season with a bit of balsamic vinegar. Spread over pizza crust.

Pillow Pizza

Sharon Miller,
Holmesville, OH

Makes 8 servings
Prep. Time: 20 minutes
Baking Time: 20 minutes

2 tubes refrigerated biscuits (10 biscuits per tube)

1½ lbs. ground beef

16-oz. can pizza sauce

Optional toppings:
chopped onions

chopped peppers

canned mushrooms

pepperoni

1 lb. mozzarella cheese

1. Cut each biscuit into quarters and place in the bottom of a greased 9x13-inch baking dish.

2. In a skillet, brown beef. Drain off drippings. Add sauce to beef in skillet and stir together.

3. Pour over biscuit quarters.

4. Top with any optional ingredients as you would a pizza. Sprinkle cheese over top.

5. Bake at 400°F for 20 minutes.

Grilling

Grilling

Flank Steak

Sharon Swartz Lambert,
Harrisonburg, VA

Makes 2–4 servings
Prep. Time: 10 minutes
Marinating Time: 5–24 hours
Grilling Time: 15 minutes

½–2-lb. flank steak

1 Tbsp. cooking sherry

2 Tbsp. soy sauce

1 tsp. minced fresh garlic

1 tsp. honey

1. Diamond-cut ¼-inch-wide slashes on both sides of flank steak.

2. Mix remaining ingredients together in a small bowl.

3. Place steak in a long dish. Pour marinade over top. Cover and refrigerate 5–24 hours, or overnight.

4. Grill 5 minutes per side over high heat. (You may need a bit more time, depending on thickness of the meat.)

5. Cut into thin slices on the diagonal.

Grilling

Grilled Burgers

**Deborah Heatwole,
Waynesboro, GA**

Makes 12 servings
Prep. Time: 10-15 minutes
Grilling Time: 10-15 minutes

2 lbs. ground beef

¾ cup uncooked rolled, or quick, oats

2 eggs

⅓ cup ketchup

1½ tsp. dried onion, *optional*

1 tsp. Worcestershire sauce, *optional*

salt and pepper, to taste

1. Mix ground beef thoroughly with the rest of the ingredients.

2. Shape ⅓ cupfuls into patties.

3. Place patties on hot grill. Grill, covered, 5–7 minutes per side, or until centers of burgers are no longer pink.

4. Serve on buns with toppings of your choice.

Grilled Pork Chops

Laura R. Showalter,
Dayton, VA

Makes 4 servings
Prep. Time: 10 minutes
Marinating Time: 2 hours
Grilling Time: 16–20 minutes

1 large onion, sliced

¾ cup lime, or lemon, juice

½ tsp. cayenne pepper

1 clove garlic, minced

½ tsp. salt, *optional*

4 pork chops

1. Combine all ingredients except the pork chops in a large resealable bag or container with tight-fitting lid. Combine well.

2. Submerge chops in marinade.

3. Seal bag or container and refrigerate at least 2 hours.

4. Remove chops from marinade and grill, covered, over medium-hot heat 8–10 minutes on each side.

5. Bring the marinade to a boil in a small saucepan. Use it to baste the chops if you wish while they grill.

Grilled Tenderloin of Pork

Joyce Parker,
North Plainfield, NJ

Makes 6-8 servings
Prep. Time: 15 minutes
Marinating Time: 3-8 hours, or overnight
Grilling Time: 20-30 minutes

1-2 lbs. pork tenderloin

Marinade:

¾ cup soy sauce

¼ cup olive oil

¼ cup sherry or cooking wine

¾ cup orange juice

1-2 Tbsp. minced garlic

1 Tbsp. fresh ginger, grated, or ¼ tsp. ground
   ginger

1 bunch scallions, sliced, or green onions,
   grated

Many grocery stores sell minced
or grated fresh ginger. If you want
to buy fresh gingerroot in the
produce department, grate what
you need and freeze the rest until
you need it again.

1. In a bowl, mix all marinade ingredients
together.

2. Marinate pork for at least 3–8 hours or
overnight.

3. Grill 10–15 minutes on each side.

4. Slice thin and serve.

Sugar-Crusted Ham

Pat Bechtel,
Dillsburg, PA

Makes 6-8 servings
Prep. Time: 10 minutes
Grilling Time: 30 minutes

2 fully cooked ham slices, each about 1-inch
  thick

1 cup brown sugar, packed

1/3 cup prepared horseradish

1/4 cup lemon juice

1. Score each side of ham 1/4-inch deep in a diamond pattern.

2. Combine remaining ingredients in a small saucepan. Heat to boiling, stirring frequently.

3. Grill ham slices 3 inches from medium-hot coals, 15 minutes on each side. Baste frequently with the sugar mixture.

Marinated Grilled Chicken

**Stephanie O'Conner,
Cheshire, CT**

Makes 6 servings
Prep. Time: 15 minutes
Marinating Time: 4–8 hours
Cooking Time: 10 minutes

6 boneless, skinless chicken breast halves

½ cup orange juice

¼ cup olive oil

4-6 medium-sized garlic cloves, finely
  chopped

6-8 branches fresh rosemary, washed, or
  1 Tbsp. dried rosemary, or less if you don't
  like a strong rosemary flavor

10-12 stems fresh thyme, washed, or 2 tsp.
  dried thyme

salt and pepper, to taste

1. Wash and pat dry chicken. Pound to
½-inch thickness.

2. Combine juice, oil, garlic, rosemary,
thyme, salt, and pepper in a shallow glass
(non-reactive) or plastic container.

3. Marinate chicken in mixture for
4–8 hours.

4. Grill over low, indirect heat for about
4 minutes on each side. Baste occasionally.

TIP

This recipe is quite versatile. You
can serve the chicken as a dinner
entrée with rice and vegetables.
Or slice it over salads, especially
a Caesar. My family's favorite is
to serve it on fresh Portuguese
rolls with yummy spreads such
as roasted red pepper, pesto,
or basil mayonnaise. Be sure to
include delicious toppings such
as cheddar cheese, tomatoes,
lettuce, or more.

Barbecued Chicken

Dawn Ranck,
Lansdale, PA

Makes 8 servings
Prep. Time: 10 minutes
Grilling Time: 25-30 minutes

½ cup vinegar

½ Tbsp. salt

1 stick (8 Tbsp.) butter

8 chicken legs and thighs, or 8 whole breasts

Topping:

¼ cup lemon juice

1 Tbsp. brown sugar

1 Tbsp. Worcestershire sauce

1 tsp. salt

½ tsp. dry mustard

1 stick (8 Tbsp.) butter

¾ cup ketchup

2 Tbsp. fresh parsley, chopped

2 Tbsp. fresh, or ¾ tsp. dried, lemon thyme

2 Tbsp. chives, chopped

1. In a small saucepan, combine vinegar, salt, and 1 stick butter. Heat until butter is melted.

2. Grill chicken, brushing frequently with vinegar mixture, until chicken is almost fully cooked, 15–20 minutes.

3. In another saucepan, combine all topping ingredients. Heat until butter is melted. Stir to blend well.

4. Brush topping on chicken. Grill 5 minutes. Turn chicken over. Brush topping on other side and grill an additional 5 minutes.

Lemon Grilled Chicken Breasts

**Wilma Haberkamp,
Fairbank, IA**

Makes 4 servings
Prep. Time: 15 minutes
Grilling Time: 4-5 minutes

1¼ lbs. boneless, skinless chicken breasts

2 lemons

2 Tbsp. olive oil

½ tsp. salt

½ tsp. coarsely ground pepper

1. Prepare grill for direct grilling over medium heat.

2. Pound chicken to uniform ¼-inch thickness.

3. Grate 1½ Tbsp. lemon peel and squeeze 3 Tbsp. lemon juice into a small bowl.

4. Add oil, salt, and pepper. Whisk until well blended.

5. In large bowl, toss chicken with marinade.

6. Place on grill. Cook 2–2½ minutes.

7. Turn over. Cook 2–2½ minutes more, or until juices run clear.

Sizzlin' Chicken Skewers

**Cheryl A. Lapp,
Parkesburg, PA**

Makes 6 servings
Prep. Time: 30 minutes
Marinating Time: 1½ hours
Grilling or Broiling Time: 12 minutes

⅓ cup hot water

¼ cup barbecue sauce

¼ cup creamy peanut butter

¼ cup soy sauce

2 Tbsp. honey Dijon mustard

1 lb. boneless, skinless chicken breasts, cut
    into small pieces

1 red pepper, cut into chunks

1 yellow pepper, cut into chunks

2 15-oz. cans whole potatoes

20-oz. can pineapple chunks

1 small zucchini, cut into chunks

1. In a small mixing bowl, combine first five ingredients. Brush small amount onto chicken pieces, enough to cover. Let stand for 1½ hours.

2. Alternate chicken and vegetables and pineapple chunks on skewers and brush with remaining sauce.

3. Place skewers on the grill or under the broiler for approximately 6 minutes. Turn and grill or broil another 6 minutes.

Grilled Turkey Breast

**Naomi Ressler,
Harrisonburg, VA**

Makes 7–9 servings
Prep. Time: 15 minutes
Marinating Time: 4 hours
Grilling Time: about 10 minutes

5–7-lb. turkey breast

8-oz. bottle light Italian dressing

½ cup soy sauce

2 tsp. onion powder

2 tsp. dry mustard

1. Cut turkey off the bone, slicing down each side of the breast bone. Then cut each half crosswise into serving-size pieces.

2. Combine remaining ingredients in a sizable baking dish. Reserve ½ cup for basting turkey while grilling.

3. Marinate turkey for at least 4 hours in the fridge, pushing meat down into marinade until submerged.

4. Grill over medium heat, basting with marinade until juices run clear. Grill for 5 minutes on one side. Turn over and grill another 5 minutes or so, watching carefully so the meat doesn't dry out or burn.

TIPS

1. Turkey cuts best when it's still partially frozen.
2. I put the breast bone in a large stockpot and nearly cover it with water. I put the lid on the pot and simmer it to make a great broth for later use. There's also good meat attached, which I cut up into the broth.

Zesty Grilled Fish

**Julie McKenzie,
Punxsutawney, PA**

Makes 6 servings
Prep. Time: 5 minutes
Marinating Time: 1-2 hours
Grilling Time: 10-11 minutes

2 lbs. fresh fish steaks or thick fillets

¼ cup soy sauce

¼ cup orange juice

2 Tbsp. ketchup

2 Tbsp. vegetable oil

1 Tbsp. lemon juice

½ tsp. dried oregano

½ tsp. pepper

1 garlic clove, finely chopped

1. Arrange fish in a single layer in a glass or plastic dish. In a small bowl, combine remaining ingredients and pour over fish. Marinate 1–2 hours.

2. Grill fish over a hot fire, using foil with holes punched in it, or a fish basket. Cook approximately 6 minutes on first side; then turn over and cook another 4–5 minutes, checking to see if fish flakes easily. Do not overcook!

NOTE

You can baste the fish with the marinade while grilling the first side, if you wish.

Grilled Parmesan Potatoes

**Joanna Bear,
Salisbury, MD**

Makes 4 servings
Prep. Time: 10 minutes
Grilling Time: 18–20 minutes

1 lb. small red potatoes

¼ cup chopped green onions, *optional*

2 tsp. cooking oil

1 Tbsp. Parmesan cheese

1 tsp. dried oregano

½ tsp. garlic salt

1. Cut potatoes in ½-inch cubes. Place in medium bowl.

2. Add onions, if you wish, and oil. Toss to coat.

3. Place potatoes in center of 12x12-inch sheet of heavy-duty aluminum foil.

4. Combine cheese and spices in a small bowl. Sprinkle over potatoes.

5. Fold foil into pouch, sealing tightly to prevent leaks.

6. Place pouch on a grill over medium hot coals for 18–20 minutes, or until potatoes are tender.

Grilled Vegetables

Deborah Heatwole,
Waynesboro, GA

Makes 4 servings
Prep. Time: about 15-30 minutes
Grilling Time: 15-25 minutes

4 cups sliced fresh summer squash and/or
    zucchini

4 cups sliced sweet onions, such as Vidalia

3-4 Tbsp. olive, or canola, oil

1-2 Tbsp. red wine vinegar

salt and pepper, to taste

1. Toss all ingredients in a large bowl until vegetables are evenly coated with oil and vinegar. Season with salt and pepper, to taste.

2. Spray a grill basket with nonstick cooking spray. Place on grill rack over hot coals.

3. Pour vegetables into basket, replace grill lid, and cook 15–25 minutes, until vegetables reach desired doneness, stirring every 4–5 minutes.

TIP

This is a versatile dish. Add or substitute your favorite garden vegetables, especially those that are in season.

Grilled Asparagus Spears

**Dale and Shari Mast,
Harrisonburg, VA**

Makes 6–8 servings
Prep. Time: 7 minutes
Grilling Time: 12 minutes

Grilling

2 lbs. fresh asparagus spears

1 Tbsp. olive oil

seasoned salt, to taste

1. Break woody ends off washed asparagus.

2. In a large bowl or ziplock bag, toss asparagus spears with oil and salt to taste.

3. Place spears directly onto preheated grill on low heat.

4. Grill for 12 minutes, turning spears 2–3 times.

5. Serve hot or at room temperature.

Grilled Peach Melba

**Stacy Schmucker Stoltzfus,
Enola, PA**

Makes 4 servings
Prep. Time: 10 minutes
Grilling Time: 5–10 minutes

4 large, unpeeled peaches or nectarines

2 cups red raspberries, fresh or frozen

½ tsp. sugar, plus more to sweeten raspberries
   if needed

vanilla ice cream

1. Halve and pit peaches or nectarines.

2. Press fresh or thawed raspberries through sieve. Save juice and discard seeds. Sweeten to taste with sugar, if needed.

3. Grill unpeeled peaches cut-side down for approximately 2 minutes. Turn peaches over. With cut side up, fill each cavity with ½ tsp. sugar, and continue grilling until grill marks appear on skins.

4. Serve immediately with a scoop of vanilla ice cream and drizzle with the raspberry sauce.

Vegetables and Side Dishes

Vegetables and Side Dishes

Ranch Potato Cubes

Charlotte Shaffer,
East Earl, PA

Makes 8 servings
Prep. Time: 20 minutes
Baking Time: 1 hour 10 minutes

6 medium potatoes, cut into ½-inch cubes

½ stick (4 Tbsp.) butter, cubed

1 cup sour cream

1 packet ranch salad dressing mix

1 cup (4 oz.) shredded cheddar cheese

1. Place potatoes in a greased 7x11-inch baking dish. Dot with butter.

2. Cover. Bake at 350°F for 1 hour.

3. Combine sour cream and salad dressing mix.

4. Spoon over potatoes. Sprinkle with cheese.

5. Bake uncovered 10 minutes until cheese is melted.

Vegetables and
Side Dishes

Rosemary Roasted Potatoes

Pamela Pierce,
Annville, PA

Makes 8 servings
Prep. Time: 10 minutes
Baking Time: 45–60 minutes

8 medium red potatoes, scrubbed, dried, and cut into wedges

3 Tbsp. olive oil

1 tsp. crushed dried rosemary

1 tsp. crushed dried thyme

½ tsp. salt

⅛ tsp. pepper

1. Toss potato wedges in oil.

2. Place in shallow roasting pan and sprinkle evenly with seasonings. Stir.

3. Roast in 375°F oven for 45–60 minutes, stirring every 10–15 minutes, until golden and fork-tender.

Oven Parmesan Chips

**Erma Martin,
East Earl, PA
Nettie J. Miller,
Millersburg, OH
Robin Schrock,
Millersburg, OH
Carol L. Stroh,
Akron, NY**

Makes 4–6 servings
Prep. Time: 10 minutes
Baking Time: 15–25 minutes

½ stick (4 Tbsp.) butter, melted

⅓ tsp. garlic powder

½ tsp. salt

⅛ tsp. pepper

2-3 Tbsp. grated Parmesan cheese

4 medium-sized baking potatoes, unpeeled

1. Melt butter on baking sheet.

2. Sprinkle seasonings and grated cheese evenly over butter.

3. Cut potatoes into ¼-inch slices.

4. Lay potato slices in single layer on top of buttery mixture. Then turn each slice over so both sides are coated.

5. Bake at 425°F for 15–25 minutes, or until potatoes are tender and golden.

Variations:

1. Instead of 4 baking potatoes, use 8 medium-sized unpeeled red potatoes, cut in half.

   —Janet Oberholtzer, Ephrata, PA

2. Omit the garlic powder and add 1 finely minced garlic clove instead. For an interesting additional flavor, add ⅛ tsp. ground nutmeg to Step 2.

   —Carol L. Stroh, Akron, NY

TIP

These are decadently delicious served with sour cream as a condiment. —Nettie J. Miller, Millersburg, OH

Vegetables and Side Dishes

Oven Fries

**Sherry H. Kauffman,
Minot, ND**

Makes 6 servings
Prep. Time: 15 minutes
Baking Time: 25 minutes

3 medium unpeeled baking potatoes (1½ lbs.)

2 large carrots, peeled

2 tsp. vegetable, or canola, oil

¼ tsp. salt

¼ tsp. pepper

nonfat cooking spray

1. Scrub potatoes. Cut potatoes and carrots into 3½x½-inch strips. Pat dry with paper towel.

2. Combine oil, salt, and pepper in large bowl. Add potatoes and carrots. Toss to coat.

3. Arrange in a single layer on a baking sheet coated with nonfat cooking spray.

4. Bake at 475°F for 25 minutes, or until tender and brown, turning after 15 minutes.

Night-Before Potatoes

Susan Tjon, Austin, TX
Jennie Martin, Richfield, PA
Leona Miller, Millersburg, OH
Leona M. Slabaugh, Apple Creek, OH

Makes 6-8 servings
Prep. Time: 45 minutes
Baking Time: 35 minutes
Chilling Time: 8 hours or overnight

8-10 potatoes, peeled

8 oz. cream cheese

1 cup sour cream

1 tsp. salt

¼ tsp. pepper

2 Tbsp. butter

1 tsp. seasoned salt, garlic salt, or onion salt

1. Cook potatoes until soft. Mash.

2. Add cream cheese and sour cream. Beat until fluffy and smooth. Add salt and pepper.

3. Place in buttered 9x13-inch dish or 2-qt. casserole.

4. Dot with butter and sprinkle with seasoned salt.

5. Refrigerate 8 hours or overnight. May also be frozen at this point (just thaw before baking).

6. Preheat oven to 325°F. Cover and bake 15 minutes.

7. Uncover and bake another 20 minutes or until peaks are light brown.

Variations:

To the mashed potatoes, add 1 pkg. frozen spinach that has been cooked and well-drained. After putting the potato mixture in a greased pan, sprinkle top with 1 cup cheddar cheese.
—Arianne Hochstetler, Goshen, IN

Double the sour cream. Top with grated cheese. These potatoes can keep up to two weeks in the refrigerator before baking.
—Brittany Zimmerman, Wrightsville, PA

TIPS

1. Low-fat cream cheese and sour cream may be used.
2. These potatoes can be rewarmed in a slow cooker before serving.
3. For convenience sake, you can bake the mashed potatoes at 350°F for up to an hour. This is handy when you are serving a holiday dinner, juggling oven space and temperatures.

Guilt-Free Golden Mashed Potatoes

Sharon Wantland,
Menomonee Falls, WI

Makes 8 servings
Prep. Time: 30 minutes
Cooking/Baking Time: 40–45 minutes

2 lbs. Yukon Gold potatoes

2 reduced-sodium chicken bouillon cubes

¼ cup skim milk

4 oz. fat-free cream cheese, softened

¼ cup fat-free sour cream

½ cup low-fat shredded sharp cheddar cheese

¼ tsp. white pepper

2 tsp. chopped fresh parsley

1. Peel and cut potatoes into small cubes. Place in 4-qt. saucepan with bouillon and water to cover.

2. Cover pan. Bring to a boil and cook until very tender, about 30 minutes.

3. Drain and return potatoes to pan.

4. Preheat oven to 425°F.

5. Mash potatoes with electric mixer or handheld ricer.

6. Add all remaining ingredients to potatoes except parsley. Mix well.

7. Place 6 oval-shaped mounds of potatoes on cookie sheet, lightly covered with vegetable spray coating.

8. Bake in preheated oven 10–15 minutes, or until golden brown.

9. Garnish with parsley just before serving.

Healthy Sweet Potato Fries

**Gladys M. High,
Ephrata, PA**

Makes 4 servings
Prep. Time: 15 minutes
Roasting Time: 30 minutes

organic olive oil cooking spray

2 large sweet potatoes, peeled and cut into
   wedges

¼ tsp. salt

¼ tsp. black pepper

oregano, thyme, rosemary, garlic powder,
   optional

1. Preheat oven to 400°F.

2. Coat baking sheet with organic olive oil
cooking spray.

3. Arrange potato wedges on baking sheet
in a single layer. Coat with cooking spray.

4. Sprinkle potatoes with salt, pepper, and
any additional seasonings of your choice.

5. Roast 30 minutes, or until tender and
golden brown.

Honey Maple Sweet Potatoes

Lorraine Kratz,
Sinking Spring, PA

Makes 6-8 servings
Prep. Time: 30 minutes
Cooking/Baking Time: 50 minutes

6-8 medium sweet potatoes

½ cup honey

½ cup maple syrup

½ cup milk

4 Tbsp. butter

1. Cook sweet potatoes in a pot with water to cover. Test with a fork and remove from heat when they are becoming soft. Do not overcook.

2. Run cold water over the sweet potatoes. Peel them.

3. Place the honey, maple syrup, milk, and butter in a pan and bring to a boil for about 30 seconds.

4. Place sweet potatoes in a 9-inch square pan. Pour the sauce over them.

5. Bake at 350°F for 30 minutes.

Scalloped Fall Bake

Kathleen A. Rogge,
Alexandria, IN
Jeanette B. Oberholtzer,
Manheim, PA
Irene J. Dewar,
Pickering, ON

Makes 6–8 servings
Prep. Time: 25 minutes
Baking Time: 40 minutes

3 large tart, unpeeled apples

4 medium sweet potatoes, cooked and peeled

½ stick (4 Tbsp.) butter, *divided*

1 tsp. salt

½ cup honey, or brown sugar

1 tsp. zest of orange, *optional*

Add ½ cup pecan pieces to top of baking dish, just before pouring sauce over all.
—Jeanette B. Oberholtzer, Manheim, PA

1. Slice apples and potatoes into ½-inch thick slices.

2. In a skillet, sauté apples in 2 Tbsp. butter until light brown.

3. Arrange alternate layers of potatoes and apples in a greased 2-qt. baking dish. Sprinkle each layer with salt.

4. Melt remaining butter in skillet. Stir in honey, and orange zest if you wish, and blend.

5. Pour over potatoes and apples.

6. Bake uncovered at 375°F for 40 minutes.

Variation:

Baked Beans

**Barbara Hershey,
Lititz, PA**

Makes 8-10 servings
Prep. Time: 30 minutes plus overnight soaking time
Cooking/Baking Time: 2½ hours

1 lb. dry northern beans

1 tsp. salt

½ tsp. baking soda

2 cups V8 juice

1 small onion, minced

2 Tbsp. molasses

1 tsp. dry mustard

7-8 pieces bacon, fried (reserve grease)

½ cup ketchup

½ cup brown sugar

TIP

If you don't have time to soak dry beans, you could purchase 6 16-oz. cans of northern beans and drain before adding other ingredients.

1. Cover beans with about 3 inches water and allow to soak overnight.

2. In morning, add salt and baking soda.

3. Bring to boil. Cook about 20–25 minutes until beans are soft. Drain.

4. Pour beans into large baking dish.

5. Add juice, onion, molasses, mustard, bacon, ketchup, brown sugar, and most of the bacon grease. Mix.

6. Bake at 325°F for 2 hours or on Low in slow cooker for 5–6 hours.

Country-Style Baked Beans

Rhoda Atzeff,
Lancaster, PA

Makes 8 servings
Prep. Time: 10–15 minutes
Cooking Time: 12–15 minutes
Standing Time: 5 minutes

2 16-oz. cans pinto beans, drained

1 cup chopped ham

½ cup Bull's-Eye Original barbecue sauce

½ cup finely chopped onion

2 Tbsp.–¼ cup molasses, depending on your taste preference

1. Combine ingredients in a lightly greased 1½-qt. casserole. Cover with waxed paper.

2. Microwave on High 12–15 minutes, or until thoroughly heated, stirring every 5 minutes.

3. Let stand 5 minutes before serving.

Best-in-the-West Beans

**Lorraine Martin,
Dryden, MI**

Makes 10 servings, about ²/₃ cup per serving
Prep. Time: 20 minutes
Baking Time: 1 hour

½ lb. ground beef

5 slices bacon, chopped

½ cup chopped onion

¼ cup brown sugar

¼ cup white sugar

¼ cup no-salt ketchup

¼ cup barbecue sauce

2 Tbsp. mustard

2 Tbsp. molasses

½ tsp. chili powder

½ tsp. pepper

1-lb. can kidney beans

1-lb. can butter beans

1-lb. can pork and beans

To prepare in slow cooker, cook on High for 1 hour. Reduce heat to Low and cook for 4 hours.

1. Brown ground beef and bacon. Drain. Add onion and cook until tender. Add all other ingredients except beans and mix well.

2. Drain kidney beans and butter beans. Add all beans to meat mixture. Pour into 3-qt. casserole dish.

3. Bake at 350°F for 1 hour.

Lima Bean Supreme

Lizzie Ann Yoder,
Hartville, OH
Jean Butzer,
Batavia, NY

Makes 9 servings, about 6 oz. per serving
Prep. Time: 20 minutes
Soaking Time: 8 hours or overnight
Cooking/Baking Time: 3 hours

1 lb. lima beans, dry

⅓ cup trans-fat-free tub margarine

1 cup fat-free sour cream

¼ cup Splenda Brown Sugar Blend

1 Tbsp. dry mustard

1 tsp. molasses, or 1 Tbsp. light corn syrup

1. Soak the dried beans overnight covered in water. Drain.

2. Cook until almost tender (about an hour) in salted water. Drain, rinse, and place in a deep casserole.

3. Mix well the margarine, sour cream, sugar, mustard, and molasses. Pour over beans and mix well.

4. Bake at 300°F for 2 hours, stirring several times. Mixture will be thin when you take it from the oven, but thickens as it cools.

Variations:
Bake at 350°F for 1 hour.
—Joanne Warfel, Lancaster, PA

Vegetables and
Side Dishes

TIPS

1. To speed up this preparation, bring the beans to a boil in the salted water. Let stand a couple of hours vs. overnight. Then proceed to cook (boil) until almost tender.
2. May be served warm or cold.

Green Beans Caesar

Carol Shirk,
Leola, PA

Makes 6–8 servings
Prep. Time: 10 minutes
Cooking/Baking Time: 30 minutes

1½ lbs. green beans, trimmed

2 Tbsp. oil

1 Tbsp. vinegar

1 Tbsp. minced onion

salt, to taste

pepper, to taste

2 Tbsp. bread crumbs

2 Tbsp. Parmesan cheese

1 Tbsp. butter, melted

1. Cook the green beans until barely tender. Drain.

2. Toss with oil, vinegar, onion, salt, and pepper.

3. Pour into an ungreased 2-qt. casserole.

4. Mix bread crumbs, Parmesan cheese, and butter. Sprinkle over beans.

5. Bake at 350°F for 20 minutes.

Barbecued Green Beans

**Naomi Ressler,
Harrisonburg, VA**

Makes 6-8 servings
Prep. Time: 15 minutes
Baking Time: 20 minutes

4 slices bacon, chopped into small pieces

½ cup sliced or chopped onions

½ cup ketchup

¼ cup brown sugar

1 Tbsp. Worcestershire sauce

1½-qts. (50-oz. can) green beans, drained

1. Fry bacon and onion together until bacon is crisp.

2. Add ketchup, brown sugar, and Worcestershire sauce. Simmer several minutes.

3. Add to drained beans in a 1½-qt. casserole dish.

4. Bake at 350°F for 20 minutes or until heated throughout.

Variation:
Double the bacon and brown sugar. Increase the ketchup to ¾ cup. And you can use bacon bits instead of frying your own bacon.
—Esther A. Hershberger, Murphysboro, IL

TIPS

1. I save part of the bacon dripping in the pan with the rest of ingredients for added flavor, but discard part for health reasons.
2. I often double the recipe and put in my slow cooker on Low for 3 hours. This is a favorite at our church potlucks.

Vegetables and
Side Dishes

Green Bean and Mushroom Sauté

**Louise Bodziony,
Sunrise Beach, MO
Clara Yoder Byler,
Hartville, OH**

Makes 4 servings
Prep. Time: 10 minutes
Cooking Time: 20 minutes

Vegetables and
Side Dishes

1 lb. fresh, or frozen, green beans

³/₄–1 cup sliced fresh mushrooms

2 Tbsp. butter

2–3 tsp. onion, or garlic, powder

4 strips bacon, cooked and crumbled, *optional*

1. Cook green beans in water to cover, just until tender.

2. Meanwhile, in a skillet sauté mushrooms in butter until tender.

3. Stir in onion, or garlic, powder.

4. Drain beans. Add to skillet and toss with mushrooms and seasonings.

5. Place in serving dish. Top with crumbled bacon if you wish.

Holiday Green Beans

Joanne Kennedy,
Plattsburgh, NY
Jean Ryan,
Peru, NY

Makes 10 servings
Prep. Time: 10 minutes
Cooking Time: 20 minutes

2 lbs. (about 8 cups) fresh green beans

1 large red onion, thinly sliced

3 cloves fresh garlic, minced

1 tsp. olive oil

½ cup slivered almonds

pepper, to taste

1. Steam beans in saucepan until just slightly crisp.

2. Sauté onion and garlic in olive oil in large skillet for 3 minutes.

3. Add beans to skillet. Sauté 1 minute.

4. Add slivered almonds and pepper to beans. Toss together and then serve.

Vegetables and
Side Dishes

Glazed Carrot Coins

**Dorothy Lingerfelt,
Stonyford, CA**

Makes 4–6 servings
Prep. Time: 20 minutes
Cooking Time: 30 minutes

12 medium carrots, cut into 1-inch pieces

½ cup brown sugar, packed

3 Tbsp. butter or margarine

1 Tbsp. grated lemon peel

¼ tsp. vanilla extract

1. In saucepan, cook carrots in a small amount of water until crisp-tender. Do not overcook.

2. Drain. Remove and keep warm.

3. In the same pan, heat brown sugar and butter until bubbly. Stir in lemon peel.

4. Return carrots to pan; cook and stir over low heat for 10 minutes or until glazed.

5. Remove from heat; stir in vanilla.

Variations:

1. For horseradish carrots, melt together ½ stick (4 Tbsp.) butter, ⅓ cup honey, and 2 Tbsp. horseradish. Add to cooked carrots.

   —Janet Batdorf, Harrisburg, PA

2. Add 1 cup raisins to the cooking carrots in Step 4. Add ½ cup brown sugar, ½ stick (4 Tbsp.) butter, 2 Tbsp. lemon juice, and 1 tsp. salt also.

   —Jeanette Oberholtzer, Lititz, PA

3. Substitute 2 Tbsp. Dijon mustard for the lemon peel and vanilla.

   —Joette Droz, Kalona, IA

Roasted Baby Carrots

Melanie Mohler,
Ephrata, PA

Makes 4–5 servings
Prep. Time: 5–10 minutes
Cooking/Roasting Time: 10–15 minutes

1 lb. baby carrots

1 Tbsp. olive oil

1 Tbsp. dried dill weed

sprinkle of salt

1. Preheat oven to 475°F.

2. If using thick baby carrots, slice in half lengthwise. Otherwise leave as is.

3. In a large bowl, combine olive oil and dill. Add carrots and toss to coat.

4. In a 10×15-inch baking pan, spread carrots in a single layer.

5. Roast, uncovered, about 10 minutes or until carrots are just tender, stirring once.

6. Sprinkle with salt before serving.

Carrots with Dill

Marilyn Mowry,
Irving, TX

Makes 4 servings
Prep. Time: 5 minutes
Cooking Time: 12–15 minutes

4 cups water

2 cups fresh carrots, peeled and sliced

1 Tbsp. soft-tub margarine, non-hydrogenated

2 Tbsp. honey

¼ tsp. Lawry's lemon pepper

¼ tsp. salt, *optional*

⅛–¼ tsp. dill weed

1. Bring 4 cups water to a boil in saucepan. Add carrots. Cover and boil 1 minute.

2. Drain carrots. Add remaining ingredients to carrots in saucepan and mix well. Heat through over low heat.

3. Stir again and spoon into serving dish.

Bacon-Touched Carrots and Turnips

Becky Frey,
Lebanon, PA

Makes 6 servings
Prep. Time: 10 minutes
Cooking Time: 20 minutes

2 slices bacon, diced

1 medium onion, sliced

3 medium carrots, julienned

2 turnips, julienned (approximately 2 cups)

salt and pepper, to taste

snipped parsley, *optional*

1. Cook bacon in saucepan. Remove from pan and drain. Reserve drippings.

2. Stir-fry vegetables in bacon drippings until crisp-tender, about 5 minutes.

3. Cover and cook on low 8–10 minutes, or until as tender as you like.

4. Sprinkle with salt and pepper. Garnish with bacon, and also parsley if you wish, just before serving.

Roasted Broccoli

**Andrea Cunningham,
Arlington, KS**

Makes 4 servings
Prep. Time: 10 minutes
Baking Time: 20 minutes

Vegetables and
Side Dishes

1 head (about 5 cups) broccoli, cut into long pieces all the way through (you will eat the stems)

1 Tbsp. olive oil

2-3 cloves garlic, sliced thin

sprinkle of pepper

lemon wedges

1. Preheat oven to 400°F.

2. Place broccoli in baking pan with sides. Drizzle with olive oil. Toss to coat.

3. Sprinkle garlic and pepper over top.

4. Transfer to oven and roast 15–20 minutes, or until broccoli is crispy on the ends and a little browned.

5. Sprinkle with lemon juice.

Broccoli with Garlic and Lemon

Jan Moore,
Wellsville, KS
Leona Yoder,
Hartville, OH

Makes 4-5 servings
Prep. Time: 10 minutes
Cooking Time: 10-15 minutes

Vegetables and Side Dishes

4½ cups fresh broccoli florets

¼-½ cup water

1 Tbsp. extra-virgin olive oil

1 garlic clove, crushed, or 1½ tsp. jarred minced garlic

juice and grated peel from half a lemon

grated Parmesan cheese, *optional*

1. Place broccoli and water in a good-sized saucepan. Cover and cook over medium-high heat, stirring occasionally for several minutes until broccoli is crisp-tender. Add more water if necessary to prevent scorching, but only a small amount.

2. Drain excess liquid from skillet. Push broccoli to one side and add olive oil and garlic to the other side. Cook for about 10–20 seconds, or until garlic begins to turn color and smell fragrant.

3. Toss all together.

4. Stir in lemon juice and peel.

5. When ready to serve, top with Parmesan cheese if you wish.

Cheesy Broccoli

Esther J. Mast,
Lancaster, PA
Jan Rankin,
Millersville, PA

Makes 6–8 servings
Prep. Time: 20 minutes
Baking Time: 20 minutes

2 10-oz. pkgs. frozen broccoli

1 stick (8 Tbsp.) butter, melted, *divided*

8-oz. pkg. Velveeta cheese, grated, *divided*

36–38 Ritz crackers (about ⅔ tube), crushed

1. Place broccoli in a medium-sized saucepan, along with about ¼ cup water. Cover and steam, stirring occasionally, until crisp-tender, about 5–10 minutes.

2. Drain broccoli and place in lightly greased 1½-qt. casserole.

3. Pour half of melted butter over broccoli.

4. Stir in most of the cheese. Reserve the rest for sprinkling on top of fully mixed casserole.

5. In a mixing bowl, combine the remaining butter with the crushed crackers. Sprinkle over broccoli mixture.

6. Top with reserved cheese.

7. Bake uncovered at 325°F for 20 minutes.

Cheesy Cauliflower

Joan Erwin,
Sparks, NV

Makes 4–5 servings
Prep. Time: 5–10 minutes
Cooking Time: 10 minutes

1 head cauliflower

1 Tbsp. water

1 cup mayonnaise

1 Tbsp. prepared mustard

½ cup chopped green or red onions

1 cup shredded Monterey Jack and cheddar
    cheeses, combined, or one of the two

1. Place whole cauliflower head in microwavable glass baking dish. Add water. Cover. Microwave on High for 9 minutes, until crisp-cooked.

2. Meanwhile, combine mayonnaise, mustard, and onions in a small bowl. Spread over cooked cauliflower. Sprinkle with cheese.

3. Cover and microwave on High for 1 minute, or until cheese is melted.

Variation:
You may break the cauliflower into florets and proceed with Step 1.

Vegetables and Side Dishes

Cauliflower Mashed "Potatoes"

Anne Hummel,
Millersburg, OH

Makes 4 servings
Prep. Time: 20 minutes
Cooking Time: 20–30 minutes

1 head cauliflower

1 clove garlic

1 leek, white only, split in 4 pieces

1 Tbsp. soft-tub margarine, non-hydrogenated

pepper, to taste

1. Break cauliflower into small pieces.

2. In a good-sized saucepan, steam cauliflower, garlic, and leeks in water until completely tender, about 20–30 minutes.

3. While cauliflower is hot, puree until the vegetables resemble mashed potatoes. (Use a food processor, or if you prefer a smoother texture, use a blender. Process only a small portion at a time, holding the blender lid on firmly with a tea towel.)

4. Add a little hot water if vegetables seem dry.

5. Stir in margarine, and pepper to taste.

Baked Corn

Phyllis Good,
Lancaster, PA

Makes 6 servings
Prep. Time: 20 minutes
Baking Time: 30-45 minutes

3 eggs

2 cups fresh or frozen corn, creamed or simply
   cut off the cob

2 cups milk

1 Tbsp. butter, melted

salt and pepper, to taste

1. In a large mixing bowl, beat eggs well.

2. Stir in the remaining ingredients.

3. Pour into a lightly greased 1½- or 2-qt. greased casserole.

4. Bake uncovered at 325°F for 30–45 minutes, or until knife inserted in center comes out clean.

Corn with Bacon

**Mary Jane Musser,
Narvon, PA**

Makes 6 servings
Prep. Time: 10 minutes
Baking Time: 35 minutes

4 cups fresh, or frozen, corn

1 tsp. salt

¼ tsp. pepper

1½ tsp. sugar

1 cup finely diced uncooked bacon

1. Place corn in a 1½-qt. greased baking dish.

2. Stir in salt, pepper, and sugar.

3. Spread bacon over top of corn.

4. Bake uncovered at 350°F for 35 minutes, or until bacon is crisp.

Corn Extraordinary

Judy Newman,
Saint Mary's, ON

Makes 6 servings
Prep. Time: 5-7 minutes
Cooking Time: 4-6 minutes

2 garlic cloves

¼ cup chives

2 tsp. olive oil

4 cups corn (best if cut straight off the cob; if you use canned, it should be without added salt)

pinch of pepper

1. Chop garlic and chives.

2. Heat oil in large skillet over medium heat. Gently sauté garlic. (Reserve chives.)

3. Add corn. Sauté 3–5 minutes.

4. Season to taste with pepper and chives.

Peas with Bacon and Crispy Leeks

**J. B. Miller,
Indianapolis, IN**

Makes 12 servings
Prep. Time: 15 minutes
Cooking Time: 45 minutes

Vegetables and
Side Dishes

3 large leeks, *divided*

vegetable oil

salt and pepper, to taste

6 thick slices of bacon

4 fresh thyme springs, or ½ tsp. ground thyme

1 cup chicken broth, *divided*

¾ cup light cream or half-and-half

30 oz. frozen baby peas, thawed

1 tsp. cornstarch

1 Tbsp. water

1. Using only the white and tender green part of the leeks, slice the leeks crosswise into ¼-inch thick pieces. Separate into rings. Wash and pat dry.

2. Heat ¼-inch of oil in a large saucepan until shimmering. Add all but ½ cup of leeks. Cook over moderate heat, stirring until golden brown.

3. Using a slotted spoon, transfer leeks to a paper towel–lined plate to drain. Discard oil. Season leeks with salt and pepper.

4. In the same saucepan, cook bacon until brown and crispy. Remove bacon, but reserve its drippings. Place bacon on paper towels. When drained, crumble.

5. Add remaining ½ cup leeks and the thyme to the skillet. Cook until soft.

6. Add ½ cup chicken broth and cook uncovered until broth is reduced by half.

7. Add cream. Cook until the creamy broth is reduced by half.

8. Stir in peas, crumbled bacon, and the remaining ½ cup broth. Bring to a boil.

9. If using fresh thyme sprigs, discard. Season cooked mixture with salt and pepper.

10. In a small bowl, stir cornstarch into water until smooth. Stir into hot sauce. Continue stirring until it thickens slightly.

11. Spoon the peas into a serving dish and top with the reserved crispy leeks just before serving.

Sugar Snap Pea Crunchies

Joy Uhler,
Richardson, TX

Makes 4–12 servings (salad/side or snack/appetizer)
Prep. Time: 6–8 minutes

Vegetables and Side Dishes

½ lb. fresh sugar snap peas, washed

1 Tbsp. sesame oil

2 tsp. toasted sesame seeds

¼ tsp. salt, *optional*

1. Pinch off ends and any strings from each pea pod.

2. Place in mixing bowl.

3. Toss raw peas with sesame oil.

4. Sprinkle toasted sesame seeds, and salt if using, over all and toss together.

5. Serve as a vegetable side dish, a salad, or as finger food for a snack or appetizer.

TIPS

1. Store these peas in an airtight container. Just take the lid off and eat or serve. Refrigerate if you won't be eating the peas immediately. Serve chilled or at room temperature.
2. You can find the oil and seeds in the Asian food section of your grocery store.

Snow Peas with Sesame Seeds

**Sylvia Beiler,
Lowville, NY**

Makes 6 servings
Prep. Time: 15 minutes
Baking Time: 10 minutes

3 cups trimmed fresh snow peas

2 Tbsp. diced onions

1 Tbsp. canola oil

3 Tbsp. sesame seeds

¼ tsp. freshly ground pepper

1. Slice each snow pea diagonally into 2–3 pieces.

2. Sauté onions and peas in oil in large skillet until tender.

3. Meanwhile, place sesame seeds in baking pan. Toast in 350°F oven for 8 minutes, or until lightly browned.

4. Add sesame seeds to onions and peas. Sauté 1 minute until peas are coated with seeds.

5. Sprinkle with freshly ground pepper.

Creamed Peas and Mushrooms

Diena Schmidt,
Henderson, NE

Makes 8 servings
Prep. Time: 15 minutes
Cooking Time: 25 minutes

20-oz pkg. frozen peas

½ cup mushroom caps

1 Tbsp. minced onion

2 Tbsp. trans-fat–free tub margarine

2 Tbsp. flour

1½ cups fat-free half-and-half

3 Tbsp. reduced-fat Velveeta cheese

1. Cook peas in boiling salted water until tender.

2. Sauté mushrooms and onion in margarine until lightly browned. Add to peas.

3. Stir flour into remaining drippings. Add half-and-half gradually, cooking and stirring until slightly thickened.

4. Turn heat to low and add cheese. Stir until dissolved. Combine with peas and mushrooms.

Garlic Mushrooms

Lizzie Ann Yoder,
Hartville, OH

Makes 4 servings
Prep. Time: 20 minutes
Cooking Time: 15–20 minutes

3 Tbsp. trans-fat-free tub margarine

2 cloves garlic, minced

1 lb. mushrooms, sliced

4 scallions, chopped

1 tsp. lemon juice

1. In a skillet, melt the butter and sauté the garlic briefly.

2. Add mushrooms, scallions, and lemon juice and cook, stirring, about 10 minutes.

Spinach Soufflé

Orpha Herr,
Andover, NY

Makes 6–8 servings
Prep. Time: 20 minutes
Baking Time: 45 minutes
Standing Time: 5–10 minutes

2 cups cottage cheese

3 eggs, beaten

3 10-oz. pkgs. frozen spinach, thawed and
squeezed dry

1½ cups shredded cheddar cheese, *divided*

½ tsp. salt

dash of ground nutmeg, *optional*

1. In large mixing bowl, beat together cottage cheese and eggs.

2. Stir in spinach, 1¼ cups cheddar cheese, salt, and nutmeg if you wish.

3. Spoon into a lightly greased 8x12-inch baking pan.

4. Bake uncovered at 350°F until set, about 45 minutes.

5. Sprinkle with remaining cheese. Let stand 5–10 minutes so cheese can melt and soufflé can firm up.

Absolutely Creamy Spinach

Vicki J. Hill,
Memphis, TN

Makes 9 servings
Prep. Time: 5 minutes
Cooking/Baking Time: 8–30 minutes

4 10-oz. pkgs. frozen chopped spinach, thawed and squeezed dry

8-oz. pkg. cream cheese

1 stick (8 Tbsp.) butter

fine bread crumbs

sprinkle of paprika, *optional*

1. Place spinach in lightly greased 2-qt. baking dish.

2. Soften cream cheese and butter in microwave for 1 minute. Beat until combined. Pour over spinach.

3. Sprinkle with crumbs, and paprika if desired.

4. Heat uncovered in oven at 350°F for 20–30 minutes, or in the microwave, covered, for 8–10 minutes.

Bacon Cabbage Surprise

**Jonathan Gehman,
Harrisonburg, VA**

Makes an adaptable number of servings!
Prep. Time: 10 minutes if cooking for
3-4 persons
Cooking Time: 15 minutes

bacon, 1 or 2 strips per person

onion, cut in thick slices, ¼ cup per person

garlic, minced, 1 small clove per person

cabbage, cut in thin strips, 1 cup per person

carrots, shredded, ¼ cup per person

1. Cut bacon in ½-inch wide squares. Place in nonstick pan large enough to hold all ingredients. Sauté over medium heat until browned but not crispy. Drain off all but 2 Tbsp. drippings.

2. Turn heat to low. Add onion and garlic and cook until transparent.

3. Add cabbage and carrots, stirring to coat with bacon drippings. Mix all ingredients together well.

4. The dish is done when the cabbage begins to wilt.

Red Cabbage with Apples

Jean Butzer,
Batavia, NY
Louise Thieszen,
North Newton, KS

Makes 8 servings
Prep. Time: 15 minutes
Cooking Time: 40 minutes

1 medium head red cabbage, shredded

1 large onion, chopped

2 Tbsp. canola oil

2 medium apples, unpeeled, cored, and sliced

¼ cup cider vinegar

¼ tsp. pepper

1 Tbsp. caraway seeds, *optional*

1. In a large skillet, sauté cabbage and onion in oil 5–8 minutes, or until crisp-tender.

2. Add apples, vinegar, pepper, and caraway seeds if you wish. Bring to a boil.

3. Reduce heat. Cover and simmer 25 minutes, or until cabbage is tender.

Vegetables and
Side Dishes

Oven Brussels Sprouts

**Gail Martin,
Elkhart, IN**

Makes 8 servings
Prep. Time: 15 minutes
Baking Time: 15–20 minutes

1½ lbs. Brussels sprouts, halved

¼ cup plus 2 Tbsp. olive oil

juice of 1 lemon

½ tsp. salt

½ tsp. pepper

½ tsp. crushed red pepper flakes

1. In a large bowl, toss halved sprouts with 2 Tbsp. olive oil.

2. Place them on a single layer on a rimmed cookie sheet.

3. Roast sprouts in the oven at 450°F, stirring twice, until crisp and lightly browned, about 15–20 minutes.

4. Whisk together in a large bowl ¼ cup oil, lemon juice, salt, pepper, and crushed red pepper.

5. Toss sprouts with dressing and serve.

TIP

Don't overcook the sprouts.

Stir-Fried Asparagus

Sylvia Beiler,
Lowville, NY

Makes 6 servings
Prep. Time: 5 minutes
Cooking Time: 2–3 minutes

1 Tbsp. canola oil

3 cups asparagus, sliced diagonally

4 scallions, or green onions, sliced diagonally

1 garlic clove, minced, *optional*

1 tsp. lemon juice

1. Heat oil in pan. Add sliced vegetables and garlic, if using.

2. Stir-fry until crisp-tender.

3. Sprinkle with lemon juice. Serve immediately.

Roasted Asparagus

Barbara Walker,
Sturgis, SD

Makes 6 servings
Prep. Time: 5 minutes
Cooking Time: 12 minutes

Vegetables and Side Dishes

1 lb. fresh asparagus spears

2–3 Tbsp. olive oil

⅛ tsp. pepper

2 Tbsp. balsamic vinegar

1. Place asparagus in bowl with olive oil. Toss together to coat asparagus.

2. Place asparagus spears on a baking sheet in a single layer. Sprinkle with pepper.

3. Roast uncovered at 450°F. Shake pan once or twice to turn spears after about 6 minutes.

4. Roast another 6 minutes, or until asparagus is tender-crisp.

5. Put on a plate and drizzle with balsamic vinegar. Serve immediately

Asparagus Bake

Leona M. Slabaugh,
Apple Creek, OH

Makes 6 servings
Prep. Time: 20 minutes
Baking Time: 45-60 minutes

5 medium potatoes, sliced

salt and pepper, to taste

2 medium onions, diced

2 cups fresh, chopped asparagus

2 Tbsp. trans-fat-free tub margarine

3 oz. 75%-less-fat cheddar cheese slices

1. Lay potatoes in greased 2-qt. casserole dish. Sprinkle with salt and pepper.

2. Sprinkle diced onions over potatoes.

3. Add asparagus.

4. Add salt and pepper to taste.

5. Dot top with pieces of margarine.

6. Cover tightly.

7. Bake at 325°F for 45–60 minutes, or until potatoes are tender when poked with a fork.

8. Remove from oven and lay sliced cheese over hot vegetables to melt.

TIP

Experiment with adding garlic, fresh parsley or other herbs, or even a dash of cayenne.

Baked Asparagus Roll-Ups

Peggy C. Forsythe,
Memphis, TN

Makes 12 servings, 1 roll-up per serving
Prep. Time: 20 minutes
Baking Time: 15 minutes

Vegetables and Side Dishes

12 slices white bread, crusts removed

½ cup reduced-fat crumbled blue cheese

1–2 Tbsp. mayonnaise

12 asparagus spears, canned and patted dry, or fresh and lightly steamed, dried, and cooled

2 Tbsp. trans-fat-free tub margarine, melted

4 Tbsp. freshly grated Parmesan cheese

paprika

1. Flatten bread with a rolling pin. Set aside.

2. In a small bowl, mix blue cheese and mayonnaise to a spreading consistency, starting with 1 Tbsp. mayonnaise and adding by teaspoons as needed. Set aside.

3. Divide cheese mixture among bread slices and spread evenly.

4. Place an asparagus spear on one end of a bread slice. Starting with the spear end, roll up the bread with the spear inside. Pinch seam a little bit to hold in place.

5. Place roll-up seam side down on greased cookie sheet. Roll up remaining bread and asparagus.

6. Brush each roll-up with melted margarine. Sprinkle each roll-up with 1 tsp. Parmesan cheese and a sprinkle of paprika.

7. Bake for 15 minutes at 375°F or until golden brown.

Roasted Onions

Elaine Gibbel,
Lititz, PA

Makes 4 servings
Prep. Time: 10 minutes
Baking Time: 1 hour

2 large Vidalia, or sweet, onions

1 Tbsp. water

3 Tbsp. honey

1 Tbsp. soft-tub non-hydrogenated margarine, melted

1 tsp. paprika

½ tsp. salt

½ tsp. curry powder

⅛–¼ tsp. ground red pepper, according to your taste preference

1. Preheat oven to 350°F.

2. Peel onions and cut in half crosswise. Place onions, cut side down, in 8-inch square baking dish.

3. Sprinkle with water. Cover with foil.

4. Bake at 350°F for 30 minutes.

5. Meanwhile, combine remaining ingredients in small bowl.

6. Turn onions over and brush with half of honey mixture.

7. Bake 30 minutes more, uncovered, until tender, basting with remaining honey mixture after 15 minutes.

Vidalia Casserole

Mary Lynn Miller,
Reinholds, PA

Makes 4-6 servings
Prep. Time: 15 minutes
Baking Time: 20-25 minutes

4-5 Vidalia, or sweet, onions, sliced ¼-inch thick

½ stick (4 Tbsp.) butter

¼ cup sour cream

¾ cup grated Parmesan cheese

10 butter-flavored crackers, crushed

1. In a skillet over medium heat, sauté onions in butter until tender. Remove from heat.

2. Stir in sour cream.

3. Spoon half of mixture into a lightly greased 1-qt. baking dish. Sprinkle with cheese.

4. Top with remaining onion mixture and crackers.

5. Bake uncovered at 350° for 20–25 minutes.

Simply Beets

**Colleen Konetzni,
Rio Rancho, NM**

4 servings
Prep. Time: 30 minutes
Cooking Time: 30–45 minutes

6 fresh red beets

water

1 tsp. olive oil

dill weed

pepper

1. Wash beets and cut off roots and leafy stems. Place in saucepan and cover with water.

2. Boil until beets are fork-tender.

3. Remove from pan and cool. The beets' peels should slip right off.

4. Slice beets ¼-inch thick. Place back in pan, along with oil.

5. Heat through over low heat.

6. To serve, sprinkle with dill weed and pepper.

Sweet and Sour Beets

Shirley Taylor,
Yuba City, CA

Makes 6 servings
Prep. Time: 10 minutes
Cooking Time: 30 minutes

½ cup sugar

1 Tbsp. cornstarch

½ tsp. salt

2 whole cloves

½ cup vinegar

3 15-oz. cans sliced beets, drained

3 Tbsp. orange marmalade

2 Tbsp. butter or margarine

1. Combine sugar, cornstarch, salt, and cloves in a large heavy saucepan. Stir in vinegar. Cook over medium heat, stirring constantly, until thickened and bubbly.

2. Add beets to sauce. Cover and cook 15 minutes.

3. Stir in marmalade and butter until both melt.

Zucchini Ribbons

**Delores Gnagey,
Saginaw, MI**

Makes 4 servings
Prep. Time: 15 minutes
Cooking Time: 9 minutes

1 large zucchini, unpeeled, ends trimmed

1 Tbsp. olive oil

3 garlic cloves, minced

1 cup cherry tomato halves

½ tsp. dried basil

pepper, to taste

1. With vegetable peeler, slice zucchini into long, lengthwise strips, thick enough not to bend. (If strips are too thin, they'll get mushy while sautéing.)

2. Heat oil in large skillet over medium heat. Add zucchini ribbons. Sauté 4 minutes.

3. Add garlic and sauté 2 more minutes.

4. Add cherry tomatoes and sauté 2 additional minutes.

5. Sprinkle with basil and pepper to taste. Cook 1 minute.

Zucchini Casserole

**Virginia R. Bender,
Dover, DE**

Makes 6 servings
Prep. Time: 30 minutes
Baking Time: 1 hour

4 cups grated fresh zucchini

1 medium onion, grated

2 Tbsp. flour

4 eggs

½–¾ cup grated cheddar cheese

black pepper, or other seasoning

salt, to taste, *optional*

1. Place grated zucchini and onion into lightly greased 2-qt. baking dish and mix together gently.

2. Sprinkle flour over all.

3. Beat eggs in a mixing bowl. Pour over all. Stir.

4. Sprinkle with grated cheese, and seasonings if you wish.

5. Bake uncovered at 350°F for 1 hour.

Maple-Glazed Squash

Jean Turner,
Williams Lake, BC

Makes 6-8 servings
Prep. Time: 10-15 minutes
Baking Time: 50-55 minutes

2 acorn squash

salt and pepper

⅔ cup maple syrup

½ cup soft bread crumbs

½ stick (4 Tbsp.) butter, softened

1. Trim off ends of acorn squash, then cut crosswise into 1-inch slices. Discard seeds.

2. Season squash with salt and pepper.

3. Arrange a single layer of squash in a large shallow baking pan. Cover and bake at 350°F for 30–35 minutes.

4. Combine syrup, crumbs, and butter in a small mixing bowl. Spread over squash.

5. Bake uncovered for 15–20 minutes, basting occasionally.

Broiled Eggplant

Carol L. Stroh,
Akron, NY

Makes 4 servings
Prep. Time: 15 minutes
Cooking Time: 5–6 minutes

2 beaten eggs

2 tsp. canola oil

1 medium-sized eggplant, peeled and sliced
   ¼-inch thick

1⅓ cups flavored bread crumbs

2 cups shredded mozzarella, or Monterey
   Jack, cheese, *optional*

2 cups tomato sauce, *optional*

1. Lightly oil unheated broiler pan.

2. Beat eggs and 2 tsp. oil together in a shallow dish.

3. Dip eggplant in egg mixture, then coat with bread crumbs.

4. Place on greased broiler pan. Broil 4 inches from heat, 2 minutes per side, or until golden.

5. If desired, spread cheese on top and broil for another minute, or until cheese melts.

6. Serve plain or with tomato sauce.

Scalloped Cheesy Tomatoes

Scarlett Von Bernuth,
Canon City, CO

Makes 6 servings
Prep. Time: 15 minutes
Baking Time: 35 minutes

4 fresh tomatoes, sliced, *divided*

1 cup soft bread cubes, *divided*

1 Tbsp. fresh parsley, *divided*

2 Tbsp. olive oil, *divided*

½ cup cracker crumbs (made from crackers with unsalted tops)

¼ cup low-sodium, low-fat grated cheese

1. Fill a lightly greased baking dish with alternate layers of tomatoes and bread cubes.

2. Sprinkle parsley and olive oil over each layer.

3. Cover top with cracker crumbs. Sprinkle with cheese.

4. Bake uncovered in 350°–375°F oven for 35 minutes.

Fried Ripe Tomatoes

**Mary W. Stauffer,
Ephrata, PA**

Makes 4 servings
Prep. Time: 10 minutes
Cooking Time: 10 minutes

Vegetables and
Side Dishes

2 firm ripe, or partly ripe, tomatoes

2 Tbsp. sugar

2 Tbsp. flour

2 Tbsp. fine bread crumbs

1-2 Tbsp. olive oil

1. Core and slice, but do not peel, tomatoes.

2. Mix sugar, flour, and crumbs together in a low mixing bowl.

3. Dip tomato slices, one by one, into this mixture. Sauté in a large skillet in oil until browned.

4. Flip and brown on the other side.

Cheesy Veggies

Judy Wantland,
Menomonee Falls, WI

Makes 6 servings
Prep. Time: 5 minutes
Baking Time: 35 minutes

16-oz. bag frozen vegetable medley, thawed

10¾-oz. can cream of mushroom soup

⅓ cup sour cream

2 cups shredded mozzarella, or cheddar, cheese

6-oz. can fried onion rings, *divided*

1. Preheat oven to 350°F.

2. In a large mixing bowl, mix all ingredients together using only half the fried onion rings.

3. Spoon into a lightly greased 2-qt. baking dish.

4. Bake covered for 30 minutes.

5. Sprinkle remaining onion rings on top. Bake uncovered an additional 5 minutes, or until onions are crispy.

Healthy Veggie Stir-Fry

**Joy Uhler,
Richardson, TX**

Makes 2–3 servings
Prep. Time: 5–10 minutes
Cooking Time: 9–10 minutes

¼ cup chopped onion

1 clove garlic, minced

12-oz. pkg. frozen vegetable mix of broccoli, carrots, sugar snap peas, and water chestnuts

7-oz. block firm tofu, cubed

1½ Tbsp. low-sodium teriyaki marinade and sauce

1. Use a large nonstick skillet or spray another skillet with nonstick cooking spray.

2. Heat skillet over medium heat.

3. Stir-fry onion and garlic for a few minutes until onion begins to wilt.

4. Stir in frozen vegetables. Cover and allow to steam, about 5 minutes.

5. Stir in tofu and sauce. Stir until heated through.

6. Serve over prepared brown rice.

Oven Roasted Vegetables

Martha G. Zimmerman,
Lititz, PA

Makes 4 servings
Prep. Time: 20 minutes
Baking Time: 25–35 minutes

1 medium zucchini

1 medium summer squash or another zucchini

1 medium red bell pepper

1 medium yellow bell pepper

1 lb. fresh asparagus

1 sweet potato, *optional*

1 red onion

3 Tbsp. olive oil

1-3 garlic cloves, minced

salt and pepper, to taste

Italian seasoning, to taste

1. Cut vegetables into bite-size pieces.

2. Place on two large rimmed baking sheets.

3. Drizzle olive oil evenly over vegetables. Sprinkle evenly with garlic, salt, pepper, and Italian seasoning.

4. Mix well. (Hands work well for this!)

5. Bake at 400°F for 25–35 minutes, stirring and flipping every 5–10 minutes. Test a few vegetables at 25 minutes to see if they are done to your preference. Keep roasting and stirring as needed.

Italian Veggie Bake

Orpha Herr,
Andover, NY

Makes 8 servings
Prep. Time: 20 minutes
Baking Time: 45–50 minutes

⅓ cup reduced-fat Italian dressing

1 large onion, chopped

1 small unpeeled eggplant, cubed

2 medium zucchini, sliced thin

1 large red bell pepper, chopped

6-oz. pkg. fresh mushrooms, sliced

2 cups freshly diced tomatoes

⅓ cup shredded Parmesan cheese

1 Tbsp. chopped fresh parsley

1. Heat dressing in large skillet over medium-high heat.

2. Add onion and steam or stir-fry 5 minutes, or until just tender.

3. Add eggplant and steam or stir-fry 5 minutes.

4. Add zucchini, pepper, and mushrooms. Steam or stir-fry 5 minutes more.

5. Add tomatoes and bring to a boil.

6. Pour mixture into lightly greased baking dish. Sprinkle with cheese.

7. Bake uncovered at 350°F for 25–30 minutes, or until bubbly.

8. Sprinkle with parsley just before serving.

Homemade Seasoned Rice Mix

Doris Beachy,
Stevens, PA

Makes 3¼ cups mix
Prep. Time: 10 minutes
Cooking Time: 15–20 minutes

3 cups uncooked long-grain rice

6 tsp. instant bouillon granules

¼ cup dried parsley flakes

2½ tsp. onion powder

¼ tsp. dried thyme

1. Combine all ingredients in a storage container with a tight lid.

2. To prepare rice as a side dish, combine 2 cups water and 1 Tbsp. butter in a saucepan.

3. Bring to a boil. Stir in 1 cup mix.

4. Reduce heat, cover, and simmer for 15–20 minutes, or until liquid is absorbed.

Uptown Rice

Judy Buller,
Bluffton, OH

Makes 8 servings
Prep. Time: 15–20 minutes
Cooking/Baking Time: 55 minutes

1½ cups uncooked white rice

½ lb. sliced fresh, or 4-oz. can sliced, mushrooms

½ cup slivered almonds

2 Tbsp. chopped onions

1 stick (8 Tbsp.) butter

3 cups chicken broth

1 Tbsp. parsley

Variations:

1. Add ½ cup chopped celery to Step 1.

2. Instead of 3 cups chicken broth, use 14-oz. can chicken broth, ⅓ cup water, and 1–2 Tbsp. soy sauce.

—Amber Swarey, Honea Path, SC

1. Sauté rice, mushrooms, almonds, and onions in butter for 10–15 minutes on medium heat, stirring constantly. When almonds look slightly toasted and rice has a yellow cast, remove from heat.

2. Add broth and parsley and mix well. Pour into a greased 3-qt. casserole dish.

3. Cover and bake at 325°F for 40 minutes.

4. Stir before serving.

Corn Bread Stuffing

Janice Muller,
Derwood, MD

Makes 4 servings
Prep. Time: 15 minutes
Baking Time: 30 minutes

1 cup chopped onions

1 cup chopped celery

1 stick (8 Tbsp.) butter

8-oz. pkg. corn bread stuffing

16-oz. jar applesauce

½ tsp. dried thyme

½ tsp. dried marjoram

½ tsp. poultry seasoning

¼ tsp. lemon-pepper

⅓ cup boiling water

1. In a large skillet, sauté onions and celery in butter until soft.

2. Add stuffing mix, applesauce, herbs, seasonings, and boiling water. Toss until evenly moist.

3. Stuff turkey, or if baking separately, spoon into a buttered 1-qt. baking dish.

4. Cover with foil. Put in a 325°F oven during the last 30 minutes that your turkey is baking. Or bake at 325°F for 30 minutes on its own.

Salads

Salads

Dried Cherry Salad

**Stacy Schmucker Stoltzfus,
Enola, PA**

Makes 12 servings
Prep. Time: 20 minutes
Cooking Time: 10 minutes

half a head of romaine lettuce, chopped

half a head of red leaf lettuce, chopped

half a large red onion, sliced

1 cup dried cherries

1 cup feta cheese

⅓ cup sugar

1 cup pecan halves

Raspberry Dressing:

4 Tbsp. raspberry vinegar

½ tsp. Tabasco sauce

½ tsp. salt

4 Tbsp. sugar

pepper, to taste

1 Tbsp. chopped parsley

½ cup vegetable oil

1. Place lettuces in a large salad bowl.
Sprinkle with onion slices, dried cherries,
and feta cheese.

2. In skillet, over medium heat, combine
⅓ cup sugar and pecans. Stir constantly
until sugar melts and pecans are coated.
Immediately pour pecans onto waxed paper
to cool.

3. Sprinkle cooled nuts over salad.

4. To make dressing, combine vinegar,
Tabasco sauce, salt, 4 Tbsp. sugar, pepper,
and parsley in a small mixing bowl. While
whisking, slowly pour in oil until emulsified.
Just before serving, pour over salad.

Caesar Salad

**Colleen Heatwole,
Burton, MI**

Makes 8 servings
Prep. Time: 15–20 minutes

8–12 cups romaine lettuce, or spring mix, torn into bite-sized pieces

⅓ cup oil

3 Tbsp. red wine vinegar

1 tsp. Worcestershire sauce

½ tsp. salt

¾ tsp. dry mustard powder

1 large garlic clove, minced

1½–2 Tbsp. fresh lemon juice

dash of pepper

¼–½ cup grated Parmesan cheese

2 cups Caesar-flavored, or garlic, croutons

1. Place lettuce in a large bowl.

2. Combine next six ingredients in a blender or food processor.

3. Add fresh lemon juice and process until smooth.

4. Just before serving, toss with lettuce.

5. Sprinkle with pepper. Add Parmesan cheese and toss well. Serve croutons separately.

TIPS

1. I have made this on more Sundays than I can count. I prepare the lettuce, blend the six ingredients, and get the hard cheese ready for my son to grate. I always use fresh lemon or fresh lime.
2. My family prefers a tart dressing. My friend adds 1 Tbsp. sugar.

Salads

Greek Salad

Ruth Feister, Makes 8 servings
Narvon, PA Prep. Time: 20 minutes

Dressing:

¼ cup chicken stock

2 Tbsp. red wine vinegar

2 tsp. lemon juice

1 tsp. sugar

½ tsp. dried basil

½ tsp. dried oregano

head of romaine lettuce, torn

1 medium-sized cucumber, sliced thin

2 medium-sized tomatoes, cut in pieces

half a red onion, finely chopped

parsley

4-oz. can sliced black olives, drained

3-4 oz. crumbled feta cheese

several artichoke hearts, quartered

1. Combine dressing ingredients in a jar with a tightly fitting lid. Shake until mixed well.

2. Place lettuce, cucumber, tomatoes, onion, and parsley in a large serving bowl.

3. Just before serving, drizzle with dressing and toss.

4. Top with olives, cheese, and artichoke hearts.

Olive Garden Salad

**Erma Martin,
East Earl, PA**

Makes 8–10 servings
Prep. Time: 15–20 minutes

1 head iceberg lettuce, torn

1 head romaine lettuce, torn

Add to taste:

black olives

diced red onion

grape tomatoes, halved

croutons

sliced banana peppers

Parmesan cheese

Dressing:

½ cup white vinegar

½ cup mayonnaise

1 tsp. olive oil

4 Tbsp. corn syrup

2 Tbsp. Parmesan cheese

2 Tbsp. Romano cheese

½ tsp. garlic salt

½ tsp. parsley

½ tsp. Italian seasoning

1 Tbsp. lemon juice

1. Combine lettuces and desired amount of olives, onion, tomatoes, croutons, peppers, and Parmesan cheese. Toss lightly.

2. Mix dressing ingredients.

3. Just before serving, pour dressing over salad and toss lightly.

Festive Tossed Salad

Cheryl A. Lapp,
Parkesburg, PA
Yvonne Kauffman Boettger,
Harrisonburg, VA
Sally Holzem,
Schofield, WI

Makes 8–10 servings
Prep. Time: 30 minutes

½ cup sugar

⅓ cup cider or red wine vinegar

2 Tbsp. lemon juice

2 Tbsp. finely chopped onions

½ tsp. salt

⅔ cup olive oil

2 tsp. poppy seeds

10 cups torn romaine lettuce

1 cup shredded Swiss cheese

1 medium-sized apple, cored and cubed

1 medium-sized pear, cored and cubed

¼ cup dried cranberries

½ cup chopped cashews

1. In a blender, combine first five ingredients until well blended.

2. With a blender running, gradually add oil. Add poppy seeds and blend.

3. In salad bowl, combine lettuce, cheese, apple, pear, and cranberries.

4. Just before serving, drizzle salad with desired amount of dressing. (You'll have more dressing than you need, so save what's left for a future salad.) Add cashews and toss to coat.

Variation:
Add 1 tsp. Dijon mustard to the dressing in Step 1. —Jennifer Eberly, Harrisonburg, VA

Apple Blue Cheese Salad

Judy Hauser,
Hershey, PA

Makes 6 servings
Prep. Time: 15–20 minutes

⅓ cup broken walnuts, or pecans

1 bunch red or green leaf lettuce

1–2 apples

3 oz. crumbled blue cheese

⅓ cup raisins, *optional*

Greek salad dressing

1. Toast coarsely chopped nuts in dry skillet over medium heat. Stir frequently to prevent burning. Set toasted nuts aside to cool.

2. Wash lettuce and tear into salad bowl.

3. Dice unpeeled apples.

4. Add apples to lettuce, along with nuts and crumbled cheese, and raisins if you wish.

5. Drizzle with Greek dressing when ready to serve.

Ed's Blue Cheese Salad

**Andrea Zuercher,
Lawrence, KS**

Makes 4 servings
Prep. Time: 15 minutes

1 small bunch Romaine lettuce

2 Tbsp. olive oil, or more or less to taste

salt and pepper, to taste

4 oz. blue cheese, crumbled

juice of half a lemon, or more to taste

¼ cup grated Parmesan cheese, *optional*

1. Wash lettuce and tear into bite-size pieces. Place in salad bowl.

2. Drizzle with olive oil. Toss.

3. Season leaves with salt and pepper to taste.

4. Add blue cheese. Toss. Set aside until near serving time. (Refrigerate if more than 15 minutes.)

5. When ready to serve, add lemon juice, and Parmesan cheese if you wish, and toss again.

TIP

If you want to use prepackaged greens, this recipe works for one regular-size bag. Adjust proportions for more or less lettuce.

Salads

Crunchy Romaine Toss

**Jolene Schrock,
Millersburg, OH
Jamie Mowry,
Arlington, TX
Lucille Hollinger,
Richland, PA**

Makes 4-6 servings
Prep. Time: 20-30 minutes
Cooking Time: 10 minutes

Dressing:

½ cup sugar

½ cup vegetable oil

¼ cup cider vinegar

2 tsp. soy sauce

salt and pepper, to taste

3-oz. pkg. ramen noodles, broken up,
    seasoning packets discarded

2 Tbsp. butter

1½ cups chopped broccoli

1 small head romaine lettuce, torn up

4 green onions, chopped

½ cup chopped walnuts

1. In the blender, combine sugar, oil, vinegar, soy sauce, salt, and pepper. Blend until sugar is dissolved.

2. In a skillet, sauté ramen noodles in butter until golden brown.

3. In a large bowl, combine broccoli, lettuce, onions, and noodles.

4. Just before serving toss with nuts and dressing.

TIP

Sometimes I serve the dressing on the side and let everybody put their own dressing on. Plus, if you have any leftover salad, it won't get soggy.

Variations:

1. Use 2 cups sliced fresh strawberries in place of broccoli. Increase walnuts to 1 cup.

    —Janice Nolt, Ephrata, PA

2. Add 1 small can mandarin oranges, drained.

    —Janet Derstine, Telford, PA

3. Wash and dry whole lettuce leaves. Put a scoop of tuna or egg salad in each one. Enjoy your lettuce boats! You can also slip these into wraps or pitas.

    —Donna Conta, Saylorsburg, PA

Salads

Salad with Hot Bacon Dressing

**Joanne E. Martin,
Stevens, PA**

Makes 8–10 servings (2 cups dressing)
Prep. Time: 15 minutes
Cooking Time: 7 minutes

6–8 strips of bacon

1½ cups sugar

2 eggs, beaten

⅓ cup vinegar

⅔ cup water

salad greens

grated carrots

hard-cooked eggs

1. In a skillet, brown bacon. Drain off drippings. Crumble and set aside.

2. In the same skillet, mix sugar, beaten eggs, vinegar, and water. Bring to boil, stirring up browned bacon drippings. Stir dressing until slightly thickened.

3. Stir in bacon.

4. Just before serving, toss warm salad dressing with mixture of salad greens, grated carrots, and hard-cooked eggs.

Mexican Salad

Jan Pembleton,
Arlington, TX

Makes 10 servings
Prep. Time: 20 minutes
Cooking Time: 15 minutes
Cooling Time: 30 minutes

1 head lettuce

¾ lb. 93%-lean ground beef

2 tomatoes, chopped

16-oz. can kidney beans, drained

¾ cup freshly grated cheddar cheese

¼ cup diced onion

¼ cup sliced black olives, sliced

1 avocado, diced

2 oz. taco chips, crushed

Sauce:

8 oz. fat-free Thousand Island dressing

1 Tbsp. dry low-sodium taco seasoning

1 Tbsp. hot sauce

1 Tbsp. sugar

1. Wash lettuce and tear into bite-sized pieces.

2. Brown, drain, and cool ground meat.

3. Combine all salad ingredients except taco chips. Set aside.

4. Combine all sauce ingredients. Pour sauce over salad and toss thoroughly.

5. Immediately before serving, add taco chips.

Simple Gluten-Free Tabbouleh

Hope Comerford,
Clinton Township, MI

Makes about 8 servings
Prep. Time: 25 minutes

1 small onion, finely chopped

½ bunch green onions, finely chopped

⅛ tsp. cinnamon

2–3 tsp. salt

¼ tsp. pepper

¾ cup cooked and cooled quinoa

2 large bunches of curly leaf parsley, finely chopped

2 large tomatoes, finely chopped

½–⅔ cup lemon juice

½ cup olive oil

1. In the bottom of a medium-sized mixing bowl, mix together the onion, green onions, cinnamon, salt, and pepper.

2. Add the remaining ingredients and toss together. Taste to be sure you have enough lemon juice and olive oil.

TIP

I like to let this sit for a couple hours in the refrigerator before serving. The flavors really start to come together then!

Salads

Tabbouleh with Mint and Blueberries

Pat Bechtel,
Dillsburg, PA

Makes 4 main-dish servings
Prep. Time: 20–25 minutes
Marinating Time: 2 hours

2 cups water

1 cup uncooked bulgur wheat, medium grind

½ lb. (about 2) fresh tomatoes, peeled and
diced

half a cucumber, diced

4 green onions, white and green parts, minced

2 cups fresh blueberries

5 Tbsp. fresh lemon juice

¼ cup olive oil

½ cup shredded fresh mint leaves

1 Tbsp. chopped fresh parsley

¼ tsp. ground cumin

¼ tsp. salt

¼ tsp. freshly ground black pepper

1. Bring 2 cups water to a boil. Add bulgur and allow to stand 5 minutes.

2. Turn soaked bulgur onto a cloth. Pick up cloth with bulgur inside and squeeze out excess moisture.

3. Combine all ingredients in a large bowl, tossing gently.

4. Cover and refrigerate. Allow to marinate 2 hours before serving.

5. Serve at room temperature.

Orange-Spinach Salad

Esther Shisler,
Lansdale, PA

Makes 6–8 servings
Prep. Time: 25 minutes

Honey-Caraway Dressing:

¾ cup mayonnaise

2 Tbsp. honey

1 Tbsp. lemon juice

1 Tbsp. caraway seeds

10-oz. bag spinach or romaine

1 medium head iceberg lettuce, shredded

2 Tbsp. diced onion

2 Tbsp. diced canned pimento, or red bell
   pepper

2 large oranges, peeled and chopped

1 small cucumber, sliced

1. In small bowl, whisk mayonnaise, honey, lemon juice, and caraway seeds until blended. Cover and refrigerate. Stir before using.

2. Into large salad bowl, tear spinach into bite-size pieces.

3. Add lettuce, onion, pimento, oranges, and cucumber. Toss gently with dressing.

TIP

A 15-oz. can mandarin oranges, drained, can be used instead of the 2 oranges. I use romaine and spinach instead of the iceberg lettuce sometimes.

Salads

Spinach Salad Caprese

Jan Moore,
Wellsville, KS

Makes 4 servings
Prep. Time: 10-20 minutes

6 cups fresh spinach

12 cherry tomatoes, halved

½ cup chopped fresh basil

4 oz. fresh mozzarella cheese, cubed

¼ cup light olive oil

1. Gently combine all ingredients.

2. Toss to mix.

3. Serve immediately.

Greek Pasta Salad

Edie Moran,
West Babylon, NY
Judi Manos,
West Islip, NY

Makes 8 servings
Prep. Time: 15 minutes
Cooking Time for pasta: 15 minutes

2 cups cooked pasta, rinsed and cooled (1 cup dry)

4 medium plum tomatoes, chopped

15-oz. can garbanzo beans, rinsed and drained

1 medium onion, chopped

6-oz. can pitted black olives, drained

4-oz. pkg. crumbled feta cheese

1 garlic clove, minced

½ cup olive oil

¼ cup lemon juice

1 tsp. salt

½ tsp. pepper

1. In a large bowl, combine pasta, tomatoes, garbanzo beans, onion, olives, feta cheese, and garlic.

2. In a small bowl, whisk together oil, lemon juice, salt, and pepper. Pour over salad and toss to coat.

3. Cover and chill in refrigerator. Stir before serving.

TIPS

1. I like to serve this salad in a clear glass salad bowl.
2. Add some baby spinach leaves. Combine vegetables with hot pasta right after draining it.
3. Kraft Greek Vinaigrette is a good dressing too. —Judi Manos, West Islip, NY

Salads

Macaroni Salad

**Frances L. and Cathy Kruba,
Dundalk, MD
Marcia S. Myer,
Manheim, PA**

Makes 8–10 servings
Prep. Time: 30 minutes
Cooking Time for pasta: 15 minutes

1 lb. macaroni, cooked and cooled

1 cup diced celery

1 cup diced onions

1 cup diced carrots

12 hard-boiled eggs, diced

2 cups sugar

½ cup vinegar, or lemon juice

2 cups mayonnaise

Dressing:
5 eggs, whisked

1 Tbsp. mustard

1 Tbsp. butter

½–1 tsp. salt

1. Mix together macaroni, celery, onions, carrots, hard-boiled eggs, sugar, and vinegar or lemon juice. Add mayonnaise.

2. In a saucepan, mix eggs, mustard, butter, and salt. Cook on medium heat until thickened and steaming, stirring constantly. Do not boil.

3. Remove from heat and cool 5 minutes. Add to macaroni mixture.

TIPS

1. Grate the carrots instead of dicing them.
2. Reduce the sugar by a ½ cup if desired.

Salads

Chicken Grape Salad

Hope Comerford,
Clinton Township, MI

Makes 6-8 servings
Prep. Time: 10 minutes
Cooling Time: 1-2 hours

16 oz. penne rigate pasta, cooked and cooled

2 cups cubed cooked chicken

1-2 cups halved grapes (green or red, or a mix of both)

½ cup chopped onion

Dressing:

½ cup mayonnaise

½ cup nonfat plain Greek yogurt

2-3 Tbsp. apple cider vinegar

2 Tbsp. sugar

1 tsp. garlic powder

1 tsp. onion powder

½ tsp. salt

⅛ tsp. pepper

1. In a large bowl, place the cooked penne, chicken, grapes, and onion.

2. In a small bowl, mix together the dressing ingredients. Pour this over the chicken and pasta mixture. Stir to coat everything well.

3. Refrigerate for 1–2 hours before serving.

Salads

Spaghetti Salad

Lois Stoltzfus,
Honey Brook, PA

Makes 6–8 servings
Prep. Time: 15 minutes
Cooking Time: 15 minutes
Cooling Time: 30 minutes

16-oz. angel-hair pasta

½ cup vegetable, or olive, oil

½ cup lemon juice

1 Tbsp. seasoned salt

½ cup mayonnaise

1 green bell pepper, chopped

1 cup grape tomatoes

1 red onion, chopped

1 cup grated cheddar cheese

½ cup black olives, sliced

pepperoni, *optional*

1. Cook pasta according to directions.

2. Mix oil, lemon juice, seasoned salt, and mayonnaise together. Add to drained pasta while it is still warm.

3. When pasta mixture has cooled at least 30 minutes, stir in pepper, tomatoes, onion, cheese, olives, and optional pepperoni. Chill.

Salads

BLT Salad

Bernadette Veenstra,
Grand Rapids, MI

Makes 12–16 servings
Prep. Time: 30 minutes
Cooking Time: 15 minutes

16-oz. pkg. rigatoni, or penne, pasta

1 lb. sliced bacon

7-oz. bag fresh spinach, roughly chopped

1 pt. cherry tomatoes, quartered

1 tsp. salt

¼ tsp. black pepper

8 oz. mozzarella cheese, cubed, *optional*

1. Cook pasta according to package directions. Drain and rinse under cold water. Transfer to a large bowl.

2. Dice bacon into small pieces. Sauté over medium heat. Place bacon on paper towel–lined plate. Pour all drippings into a small bowl.

3. Return 1 Tbsp. drippings to skillet and heat. Stir spinach into hot drippings until it wilts, about 1 minute. Transfer spinach to pasta.

4. Add ½ Tbsp. drippings to skillet and heat. Stir tomatoes into drippings in skillet. Cook for 2 minutes. Transfer tomatoes to spinach and pasta and toss.

5. If pasta seems dry, add up to 1½ Tbsp. more of the drippings.

6. Add salt, pepper, bacon, and cheese if desired. Refrigerate until serving time.

Creamy Dill Pasta Salad

Jan Mast,
Lancaster, PA

Makes 10 servings
Prep. Time: 15 minutes
Cooking Time: 12–15 minutes

3 cups uncooked tri-color spiral pasta

6-oz. can black olives, halved and drained

½ cup chopped red pepper

½ cup chopped green pepper

½ cup chopped onions

2 tomatoes, chopped

1 Tbsp. dill weed

Dressing:

¾ cup mayonnaise

2 Tbsp. prepared mustard

¼ cup vinegar

⅓ cup sugar

1. Cook pasta according to package directions, being careful not to overcook. Rinse in cool water. Drain well. Place in large mixing bowl.

2. Add olives, vegetables, and dill weed and toss.

3. In a mixing bowl, combine mayonnaise, mustard, vinegar, and sugar.

4. Pour over pasta and vegetables and stir to coat.

5. Chill and serve.

Salads

Summer Pasta Salad

**Judy Govotsos,
Frederick, MD**

Makes 15–18 servings
Prep. Time: 8–10 minutes
Cooking Time: 15 minutes

1 lb. uncooked penne or corkscrew pasta

1 yellow pepper, sliced

1 green pepper, sliced

1 red pepper, sliced

1 red onion, sliced

8 oz. crumbled feta cheese, *optional*

½ lb. pitted Kalamata olives, *optional*

cherry tomatoes, *optional*

16-oz. bottle Caesar salad dressing

10-oz. pkg. chicken strips, cooked, *optional*

1. Cook pasta according to package directions. Drain.

2. In a large mixing bowl, combine all ingredients except salad dressing and chicken.

3. Pour dressing over pasta mixture. Toss.

4. Add chicken immediately before serving.

Variations:

1. Instead of yellow and red peppers, substitute 2 cups cut-up broccoli florets in Step 2.

2. Instead of feta cheese, use 1 cup shredded cheddar cheese.

Salads

Tortellini Summer Salad

Norma P. Zehr,
Lowville, NY

Makes 4-6 servings
Prep. Time: 15 minutes
Cooking Time: 10 minutes
Cooling Time: 30 minutes

9-oz. pkg. cheese tortellini, cooked and cooled

1 cup julienned fully cooked ham

¾ cup frozen peas, thawed

½ cup Swiss cheese, cut in cubes

2 cups ranch dressing

1. Cook tortellini according to package directions until done. Drain and cool.

2. Combine all ingredients in a large mixing bowl and toss.

3. Chill until ready to serve.

Variation:
Add several tablespoons minced onion in Step 2 for extra flavor.

Crab Pasta Salad

Lauren Eberhard,
Seneca, IL

Makes 8–10 servings
Prep. Time: 20 minutes
Cooking Time: 10–15 minutes
Chilling Time: 1 hour

1-lb. pkg. rotini, or your choice of pasta

8-oz. pkg. crabmeat

1 cup frozen peas

2 carrots

1 bottle favorite salad dressing, or coleslaw dressing

1. Prepare pasta as directed on package. Rinse and cool.

2. Cut crabmeat into 1-inch pieces.

3. Thaw peas and grate carrots.

4. Mix all together in a large bowl.

5. Stir in dressing one hour before serving. Refrigerate and allow flavors to blend.

TIP

If you wish, place lettuce leaves in large salad bowl and put salad on top. Or put 1 Bibb lettuce leaf on each dinner or salad plate and top with a scoop of salad.

Salads

Pasta Salad with Tuna

Sheila Soldner,
Lititz, PA

Makes 6–8 servings
Prep. Time: 15 minutes
Cooking Time: 15 minutes

½ lb. uncooked rotini pasta

12½-oz. can solid white tuna, drained and
   flaked

2 cups thinly sliced cucumber

1 large tomato, seeded and sliced, or
   ½ pt. cherry or grape tomatoes

½ cup sliced celery

¼ cup chopped green pepper

¼ cup sliced green onions

1 cup bottled Italian dressing

¼ cup mayonnaise

1 Tbsp. prepared mustard

1 tsp. dill weed

1 tsp. salt

⅛ tsp. pepper

1. Prepare rotini according to package
directions. Drain.

2. In a large bowl, combine rotini, tuna,
cucumbers, tomato, celery, green pepper, and
onions.

3. In a small bowl, blend together
Italian dressing, mayonnaise, mustard, and
seasonings. Add to salad mixture. Toss to
coat.

4. Cover and chill. Toss gently before
serving.

Salads

Greek Orzo Salad

**Lavina Hochstedler,
Grand Blanc, MI**

Makes 8 servings
Prep. Time: 20 minutes
Cooking Time: 12 minutes
Chilling Time: 2–24 hours

1 cup uncooked orzo pasta

6 tsp. olive oil, *divided*

1 medium-sized red onion, finely chopped

½ cup minced fresh parsley

⅓ cup cider vinegar

1½ tsp. dried oregano

1 tsp. salt

1 tsp. sugar

⅛ tsp. pepper

1 large tomato, chopped

1 large red pepper, chopped

1 medium-sized cucumber, peeled, seeded, and chopped

½ cup black olives, sliced and drained, *optional*

½ cup crumbled feta cheese

1. Cook pasta according to directions. Drain.

2. In a large mixing bowl, toss cooked orzo with 2 tsp. olive oil.

3. In a separate bowl, combine the onion, parsley, vinegar, oregano, salt, sugar, pepper, and remaining oil. Pour over orzo and toss to coat.

4. Cover and refrigerate 2–24 hours.

5. Just before serving, gently stir in tomato, red pepper, cucumber, olives, and cheese.

Tomato Basil Couscous

Amber Martin,
Mount Joy, PA

Makes 6 servings
Prep. Time: 25 minutes
Cooking Time: 10 minutes, for couscous
Chilling Time: 2 hours

2 cups cooked couscous, cooled

1 cup chopped tomato

2 Tbsp. chopped fresh basil

2-oz. feta cheese, crumbled fine

¼ cup olive oil

2 Tbsp. lemon juice

1 tsp. Dijon mustard

1 clove garlic, crushed

fresh black pepper, to taste

1. Mix together couscous, tomato, basil, and feta cheese.

2. In separate bowl, mix together olive oil, lemon juice, mustard, garlic, and black pepper. Pour over couscous mixture and toss.

3. Chill at least 2 hours before serving.

TIP

To cook couscous, boil 1½ cups water and ½ tsp. salt. Remove from heat. Add 1 cup couscous, stir, and cover. Let stand 5 minutes. Fluff couscous lightly with fork. Cool before using in salad.

Salads

Tuna Salad

Vera Martin,
East Earl, PA

Makes 2–3 servings
Prep. Time: 15 minutes

6-oz. can tuna, drained and flaked

1 Tbsp. mayonnaise

1½ tsp. onion flakes

salt and pepper, to taste

lettuce leaves

green pepper, *optional*

radish, *optional*

1. Combine tuna, mayonnaise, onion flakes, and salt and pepper to taste in a medium-sized bowl.

2. When ready to serve, place lettuce leaves on a plate and put tuna mixture in center of lettuce.

3. If you wish, place pepper rings and radish roses around the tuna salad.

Salads

Albacore Tuna-Stuffed Tomatoes

Joe Barker,
Carlsbad, NM

Makes 6-8 servings
Prep. Time: 1 hour

6-8 Roma tomatoes

2 6-oz. cans albacore tuna, drained

1 Tbsp. mayonnaise

½ tsp. prepared mustard

1½ tsp. blue cheese dressing

2 tsp. thinly sliced green onion

1½ tsp. chopped chives

1½ tsp. chopped black olives

1½ tsp. chopped cucumber

1½ tsp. chopped red bell pepper

1½ tsp. chopped yellow bell pepper

celery leaves

sprinkle of paprika

6-8 mint leaves

1. Cut tomatoes in half and remove seeds and veins. Keep for another use. Keep the tomato shells cool.

2. Mix remaining ingredients except paprika and mint together in a bowl.

3. Stuff tomato halves with tuna mixture.

4. Sprinkle paprika lightly over top.

5. Garnish each tomato with a mint leaf.

6. Keep cold until ready to serve.

Exotic Chicken Salad

**Mable Hershey,
Marietta, PA**

Makes 6 servings
Prep. Time: 30 minutes
Cooking Time: 15–20 minutes, if cooking the chicken
Chilling Time: 2–3 hours

1 lb. green seedless grapes, halved

1-1½ cups slivered almonds

4 cups cooked chicken, cut in pieces, or 2 5-oz. cans cooked chicken

4-oz. can sliced water chestnuts, drained

1 cup sliced celery

1½ cups mayonnaise

1½ tsp. curry powder

1 Tbsp. soy sauce

1 Tbsp. lemon juice

lettuce leaves

1. Cut grapes in half.

2. Toast almonds by spreading them in a large dry skillet. Place over medium-high heat, stirring them frequently so they brown on both sides and don't burn.

3. Combine grapes, 1 cup almonds, chicken, water chestnuts, and celery in a large mixing bowl.

4. In a smaller bowl, mix together mayonnaise, curry powder, soy sauce, and lemon juice. Add to chicken mixture.

5. Chill several hours.

6. Sprinkle with remaining almonds.

7. Serve over lettuce leaves.

Variations:

1. Add ⅓ cup minced onions to Step 3.

2. Replace mayonnaise, curry powder, and lemon juice with 1½ cups peach or lemon yogurt. Increase the soy sauce to 2 Tbsp.

3. In Step 7, garnish prepared plates with melon wedges before serving.
   —Donna Treloar, Hartford City, IN

Cabbage Slaw with Vinegar Dressing

Betty Hostetler,
Allensville, PA

Makes 10-12 servings
Prep. Time: 30-45 minutes
Chilling Time: 3-4 hours

8 cups grated cabbage

¼ cup grated carrots

¼ cup diced celery

¼ cup chopped red pepper

¼ cup chopped yellow pepper

⅛ cup chopped green pepper

1 Tbsp. celery seed

¾-1 cup sugar

1 tsp. salt

½ cup white vinegar

¼ cup plus 2 Tbsp. oil

1. Combine vegetables, celery seed, sugar, and salt in a large mixing bowl. Mix well.

2. In a small saucepan, bring vinegar to a boil. Add oil. Pour over vegetables. Mix well.

3. Refrigerate for 3–4 hours before serving.

Variations:

1. Add 1 medium-sized onion, chopped, to the vegetables in Step 1.

2. Reduce celery seed to 1 tsp. and add 1½ tsp. mustard seed and ½ tsp. turmeric.
—Emilie Kimpel, Arcadia, MI

Salads

Poppy Seed Coleslaw

**Esther Becker,
Gordonville, PA**

Makes 8–10 servings
Prep. Time: 10–15 minutes
Chilling Time: 1 hour

16-oz. bag tri-color coleslaw mix

8¼-oz. can mandarin oranges, drained

8-oz. can pineapple chunks, drained

½ cup poppy seed salad dressing

½ cup sour cream

1. In a large mixing bowl, combine coleslaw mix and fruit.

2. In a small bowl, stir together poppy seed dressing and sour cream.

3. Pour over slaw. Mix and toss.

4. Chill in refrigerator for an hour.

Cranberry Coleslaw

**Carolyn Baer,
Conrath, WI**

Makes 6–7 servings
Prep. Time: 15 minutes
Chilling Time: 45 minutes

½ cup mayonnaise

2 Tbsp. honey

2 Tbsp. vinegar

¼ cup fresh cranberries, chopped, or snipped
dried cranberries

5 cups shredded cabbage (1 small head)

This salad is very pretty for holiday parties,
but it is delicious anytime.

1. Combine mayonnaise, honey, and
vinegar. Stir in cranberries.

2. Place shredded cabbage in a large bowl.

3. Pour dressing over cabbage. Toss to coat.

4. Cover and chill for 45 minutes.

Salads

Broccoli Slaw

**Bonnie Heatwole,
Springs, PA**

Makes 8 servings
Prep. Time: 15 minutes

16-oz. pkg. broccoli slaw

1 cup sunflower seeds

1 cup slivered almonds

2 3-oz. pkgs. chicken-flavored ramen noodles

1 cup diced green onions

Dressing:

½ cup oil

⅓ cup white vinegar

½ cup sugar

2 seasoning packets from ramen noodles

1. Combine salad ingredients in a large bowl.

2. Shake the dressing ingredients together in a jar with a tight-fitting lid. (The dressing is probably more than needed for the amount of salad, so begin by adding only half of what you've made. Add more if you need it.) Add the dressing right before serving. Toss to mix.

Variations:

1. Instead of broccoli slaw, use 10-oz. pkg. coleslaw mix, 6-oz. pkg. fresh spinach, and 2 cups shredded lettuce. Add 3 Tbsp. sesame seeds, lightly toasted, to the salad.
   —Sharon Eshleman, Ephrata, PA

2. Instead of broccoli slaw, use 6-oz. pkg. fresh spinach and half a head of torn romaine lettuce. Substitute walnuts or pecans for the almonds, if you wish.

Salads

Simple Broccoli Slaw

**Hope Comerford,
Clinton Township, MI**

Makes 4 cups
Prep. Time: 5 minutes
Chilling Time: 30 minutes

4 cups broccoli slaw

Dressing:

¼ cup olive oil

¼ cup apple cider vinegar

2 Tbsp. sugar

½ tsp. mustard powder

½ tsp. garlic powder

½ tsp. onion powder

1. Place slaw in bowl. Mix together all of the dressing ingredients. Pour this over the broccoli slaw.

2. Refrigerate for 30 minutes or longer.

Salads

The Best Broccoli Salad

Sandra Haverstraw, Hummelstown, PA

Makes 10–12 servings
Prep. Time: 20–25 minutes
Chilling Time: 8–12 hours

2 bunches fresh broccoli, cut or broken into florets (save stems for another use)

1 cup golden raisins

1 small onion, chopped

10 slices bacon, fried and chopped

1 cup chopped cashews

Dressing:

½ cup sugar

2 Tbsp. vinegar

1 cup Miracle Whip dressing

2 Tbsp. horseradish

¼ tsp. salt

½ tsp. prepared mustard

1. Mix broccoli florets, raisins, chopped onion, and bacon.

2. Prepare dressing by blending sugar, vinegar, Miracle Whip, horseradish, salt, and mustard until smooth.

3. Pour dressing over broccoli mix and toss gently until evenly coated.

4. Cover and refrigerate 8–12 hours. Add cashews just before serving.

TIP

Precooked bacon works well.

Salads

Waldorf Salad with Broccoli

**Frances L. Kruba,
Dundalk, MD**

Makes 2 servings
Prep. Time: 10–15 minutes
Chilling Time: 1–2 hours

3 Tbsp. mayonnaise

1 Tbsp. honey

1 tsp. cider vinegar

1½ cups chopped fresh broccoli

¾ cup chopped apple

2 Tbsp. raisins, *optional*

1 Tbsp. pecans, chopped, *optional*

1. In a medium-sized bowl, combine mayonnaise, honey, and vinegar. Whisk together until smooth.

2. Stir in broccoli and apple. Add raisins and pecans if you wish.

3. Refrigerate for an hour or two before serving.

Trees and Seeds Salad

Nanci Keatley,
Salem, OR

Makes 8–10 servings
Prep. Time: 10–20 minutes
Chilling Time: 30 minutes

4 cups cauliflower florets

3 cups cut-up broccoli

1 cup diced red onions

2 pts. cherry tomatoes, halved

½–1 lb. bacon, cooked and diced, according
    to your preference

3 Tbsp. sesame seeds

¼ cup sunflower seeds

¼ cup slivered almonds

Dressing:

1 cup mayonnaise

½ cup sugar, or sugar substitute

3 Tbsp. cider vinegar

½ tsp. salt

½ tsp. pepper

1. In a large serving bowl, combine cauliflower, broccoli, onions, tomatoes, bacon, seeds, and almonds.

2. In a separate bowl, mix together mayonnaise, sugar, vinegar, salt, and pepper. Pour over vegetables.

3. Refrigerate at least 30 minutes to blend flavors.

Variations:

1. Change the "green" base of this salad to:
   3 cups shredded cabbage or coleslaw mix;
   2 cups broken cauliflower; 2 cups chopped broccoli.
   —Teresa Martin, Gordonville, PA

2. Add ⅓ cup grated Parmesan cheese to the dressing in Step 2.
   —Phyllis Smith, Goshen, IN

3. Add 8 sliced radishes to Step 1.
   —Sara Wilson, Blairstown, MO

TIP

This is great to make ahead. Mix all ingredients together except the dressing. Chill, then add the dressing half an hour before serving. Refrigerate until serving time.

Salads

Picnic Pea Salad

**Mary Kathryn Yoder,
Harrisonville, MO**

Makes 4–6 servings
Prep. Time: 30 minutes
Chilling Time: 1 hour

10-oz. pkg. frozen peas, thawed

¼ cup chopped onion, or green onions

½ cup chopped celery

½ cup sour cream

2 Tbsp. mayonnaise

1 tsp. salt

1 tsp. dill weed

¼ tsp. pepper

1 cup Spanish peanuts

¼–½ cup fried and crumbled bacon

1 cup cherry tomatoes for garnish, *optional*

1. Mix peas, onion, celery, sour cream, mayonnaise, salt, dill weed, and pepper. Chill.

2. Just before serving, stir in peanuts. Garnish with bacon and tomatoes.

Variation:
Omit celery, peanuts, and dill weed. Add a chopped hard-boiled egg and a dash of garlic powder.

—Dorothy VanDeest, Memphis, TN

Carrot Raisin Salad

**Sheila Heil,
Lancaster, PA**

Makes 6 servings
Prep. Time: 10 minutes
Chilling Time: 4–12 hours

5 large carrots, shredded

1 cup raisins

²⁄₃ cup plain yogurt

4 Tbsp. mayonnaise

2 tsp. honey

1. Combine ingredients in a medium nonmetallic bowl.

2. Chill for several hours or overnight. Serve cold.

Salads

Carrot-Pineapple-Nut Salad

**Jeanette B. Oberholtzer,
Manheim, PA**

Makes 6–8 servings
Prep. Time: 20 minutes
Chilling Time: 1–2 hours

1 lb. carrots, grated

8-oz. can pineapple tidbits, in their own juice

½ cup raisins

lettuce leaves

sunflower seeds

1. Mix carrots, pineapple, and raisins together. Refrigerate 1–2 hours before serving.

2. Place a lettuce leaf on 6 or 8 individual salad plates.

3. Top with fruit-vegetable mixture.

4. Sprinkle generously, or to your liking, with sunflower seeds.

Variation:
We like our salads topped with a mound of cottage cheese.

Sour Cream Cucumber Salad

**Mary Jones,
Marengo, OH**

Makes 6 servings
Prep. Time: 20–30 minutes

3 medium cucumbers, sliced thinly

½ tsp. salt

½ cup finely chopped green onions

1 Tbsp. white vinegar

dash pepper, *optional*

¼ cup sour cream

1. Place cucumbers in glass bowl. Sprinkle cucumber with salt. Let stand 15 minutes. Drain liquid.

2. Add onions, vinegar, and pepper.

3. Just before serving, stir in sour cream.

Variation:
Use lemon juice instead of vinegar and make a dressing with sour cream, salt, lemon juice, and 2 tsp. sugar. Simply add the dressing to the cucumbers and onions, chilling 2 hours before serving.
—Joyce Shackelford, Green Bay, WI

Salads

Marinated Garden Tomatoes

**Bonnie Goering,
Bridgewater, VA**

Makes 10 servings
Prep. Time: 10 minutes
Chilling Time: 1 hour or more

6 large firm tomatoes, cut in wedges

½ cup sliced onions

½ cup sliced green bell pepper

¼ cup olive oil

2 Tbsp. red wine vinegar

¼ tsp. garlic powder

½ tsp. salt

¼ tsp. pepper

2 Tbsp. sugar

2 Tbsp. minced fresh, or 2 tsp., parsley flakes

1 Tbsp. snipped fresh, or 1 tsp. dried, thyme

1. Arrange tomatoes, onions, and peppers in a flat dish.

2. In a jar with a tight-fitting lid, mix together oil, vinegar, garlic powder, salt, pepper, and sugar. Pour over vegetables.

3. In a small bowl, combine parsley and thyme and sprinkle on top.

4. Refrigerate for one hour or more before serving.

Rice and Beans Salad

Esther Kraybill,
Lancaster, PA

Makes 10 main-dish servings
Prep. Time: 20 minutes
Cooking Time: 45–50 minutes
Chilling Time: 2 hours or more

1½ cups uncooked brown rice

3 cups water

½ cup fresh parsley, cut up

2 shallots or several spring onions cut up (½ cup)

15-oz. can garbanzo beans, rinsed and drained

15-oz. can dark kidney beans, rinsed and drained

¼ cup olive oil

⅓–½ cup rice vinegar, according to your taste preference

1. Place rice and water in a stockpot. Cover and cook over medium heat until rice is tender, about 45–50 minutes.

2. Cool to room temperature.

3. Stir in the remaining ingredients.

4. Chill 2 hours or longer.

German Bean Salad

**Chris Kaczynski,
Schenectady, NY**

Makes 6 servings
Prep. Time: 5 minutes
Cooking Time: 10 minutes

2 cans French-style green, or yellow, beans

2 small onions

6 slices bacon

⅓ cup vinegar

2½ Tbsp. sugar

1. Heat beans. Drain and keep warm.

2. Cut onions into slices. Separate into rings, and put in bowl with beans.

3. Dice bacon and fry until crisp. Remove bacon, but reserve drippings.

4. Add vinegar and sugar to drippings in skillet. Heat to boiling, stirring well.

5. Meanwhile, crumble bacon and stir into beans and onions.

6. Pour vinegar-sugar mixture over vegetables and bacon. Toss lightly to coat thoroughly.

7. Serve warm or at room temperature.

Five Bean Salad

Jeanne Heyerly,
Shipshewana, IN

Makes 8–10 servings
Prep. Time: 20 minutes
Chilling Time: 12 hours

15-oz. can green beans

15-oz. can wax beans

15-oz. can lima beans

15-oz. can kidney beans

15-oz. can garbanzo beans

½ cup canola or light olive oil

½ cup apple cider vinegar

¾ cup sugar

1 tsp. salt

1 tsp. pepper

1 tsp. dry mustard

1½ tsp. celery seed

1 medium onion, chopped

1 green or red bell pepper, chopped

1 large clove garlic, minced

1. Drain all beans and combine in a large nonmetallic bowl.

2. Heat (but do not boil) the oil, vinegar, sugar, salt, pepper, mustard, and celery seed in microwave or on stovetop.

3. Mix with bean mixture and let stand overnight.

4. Add onion, green pepper, and garlic about 1 hour before serving.

TIPS

1. Omit dry mustard, celery seed, and garlic.
2. If there is another type of bean you like, add it; or you could double up on the kinds you do like. There is enough dressing to cover it. —Jean Halloran, Green Bay, WI
3. Add ½ cup chopped celery and 2-oz jar pimentos.
   —Joyce Kaut, Rochester, NY

Salads

Black Bean Fiesta Salad

**Lorraine Pflederer,
Goshen, IN**

Makes 6 servings
Prep. Time: 30 minutes
Chilling Time: 2–8 hours, or overnight

15-oz. can black beans, rinsed and drained

1 cup frozen corn, thawed

1 green pepper, diced

1 sweet red pepper, diced

1 cup diced red onions

2 celery ribs, chopped

¾ cup cubed Monterey Jack cheese

3 Tbsp. lemon juice

3 Tbsp. red wine, or cider, vinegar

2 Tbsp. olive oil

2 garlic cloves, minced

1 Tbsp. Italian seasoning

1 tsp. pepper

½ tsp. ground cumin

1. In a large bowl, combine beans, corn, peppers, onions, celery, and cheese.

2. In a jar with a tight-fitting lid, combine the remaining ingredients. Shake well.

3. Pour over vegetable mixture and toss gently.

4. Cover and chill for 2 hours or overnight.

Roasted Potato Salad

Mary Puskar,
Forest Hill, MD

Makes 10 servings
Prep. Time: 30 minutes
Baking Time: 30–35 minutes

5 lbs. potatoes, unpeeled, quartered

1 lb. bacon

2-3 chopped hard-cooked eggs

1 bunch spring onions, chopped

16-oz. jar Miracle Whip salad dressing

1. Bake potatoes at 425°F in a baking pan sprayed with nonstick cooking spray for 30–35 minutes, or until tender.

2. Meanwhile, cook bacon in a large skillet until crisp. Do in several batches so as not to crowd skillet. Drain bacon. When cooled, crumble. Set aside.

3. Mix all ingredients in a large mixing bowl. Toss well and serve.

TIPS

1. I like to microwave the bacon. Put pieces one-layer deep on a paper plate. Cover with another paper plate. Microwave on High, 1 minute per slice of bacon.
2. As you finish one batch, drain off drippings, set bacon aside to cool, and continue with the rest.

Salads

Grandpa Steve's Potato Salad

Nanci Keatley,
Salem, OR

Makes 6-8 servings
Prep. Time: 20 minutes
Cooking Time: 20 minutes , for potatoes

6 russet potatoes, peeled, cooked, and cubed

1 cup finely chopped onion

1 cup thinly sliced celery

1 cup sliced black olives (reserve 1 Tbsp. for top of salad)

1 large carrot, grated

6 hard-boiled eggs (4 chopped, 2 sliced for top of salad)

1 pt. Best Foods, or your choice of, mayonnaise

salt and pepper, to taste

Tabasco sauce, *optional*

1. Gently mix potatoes, onion, celery, olives, carrot, and chopped eggs together.

2. Add the mayonnaise and blend.

3. Season with salt and pepper to taste. Add Tabasco sauce to taste, if desired. Garnish with egg slices and olives.

Sweet Potato Salad

Jean Johnson,
Dallas, OR

Makes 6 servings
Prep. Time: 10 minutes
Cooking Time: 20 minutes
Chilling Time: 3 hours

4 medium-sized sweet potatoes

½ cup mayonnaise

½ cup plain yogurt

1–1½ tsp. curry powder

salt, to taste

2 medium-sized Granny Smith apples, chopped

2 medium-sized oranges, peeled and chopped, or 2 11-oz. cans mandarin oranges, drained

½ cup raisins

½ cup chopped dates

20-oz. can pineapple chunks, drained

1 cup sliced celery

1. Place whole, unpeeled sweet potatoes in a saucepan. Add 2 inches of water. Cover and cook over medium-high heat until tender in the middle, but not mushy.

2. Meanwhile, combine mayonnaise, yogurt, curry powder, and salt in a large bowl. Mix well.

3. When the cooked sweet potatoes are cool enough to handle, peel them. Then cut into chunks about the size of the pineapple chunks. Add to mayonnaise mixture.

4. Add remaining ingredients. Toss well.

5. Refrigerate at least 3 hours.

Salads

Double Apple Salad

Anne Nolt,
Thompsontown, PA

Makes 10–12 servings
Prep. Time: 20 minutes
Chilling Time: 1 hour

1 large Golden Delicious apple, unpeeled and diced

1 large Red Delicious apple, unpeeled and diced

1 tsp. lemon juice

20-oz. can pineapple chunks, drained

1 cup miniature marshmallows

²/₃ cup flaked coconut

½ cup chopped walnuts

¼ cup raisins

¼ cup mayonnaise

2 Tbsp. thinly sliced celery

1. In a large mixing bowl, toss apples with lemon juice until coated.

2. Add pineapple, marshmallows, coconut, walnuts, raisins, mayonnaise, and celery.

3. Mix well and transfer to a serving bowl. Cover and chill for 1 hour before serving.

Festive Apple Salad

**Susan Kasting,
Jenks, OK**

Makes 8 servings
Prep. Time: 15 minutes

Dressing:

2 Tbsp. olive oil

2 Tbsp. vinegar, or lemon juice

2 Tbsp. Dijon mustard

1½–3 Tbsp. sugar

salt and pepper, to taste

4-6 Tbsp. chopped walnuts, or cashews

1 Granny Smith apple, chopped

1 large head romaine lettuce, chopped

4 Tbsp. crumbled blue cheese, or shredded
baby Swiss, *optional*

1. In the bottom of a large salad bowl, make dressing by mixing together the oil, vinegar, mustard, sugar, salt, and pepper.

2. Add the nuts and apple and stir to coat. Put lettuce and blue cheese on top without stirring.

3. Mix it all together when ready to serve.

TIPS

1. This is so nice to take places because it has the dressing in the bottom so the salad doesn't wilt. You can also serve the dressing on the side.
2. You can add a little chopped onion and 1 Tbsp. poppy seeds to the dressing. Add ¼ cup Craisins and one diced pear to the salad. —Mary Ann Bowman, Ephrata, PA

Favorite Blueberry Salad

Vicki J. Hill,
Memphis, TN

Makes 10–12 servings
Prep. Time: 10–20 minutes
Chilling Time: 4 hours

6-oz. pkg. raspberry gelatin

1½ cups boiling water

16½-oz. can blueberries, undrained

20-oz. can crushed pineapple, undrained

8-oz. pkg. cream cheese, softened

1 cup sour cream

¼ cup sugar

½ cup chopped nuts

1. In a large saucepan or mixing bowl, dissolve gelatin in water.

2. Stir in blueberries and pineapple. Pour into a 9x13-inch pan. Chill until set, about 4 hours.

3. Meanwhile, cream together cream cheese, sour cream, and sugar, either by hand, or with an electric mixer or food processor. Spread on top of congealed salad.

4. Sprinkle with nuts.

Salads

Cranberry Salad

Mary Lynn Miller,
Reinholds, PA

Makes 6-8 servings
Prep. Time: 30-40 minutes
Chilling Time: 6-8 hours, or overnight

4 cups fresh cranberries, rinsed and drained

4 oranges (2 peeled, 2 unpeeled)

4 apples, peeled and quartered

2 cups sugar

1. Grind cranberries, oranges, and apples. Mix well.

2. Pour sugar over fruit and mix well.

3. Refrigerate for 6–8 hours before serving.

Salads

Five-Minute Salad

Jane Geigley,
Lancaster, PA
Becky Frey,
Lebanon, PA
Heidi Hunsberger,
Harrisonburg, VA

Makes 4-6 servings
Prep. Time: 5-10 minutes
Chilling Time: 5-60 minutes

1 pt. cottage cheese

3-oz. pkg. orange gelatin

11-oz. can mandarin oranges, drained

2 cups frozen whipped topping, thawed

1. Mix cottage cheese and gelatin powder.

2. Add orange slices and whipped topping.

3. Allow to stand at least 5 minutes or can
be refrigerated to chill completely.

Variations:
Use lemon gelatin and crushed pineapple.
—Carla Koslowsky, Hillsboro, KS

Substitute 20-oz. can crushed pineapple or
pineapple tidbits for mandarin oranges.
—Christine Lucke, Aumsville, OR

TIPS

1. This can be either a salad or a
   light dessert.
2. You can use other flavors of
   gelatin. Strawberry or lime is
   also delicious.

Salads

Strawberry Velvet Salad

Colleen Heatwole,
Burton, MI

Makes 6–8 servings
Prep. Time: 30 minutes
Chilling Time: 6 hours

6-oz. pkg. strawberry gelatin

2 cups boiling water

2 cups frozen strawberries, drained and thawed (syrup reserved)

8-oz. cream cheese, softened

¼ cup mayonnaise

¼ cup orange juice

1. Dissolve gelatin in boiling water. Set aside.

2. Add syrup drained from strawberries.

3. Meanwhile in a small bowl beat cream cheese until creamy.

4. Add mayonnaise and orange juice and whisk or beat to combine well.

5. Whip thickened, but not set, gelatin.

6. Add cream cheese mixture and combine again.

7. Stir in strawberries.

8. Pour into 6–8 cup mold or pretty dish. Chill until firm.

Desserts

Desserts

Raspberry Angel Food Cake

Hope Comerford,
Clinton Township, MI

Makes about 20 servings
Prep. Time: 1½ hours
Chilling Time: 1¼ hours

1 cup boiling water

3-oz. pkg. raspberry gelatin

½ cup cold water

1 pt. raspberries

8 oz. frozen whipped topping, thawed, *divided*

10-inch angel food cake

1. In a medium size bowl, pour the 1 cup of boiling water into gelatin and stir until dissolved. Then, pour in the ½ cup cold water.

2. Refrigerate for 1 hour.

3. Fold in most of the raspberries and ½ (4 oz.) of the whipped topping. (You'll want a few raspberries to decorate with at the end.)

4. Split the angel food cake into 3 layers. Spread ½ of the gelatin mixture over the bottom layer. Repeat this process once more, ending with the top layer.

5. Spread the remaining whipped topping over the cake and decorate with remaining raspberries.

Chocolate Sheet Cake

Robin Schrock,
Millersburg, OH

Makes 18 servings
Prep. Time: 30 minutes
Baking Time: 20 minutes
Cooling Time: 1½ hours

Cake:

2 sticks (16 Tbsp.) butter

5 Tbsp. unsweetened cocoa powder

1 cup water

2 eggs, beaten

1 Tbsp. vinegar

1 tsp. baking soda

1 tsp. baking powder

½ cup sour milk, or buttermilk

1 Tbsp. vanilla extract

2 cups sugar

2 cups flour

½ tsp. salt

Frosting:

1 stick (8 Tbsp.) butter

5 Tbsp. unsweetened cocoa powder

½ cup milk

1 tsp. vanilla extract

confectioners' sugar

1. To make cake, combine butter, cocoa powder, and water in a small saucepan. Bring to a rolling boil, stirring occasionally. Remove from heat and cool.

2. When cooled, pour slowly into mixing bowl. Add eggs, vinegar, baking soda, baking powder, sour milk, and vanilla. Mix well.

3. In a separate bowl, mix together sugar, flour, and salt. Add to liquid mixture and blend thoroughly.

4. Pour into a 13x16x1½-inch cake pan. Bake at 350°F for 20 minutes.

5. Allow cake to cool to room temperature.

6. When ready to ice, make frosting by combining butter, cocoa powder, and milk in the saucepan. Bring to a rolling boil.

7. When slightly cool, add vanilla. Gradually add confectioners' sugar, ½ cup at a time, beating to make a spreadable consistency.

8. Ice cooled cake with frosting.

Angel Food Cake

**Pauline Hindal,
Grandin, MI**

Makes 16 servings
Prep. Time: 10–15 minutes
Baking Time: 35–40 minutes

2 cups egg whites, at room temperature

1⅛ cups flour

2 cups sugar, *divided*

½ tsp. salt

1½ tsp. cream of tartar

1 tsp. vanilla extract

1. Place egg whites in the large bowl of an electric mixer.

2. In a separate bowl, sift flour and 1 cup sugar together. Set aside.

3. Add salt to egg whites and beat on high speed until foamy, about half a minute.

4. Beat cream of tartar into egg whites. Continue beating until whites are stiff, but not dry, approximately 2½–3 minutes.

5. Quickly sprinkle 1 cup sugar into whites. Beat on a slower speed while sprinkling in the sugar. Then increase mixer to the highest speed, just until the sugar is blended in and very stiff peaks form.

6. Sprinkle in the flour/sugar mixture and vanilla. Blend in quickly by hand, using a spatula and a gentle folding motion from the sides toward the center of the bowl.

7. Spoon gently into an ungreased tube pan. Cut carefully through the batter—going the whole way around the pan—with a knife to release large bubbles.

8. Bake at 350°F for 35–40 minutes, or until the top is springy when touched.

TIPS

1. Do not open the oven door while the cake is baking.
2. I like to use an electric knife to cut angel food cakes.

Desserts

Apple German Chocolate Cake

Sue Pennington,
Bridgewater, VA

Makes 12–15 servings
Prep. Time: 10–15 minutes
Baking Time: 40–45 minutes

21-oz. can apple pie filling

18¼-oz. pkg. German chocolate cake mix

3 eggs

¾ cup coarsely chopped walnuts

½ cup miniature semisweet chocolate chips

1. Place pie filling in blender. Cover and process until the apples are in ¼-inch chunks.

2. Pour into mixer bowl.

3. Add dry cake mix and eggs. Beat on medium speed for 5 minutes.

4. Pour into a greased 9x13-inch baking pan.

5. Sprinkle with nuts and chocolate chips.

6. Bake at 350°F for 40–45 minutes, or until a toothpick inserted in the center comes out clean. Cool completely on rack before cutting.

Whoopie Pie Cake

Sheila Plock,
Boalsburg, PA

Makes 20-24 servings
Prep. Time: 20 minutes
Cooking/Baking Time: 20-25 minutes
Cooling Time: 1 hour

1 chocolate cake mix

1 extra egg

Filling:

1 stick (8 Tbsp.) margarine, softened

½ cup shortening

1 cup sugar

pinch of salt

1 tsp. vanilla extract

½ cup milk

4 Tbsp. flour

1. Mix cake mix as directed on package with the addition of one extra egg.

2. Grease one 9x13-inch pan. Pour in half the batter.

3. Line another 9x13-inch pan with waxed paper on the bottom and up the sides to use as handles after the cake is baked.

4. Pour the other half of the batter in the waxed paper pan.

5. Bake according to package directions, possibly decreasing baking time because the mix is halved per pan. Check for doneness by inserting toothpick near center of cake. If toothpick is clean, cake is done. Cool at least 1 hour.

6. Make the filling by creaming margarine, shortening, sugar, and pinch of salt in a medium mixing bowl.

7. Slowly add vanilla and milk.

8. Add flour, 1 Tbsp. at a time. Beat on high 5 minutes until sugar dissolves.

9. Spread filling on bottom cake layer in greased pan.

10. To make the top layer, lift the other cake out of pan with waxed paper. Remove waxed paper. Place on top of filling.

Unbelievable Carrot Cake

Sue Hamilton,
Minooka, IL

Makes 16 servings
Prep. Time: 5–10 minutes
Baking Time: 30 minutes
Cooling Time: 1 hour

Cake:

1 2-layer spice cake mix

2 cups (½ lb.) shredded carrots

1 cup crushed pineapples with juice

3 egg whites

½ cup All-Bran cereal

Frosting:

2 3-oz. pkgs. fat-free or light cream cheese,
   softened

1 cup Splenda

1 tsp. vanilla extract

4 oz. (⅓ of a 12-oz. container) fat-free frozen
   whipped topping, thawed

1. Combine all cake ingredients thoroughly.

2. Pour into a 9x13-inch baking pan sprayed with nonfat cooking spray.

3. Bake at 350°F for 30 minutes. Cool completely.

4. Beat together cream cheese, Splenda, and vanilla.

5. Fold in the whipped topping. Frost cake and refrigerate.

TIP

There is no need to shred
carrots yourself anymore,
because you can now buy
them in a bag all ready to use.

Desserts

Blueberry Swirl Cake

Lori Lehman,
Ephrata, PA

Makes 15 servings
Prep. Time: 15 minutes
Baking Time: 30–40 minutes

3-oz. pkg. cream cheese, softened

18¼-oz. box white cake mix

3 eggs

3 Tbsp. water

21-oz. can blueberry pie filling

1. Beat cream cheese in a large mixing bowl until soft and creamy.

2. Stir in dry cake mix, eggs, and water. Blend well with cream cheese.

3. Pour into a greased 9x13-inch baking pan.

4. Pour blueberry pie filling over top of batter.

5. Swirl blueberries and batter with a knife by zigzagging through batter.

6. Bake at 350°F for 30–40 minutes, or until tester inserted in center comes out clean.

Desserts

Cheesecake

Dot Hess,
Willow Street, PA

Makes 12 servings
Prep. Time: 30 minutes
Baking Time: 1 hour 10 minutes
Chilling Time: 3 hours

Crust:

1½ cups crushed graham crackers

¼ cup sugar

½ stick (4 Tbsp.) butter, softened

Filling:

3 8-oz. pkgs. cream cheese, softened

5 eggs

1 cup sugar

1½ tsp. vanilla extract

Topping:

1½ pts. sour cream

⅓ cup sugar

1½ tsp. vanilla extract

1. Combine graham crackers, sugar, and butter. Press into bottom of 9-inch springform pan.

2. Beat cream cheese well with mixer. Add eggs, one at a time, mixing well after each one.

3. Add sugar and vanilla. Mix well.

4. Pour gently over prepared crust.

5. Bake at 300°F for 1 hour. Cool 5 minutes. Do not turn off oven.

6. As the cake cools, mix sour cream, sugar, and vanilla.

7. Spread topping on cake and bake 5 minutes more.

8. Chill for at least 3 hours before serving.

Variation:
Omit crust. Bake at 350°F for 35 minutes and proceed with topping.
                         —Renee Hankins, Narvon, PA

Desserts

Chocolate Chip Cheesecake

Chris Kaczynski,
Schenectady, NY

Makes 16 servings
Prep. Time: 15 minutes
Baking Time: 45–50 minutes
Chilling Time: 3–4 hours

3 eggs, beaten

¾ cup sugar

3 8-oz. pkgs. cream cheese, softened

1 tsp. vanilla extract

24-oz. roll refrigerated chocolate chip cookie dough

1. Preheat oven to 350°F.

2. Place all ingredients except cookie dough in large mixing bowl. With electric mixer, blend together until creamy. Set aside.

3. Slice cookie dough into ¼-inch-thick slices. Set aside 9 slices.

4. Lay remaining slices in bottom of 9x13-inch baking pan. Pat the slices together to form a solid crust.

5. Spoon in cream cheese mixture. Spread out over cookie crust.

6. Arrange the reserved nine cookie slices on top of cream cheese mixture.

7. Bake at 350°F for 45–50 minutes. Allow to cool to room temperature.

8. Chill in refrigerator. When firm, cut into squares.

9. If you wish, when serving, top with whipped cream or chocolate topping.

No-Bake Raspberry Cheesecake

Arlene M. Kopp,
Lineboro, MD

Makes 10–12 servings
Prep. Time: 30 minutes
Chilling Time: 4–5 hours

3-oz. pkg. raspberry gelatin

1 cup boiling water

8-oz. pkg. cream cheese, softened

1 cup sugar

1 tsp. vanilla extract

1⅓ cups (19–20 crackers) graham cracker crumbs

¼ cup melted butter

3 Tbsp. lemon juice

12-oz. can evaporated milk, chilled

1. Place a large mixing bowl in the fridge. (You'll need it later to whip the milk.)

2. Combine gelatin and boiling water in a small bowl, stirring until gelatin is dissolved. Cool.

3. In a medium-sized mixing bowl, cream together cream cheese, sugar, and vanilla. Mix well.

4. Add gelatin. Mix well. Chill until it begins to set.

5. Meanwhile, combine cracker crumbs and butter in a small bowl. Press ⅔ of crumbs into the bottom of a 9x13-inch pan.

6. Combine lemon juice and milk in the bowl you've been chilling. Whip until it is stiff and holds a peak.

7. Lightly fold gelatin mixture into whipped mixture.

8. Pour into crumb crust in pan, being careful not to disturb the crumbs. Sprinkle top with remaining crumbs.

9. Chill until set, about 2–3 hours.

Cherry Cheesecake Tarts

Jan Mast,
Lancaster, PA

Makes 18 servings
Prep. Time: 15 minutes
Baking Time: 15–20 minutes

18 vanilla wafers

8-oz. cream cheese, softened

3 eggs

¾ cup sugar

21-oz. can cherry pie filling

1. Fill 18 cupcake tins with paper cupcake liners.

2. Place one vanilla wafer in each paper liner. Set aside.

3. Beat cream cheese just until soft and smooth. Do not overbeat.

4. Add eggs and sugar, beating until just blended. Do not overbeat.

5. Pour cream cheese mixture evenly into 18 cupcake liners, covering vanilla wafer.

6. Bake at 325°F degrees for 15–20 minutes. Cool completely.

7. Top each cooled tart with cherry pie filling.

TIPS

1. Substitute blueberry pie filling or eliminate pie filling and use slices of assorted fresh fruits like kiwi, orange, strawberry, etc.
2. Refrigerate after preparing.
3. Do not overbeat the cream cheese mixture—it needs to be heavy enough to keep the wafers at the bottom. If too much air is beaten into it, the wafers will float to the top.

Desserts

Grandma's Apple Pie

Andrea Zuercher,
Lawrence, KS

Makes 8 servings
Prep. Time: 30 minutes
Baking Time: 45 minutes

6 cups pared and sliced apples (about 6 medium-sized tart apples; Granny Smith work well)

6-oz. can frozen 100%-juice apple juice concentrate, thawed

1½ Tbsp. cornstarch

1 Tbsp. water

1 tsp. cinnamon

10-inch double pie crust, unbaked

3 Tbsp. butter, *optional*

1. Place sliced apples in saucepan with juice concentrate.

2. Bring to a boil. Reduce heat, and then simmer, covered, for 5 minutes.

3. In a small bowl, dissolve cornstarch in water.

4. Gently stir into the apples.

5. Bring to a boil. Reduce heat. Simmer, covered, for 10–15 minutes. Apples will begin to soften as mixture becomes thickened. Stir occasionally so it does not scorch.

6. Gently stir in cinnamon.

7. Fill bottom pie crust with apples.

8. Dot with butter if you wish.

9. Cover with top crust. Pinch crusts together. With a sharp knife, cut 6–8 steam vents across the top crust.

10. Place pie pan on a baking sheet in case the filling cooks out. Bake at 350°F for about 45 minutes, or until top crust is lightly browned.

Fresh Peach Pie

Lavon Martins,
Postville, IA
Darlene E. Miller,
South Hutchinson, KS

Makes 6–8 servings
Prep. Time: 15 minutes
Cooking Time: 10 minutes
Chilling Time: 30 minutes

¾ cup sugar

½ tsp. salt

1 cup water

3 Tbsp. cornstarch

2 Tbsp. white corn syrup

3-oz. pkg. peach gelatin

4–6 peaches

9-inch baked pie crust

1. In a saucepan, combine sugar, salt, water, cornstarch, and syrup. Cook until clear, stirring constantly.

2. Add gelatin and stir until dissolved. Cool in fridge for 30 minutes.

3. Slice peaches. Place in pie crust.

4. Pour filling over peaches. Chill until ready to serve.

5. Serve with whipped cream or ice cream.

Variation:
Replace the peach gelatin with strawberry gelatin. And use 1 qt. strawberries, fresh or frozen, instead of the peaches.
—June S. Groff, Denver, PA

NOTE

If you want to make your own crust, try this:
1½ cups flour
½ tsp. salt
1½ Tbsp. sugar
2 Tbsp. milk
½ cup oil
Mix all ingredients together in a mixing bowl. When blended, simply press into a 9-inch pie plate. Jag with a fork to keep it from buckling while baking. Bake at 350°F until golden brown. Cool thoroughly before filling with fruit.
—Darlene E. Miller,
South Hutchinson, KS

Desserts

Lemon Pie for Beginners

Jean Butzer,
Batavia, NY

Makes 8 servings
Prep. Time: 10 minutes
Cooking Time: 10–12 minutes
Cooling Time: 15 minutes

1 cup sugar

4 Tbsp. cornstarch

¼ tsp. salt

½ cups water, *divided*

3 egg yolks, slightly beaten

2 Tbsp. butter

⅓ cup lemon juice

9-inch baked pastry shell

meringue or whipped cream, *optional*

1. Combine sugar, cornstarch, salt, and ¼ cup water in 1½-qt. microwave safe bowl.

2. Microwave remaining ¼ cup water on High until boiling. Stir into sugar mixture.

3. Microwave 4–6 minutes until very thick, stirring every 2 minutes.

4. Mix a little hot mixture into egg yolks. Blend yolks into sugar mixture.

5. Microwave 1 minute more.

6. Stir in butter and lemon juice.

7. Cool for 15 minutes and pour into pie shell.

8. If desired, top with meringue (instructions below) or serve with whipped cream.

TIPS

1. To make a meringue, beat 3 egg whites, adding ¼ tsp. cream of tartar and 3 Tbsp. sugar slowly. Continue beating until stiff peaks form. Cover the lemon filling with meringue to edge of crust. Bake in 350°F oven for 10–12 minutes or until meringue is golden.
2. Using the microwave is so much easier than cooking the filling on the top of the stove. You don't have to worry about it sticking or burning to the bottom of the pan.

Desserts

Butterscotch Pie Dessert

Karen Stoltzfus,
Alto, MI

Makes 12 servings
Prep. Time: 15–20 minutes
Baking Time: 20–25 minutes
Cooling Time: 30–45 minutes

1½ cups flour

2 sticks (16 Tbsp.) butter, melted

½ cup chopped walnuts

8-oz. pkg. cream cheese

1 cup confectioners' sugar

2 3.4-oz. pkgs. instant butterscotch pudding

3 cups milk

1 tsp. vanilla extract

8-oz. container frozen whipped topping, thawed

½ cup butterscotch chips

1. Combine flour, butter, and nuts in a mixing bowl. Press into a greased 9x13-inch baking pan. Bake at 350°F for 20 minutes. Cool.

2. In a mixing bowl, beat cream cheese until fluffy. Beat in sugar until creamy. Spread over crust, being careful not to pull the crust up.

3. In the same mixing bowl, beat pudding, milk, and vanilla until thickened. Spread over top of cream cheese layer.

4. Spread whipped topping over pudding. Sprinkle with butterscotch chips.

Variations:

1. Replace butterscotch pudding and butterscotch chips with chocolate pudding and chocolate chips.

2. Replace butterscotch pudding and butterscotch chips with pistachio pudding and chopped walnuts.

Desserts

Fudge Sundae Pie

Deb Martin,
Gap, PA

Makes 6 servings
Prep. Time: 30 minutes
Freezing Time: 2 hours

¼ cup plus 3 Tbsp. light corn syrup, *divided*

2 Tbsp. brown sugar

3 Tbsp. butter or margarine

2½ cups crispy rice cereal

¼ cup peanut butter

¼ cup ice cream fudge sauce

1 qt. vanilla ice cream

1. Combine ¼ cup corn syrup, brown sugar, and butter in medium saucepan.

2. Cook over low heat, stirring occasionally until mixture begins to boil. Remove from heat.

3. Add rice cereal, stirring until well coated.

4. Press evenly into a 9-inch pie plate to form crust.

5. Stir together peanut butter, fudge sauce, and 3 Tbsp. corn syrup.

6. Spread half the peanut butter mixture over crust. Freeze until firm, 1 hour.

7. Allow ice cream to soften slightly.

8. Spoon into frozen pie crust; spread evenly. Freeze until firm, 1 hour.

9. Let pie stand at room temperature for 10 minutes before cutting and serving.

10. Warm the other half of the peanut butter mixture and drizzle over the top.

TIP

Add chopped peanuts to the top, or whipped topping and maraschino cherries. Use butterscotch topping as drizzle.

Ultimate Apple Crisp

Judi Manos,
West Islip, NY

Makes 6–8 servings
Prep. Time: 15 minutes
Cooking/Baking Time: 25 minutes

6–8 apples (use baking apples if you can find them)

1 cup brown sugar

1 cup dry oats, quick or rolled (both work, but rolled have more texture)

1 cup flour

1 Tbsp. cinnamon

1½ sticks (12 Tbsp.) butter, melted

½ stick (4 Tbsp.) butter, cut in pieces

1. Core, peel if you want, and slice apples. Place in microwave- and oven-safe baking dish (a Pyrex-type pie plate works well).

2. In a separate bowl, mix together brown sugar, oats, flour, and cinnamon. Add melted butter and mix with a fork until thoroughly mixed.

3. Place mixture on top of the apples. Microwave on High, uncovered, for 10 minutes. Let stand for 2 minutes.

4. Place cut-up butter on top of heated apple mixture.

5. Place in oven and bake at 350°F for 15 minutes.

Cherry Berry Cobbler

Carol DiNuzzo,
Latham, NY

Makes 6 servings
Prep. Time: 10 minutes
Baking Time: 30 minutes

21-oz. can cherry pie filling

10-oz. pkg. frozen red raspberries, thawed and drained

1 tsp. lemon juice

½ cup flour

¼ cup sugar

⅛ tsp. salt

½ stick (4 Tbsp.) butter

1. In a saucepan, combine pie filling, raspberries, and lemon juice. Bring to a boil over medium heat.

2. Turn into a greased 1-qt. casserole.

3. In a bowl, mix together flour, sugar, and salt. Cut in butter until crumbly. Sprinkle over fruit.

4. Serve warm (not hot), alone or over ice cream.

Peach Cobbler

Eileen Eash,
Carlsbad, NM
June S. Groff,
Denver, PA
Sharon Wantland,
Menomonee Falls, WI

Makes 10 servings
Prep. Time: 30 minutes
Baking Time: 60-70 minutes

8 cups sliced fresh, or frozen, peaches

1 stick (8 Tbsp.) butter, softened

¾ cup sugar

1 cup flour

cinnamon sugar (¼ tsp. cinnamon mixed with
    ½ tsp. sugar)

1. Place peaches in ungreased 9x13-inch baking dish.

2. In a medium-sized mixing bowl, cream butter and sugar together, either with a spoon or an electric mixer.

3. Add flour and mix well. Sprinkle over peaches.

4. Top with cinnamon sugar.

5. Bake at 325°F for 60–70 minutes, or until top is golden brown.

6. Serve warm with milk or ice cream, if you wish.

Desserts

Blueberry Crinkle

Phyllis Good,
Lancaster, PA

Makes 6-8 servings
Prep. Time: 15-20 minutes
Baking Time: 20 minutes

½ cup brown sugar

¾ cup dry quick oats

½ cup flour, white or whole wheat

½ tsp. cinnamon

dash of salt

6 Tbsp. butter, at room temperature

4 cups blueberries, fresh or frozen

2 Tbsp. sugar

2 Tbsp. instant tapioca

2 Tbsp. lemon juice

½ tsp. grated lemon peel

1. In a large bowl, combine brown sugar, oats, flour, cinnamon, and salt. Cut in butter to make crumbs. Set aside.

2. In a separate bowl, stir together blueberries, sugar, tapioca, lemon juice, and lemon peel.

3. Spoon into a greased 8-inch square baking pan. Sprinkle crumbs over blueberries.

4. Bake at 375°F for 20 minutes.

Chocolate Raspberry Torte

Pam McAllister,
Wooster, OH

Makes 10–12 servings
Prep. Time: 35 minutes
Baking Time: 25–30 minutes
Cooling Time: 1 hour

18¼-oz. pkg. chocolate cake mix

3-oz. pkg. cream cheese, softened

¾ cup cold milk

3.4-oz. pkg. instant vanilla pudding

8-oz. container frozen whipped topping, thawed

2 cups fresh raspberries

confectioners' sugar

fresh mint and additional raspberries, *optional*

1. Prepare the cake according to package directions, using three greased and floured 9-inch round cake pans.

2. Bake at 350°F for 25–30 minutes, or until toothpick inserted in center comes out clean.

3. Cool for 10 minutes in pan. Remove from pans to wire racks to cool completely.

4. While the cake is baking, beat the cream cheese in a mixing bowl until fluffy.

5. In a separate bowl, combine milk and pudding. Add to cream cheese mixture and mix well.

6. Fold whipped topping and raspberries into creamy mixture.

7. Place one cake layer on a serving plate. Spread with half the creamy fruit filling. Repeat layers, ending with a cake layer.

8. Just before serving, dust with confectioners' sugar. Garnish with mint leaves and raspberries if you wish. Store in the refrigerator until the moment you're ready to serve.

TIP

You can substitute sliced fresh strawberries for raspberries.

Chocolate Chip Cookies

**Mary Martins,
Fairbank, IA**

Makes 3 dozen big cookies
Prep. Time: 15 minutes
Baking Time: 9 minutes per sheet
Chilling Time: 1 hour

2 sticks (16 Tbsp.) butter, at room temperature

1 cup brown sugar

1 cup sugar

3 eggs, beaten

3½ cups flour

2 tsp. cream of tartar

2 tsp. baking soda

½ tsp. salt

1 tsp. vanilla extract

12-oz. pkg. chocolate chips

1 cup chopped nuts, *optional*

1. In a large mixing bowl, combine butter, sugars, and eggs.

2. In a separate mixing bowl, sift together flour, cream of tartar, baking soda, and salt.

3. Add about one-third of the dry ingredients to the creamed mixture. Mix well. Add half of the remaining dry ingredients and mix well. Add the remaining dry ingredients and mix until thoroughly blended.

4. Stir in vanilla, chocolate chips, and nuts (if using). Chill in the fridge for 60 minutes.

5. Drop by spoonfuls onto a greased cookie sheet.

6. Bake at 400°F for about 9 minutes, or until lightly browned

TIPS

1. If you like smaller cookies, make the spoonfuls in Step 5 about the size of a level teaspoon.
2. I usually bake a cookie sheet full and then cover the rest of the dough and keep it in the refrigerator for a day or so, so that I can have freshly baked cookies.
3. Use macadamia nuts in Step 4 for a real treat. — Barb Yoder, Angola, IN

Desserts

Chocolate Trifle

Ruth E. Martin,
Loysville, PA

Makes 6-8 servings
Prep. Time: 15-20 minutes
Cooking Time: 20 minutes
Chilling Time: 1 hour

Chocolate Pudding:

1 egg yolk, slightly beaten

²/₃ cup sugar

3 Tbsp. unsweetened cocoa powder

3 Tbsp. cornstarch

1½ cups milk

2 tsp. instant coffee granules

1 Tbsp. butter

½ tsp. vanilla extract

3 cups chocolate cake crumbs

12 oz. frozen whipped topping, thawed

½ cup Heath English Toffee Bits

1. Put egg yolk in a medium bowl.

2. In medium saucepan, stir together sugar, cocoa, cornstarch, milk, and instant coffee.

3. Cook, stirring constantly, until mixture boils. Boil and stir 1 minute. Remove from heat.

4. Gradually stir small amount of hot mixture into egg yolk, whisking well.

5. Return to pan, stir and heat again until boiling. Remove from heat.

6. Stir in butter and vanilla. Lay plastic wrap directly on the surface. Chill at least one hour.

7. To assemble the trifle, in a clear glass bowl, put a third of the cake crumbs, then a third of the pudding, then a third of the whipped topping. Sprinkle with Heath bits. Repeat twice more, ending with Heath bits on top.

Ginger Snaps

Joan Brown,
Warriors Mark, PA

Makes 3 dozen cookies
Prep. Time: 30 minutes
Baking Time: 15 minutes per sheet

¾ cup solid shortening

1 cup sugar

1 egg

¼ cup molasses

2 cups flour

1½ tsp. baking soda

¾ tsp. allspice

1 tsp. cinnamon

1 tsp. ginger

sugar

1. In an electric mixing bowl, cream shortening and sugar together. Add unbeaten egg and molasses. Beat until smooth.

2. In a separate bowl, sift together flour, baking soda, allspice, cinnamon, and ginger. Gradually add to creamed mixture. Mix well.

3. Roll into 1-inch balls. Roll in sugar. Place on ungreased cookie sheets.

4. Bake at 350°F for 15 minutes.

Variation:
Instead of allspice, use ¾–1 tsp. ground cloves.
—Cova Rexroad, Kingsville, MD

Desserts

Peanut Butter Cookies

Juanita Lyndaker, Croghan, NY
Stacy Stoltzfus, Grantham, PA
Joleen Albrecht, Gladstone, MI
Doris Bachman, Putnam, IL

Makes 1–1½ dozen cookies
Prep. Time: 15 minutes
Baking Time: 8–10 minutes per sheet

1 cup peanut butter

1 cup sugar

1 egg

additional sugar

1. Mix the first three ingredients together in a medium-sized mixing bowl.

2. Break dough off with a teaspoon and shape into balls.

3. Roll each ball in granulated sugar.

4. Place on greased baking sheet. Press down with a fork, making a crisscross pattern.

5. Bake at 350°F for 8–10 minutes, or until golden brown.

Soft, Chewy Molasses Cookies

Martha Ann Auker,
Landisburg, PA

Makes 3 dozen cookies
Prep. Time: 10 minutes
Baking Time: 8-10 minutes per sheet

1 stick (8 Tbsp.) butter, at room temperature

1 cup brown sugar

1 egg

2 cups flour

2 tsp. baking soda

2 tsp. ginger

2 tsp. cinnamon

4 Tbsp. blackstrap molasses

sugar

1. In an electric mixing bowl, cream together butter and sugar. Add egg. Mix well.

2. In a separate bowl, mix together flour, baking soda, ginger, and cinnamon. Add to creamed mixture, alternately with the molasses, until well blended.

3. Shape batter into 1-inch balls. Roll each in sugar. Place 2 inches apart on a greased cookie sheet.

4. Bake at 350°F for 8–10 minutes.

5. Let stand on cookie sheet about 2 minutes before removing to wire rack to cool.

Variation:
Add ½ tsp. ground cloves to Step 2, if you wish.

—Marjora Miller, Archbold, OH

Lemon Chocolate Chip Cookies

Hope Comerford,
Clinton Township, MI

Makes 24 cookies
Prep. Time: 10 minutes
Baking Time: 15 minutes

1 box lemon cake mix

2 eggs

½ cup vegetable oil or coconut oil

1 cup white chocolate chips

1. Preheat oven to 325°F.

2. Mix together the lemon cake mix, eggs, and vegetable oil. Stir in the white chocolate chips.

3. On a greased cookie sheet, or parchment paper lined cookie sheet, place 1½-tsp.-sized balls of dough 1 inch apart.

4. Bake for 15 minutes.

5. Let cool slightly, then place on a cooling rack.

No-Bake Chocolate Cookies

**Penny Blosser,
Beavercreek, OH**

Makes 36 cookies
Prep. Time: 20 minutes
Cooking Time: 15 minutes
Cooling Time: 30 minutes

½ cup trans-fat-free tub margarine

½ cup fat-free milk

1 cup Splenda Blend for Baking

1 cup chocolate chips

½ cup peanut butter

1 tsp. vanilla extract

3 cups quick oats

1. Put margarine, milk, Splenda, and chocolate chips in a saucepan.

2. Bring to boil, and boil 1 minute. Remove from heat.

3. Stir in peanut butter and vanilla until melted.

4. Add rolled oats. Mix.

5. Drop by heaping tablespoonfuls onto waxed paper–lined baking sheet.

6. Let cool until set.

Chocolate Chip Meringue Drops

**Bonnie Whaling,
Clearfield, PA**

Makes 40 cookies
Prep. Time: 15-20 minutes
Baking Time: 1 hour
Standing Time: 2 hours

2 large egg whites

½ cup sugar

1 tsp. vanilla extract

3 Tbsp. cocoa powder, unsweetened

½ cup semisweet mini chocolate chips

1. Preheat oven to 250°F.

2. Line 2 baking sheets with parchment paper or aluminum foil. Set aside.

3. In large mixer bowl, beat egg whites until they hold stiff peaks.

4. Beat in sugar one tablespoon at a time.

5. Then beat in vanilla.

6. Reduce speed to low and beat in cocoa powder.

7. With a spatula, fold in chocolate chips.

8. Drop batter by rounded teaspoonfuls onto baking sheets, spacing cookies 1 inch apart.

9. Bake 1 hour.

10. Turn off oven and let cookies remain in oven 2 hours longer.

11. Remove from baking sheets and store in airtight container.

TIP

Don't make these on a humid day. The mixture will be sticky and hard to handle.

Lemon Squares

Mary Kathryn Yoder,
Harrisonville, MO

Makes 15 servings
Prep. Time: 10 minutes
Baking Time: 30 minutes
Cooling Time: 1–2 hours

1 box angel food cake mix

21-oz. can lemon pie filling

⅛ cup confectioners' sugar

1. Mix cake mix and pie filling together with an electric mixer.

2. Pour into a lightly greased 9x13-inch baking pan.

3. Bake at 350°F for 30 minutes. Let cool.

4. Sprinkle confectioners' sugar over top.

5. Cut into bars.

Cheesecake Bars

**Leona Yoder,
Hartville, OH**

Makes 12 bars
Prep. Time: 10–15 minutes
Baking Time: 40 minutes

1 cup flour

⅓ cup brown sugar

⅓ cup (5⅓ Tbsp.) butter, melted

8-oz. pkg. cream cheese, at room temperature

¼ cup sugar

1 large egg

1 Tbsp. lemon juice

2 Tbsp. milk

1 tsp. vanilla extract

1. Mix flour, brown sugar, and butter together in an electric mixing bowl. Reserve 1 cup mixture. Press remainder into a greased 8x8-inch baking pan.

2. Bake at 350°F for 15 minutes.

3. Meanwhile, in the mixing bowl, beat together the remaining ingredients. Spread on baked crust.

4. Top with reserved crumbs and bake for 25 minutes, or until set.

Pecan Pie Squares

Mary Ann Bowman,
Ephrata, PA
Arianne Hochstetler,
Goshen, IN

Makes 24 bars
Prep. Time: 15 minutes
Baking Time: 35–40 minutes

Crust:

1½ cups flour

3 Tbsp. brown sugar

¼ tsp. salt

1 stick (8 Tbsp.) butter

2 eggs

½ cup light corn syrup

½ cup brown sugar

1 cup chopped pecans

2 Tbsp. butter, melted

½ tsp. vanilla extract

1. Mix together flour, 3 Tbsp. brown sugar, and salt.

2. Cut butter into mixture with a pastry cutter or two knives until crumbly.

3. Press mixture into a greased 11x7-inch pan to form a crust.

4. Bake at 350°F for 15 minutes. Set aside, but do not turn off oven.

5. In a medium mixing bowl, beat eggs slightly.

6. Stir in corn syrup, ½ cup brown sugar, pecans, butter, and vanilla.

7. Pour over baked crust.

8. Put the pan back in the oven. Bake at 350°F for 20–25 minutes. Cool slightly. Cut into bars.

TIP

Try cutting back some of the sugar. I also use half whole wheat flour for the crust.
—Arianne Hochstetler,
Goshen, IN

Desserts

Deliciously Chocolate Brownies

**Alice Whitman,
Lancaster, PA
Michelle Martin,
Ephrata, PA**

Makes 10 servings
Prep. Time: 10-15 minutes
Baking Time: 28-30 minutes

2 sticks (16 Tbsp.) butter, melted

½ cup plus 2 Tbsp. unsweetened cocoa powder

2 cups sugar

4 eggs, beaten

1½ cups flour

pinch of salt

½ cup chopped nuts

1 cup miniature chocolate chips

1. In a mixing bowl, combine butter and cocoa powder until well blended.

2. Add sugar, eggs, flour, and salt. Stir with a fork. (Stirring with a fork keeps the brownies from becoming too cakey.)

3. Stir in chopped nuts. Spread in a greased 9x13-inch baking pan.

4. Bake at 350°F for 25 minutes. Do not overbake.

5. Sprinkle with chocolate chips. Return to oven for 3–5 minutes, or just until chocolate melts.

6. Cool completely before cutting with a plastic knife—which will cut clean.

Chocolate Chip Blonde Brownies

Vera Martin,
East Earl, PA

Makes 18–20 brownies
Prep. Time: 15 minutes
Baking Time: 25 minutes
Cooling Time: 20 minutes

10⅔ Tbsp. (⅔ cup) butter

2 Tbsp. hot water

2 cups brown sugar

2 eggs

2 tsp. vanilla extract

2 cups flour

1 tsp. baking powder

¼ tsp. baking soda

1 tsp. salt

½ cup chopped nuts, *optional*

½ cup chocolate chips

1. In a good-sized saucepan, melt butter. Add water and brown sugar. Cool for 20 minutes.

2. Add eggs and vanilla. Beat well.

3. In a mixing bowl, combine flour, baking powder, baking soda, and salt.

4. Add dry ingredients to egg/sugar mixture. Mix well and add nuts if desired.

5. Spread into a greased 9x13-inch baking pan. Sprinkle chocolate chips over the top.

6. Bake at 350°F for 25 minutes. Cool slightly. Cut into squares with a plastic knife—which will make clean cuts.

TIP

These will be chewy in the center. Don't overbake.

Desserts

Gluten-Free Pretzel Jell-O

**Hope Comerford,
Clinton Township, MI**

Makes 12 servings
Prep. Time: 1 hour
Bake Time: 10 minutes
Chilling Time: 4 hours or until set

Crust:
3 cups crushed gluten-free pretzels

1½ sticks (12 Tbsp.) butter, melted

2 Tbsp. sugar

1 cup sugar

8 oz. cream cheese, softened

16 oz. frozen whipped topping, thawed

6 oz. pkg. strawberry gelatin

2 cups hot water

20 oz. frozen strawberries, thawed

1. Preheat the oven to 375°F.

2. Mix the crust ingredients and press them into a 9x13-inch baking pan. Bake for 10 minutes and let cool.

3. Mix the sugar and cream cheese. Gently fold in the topping. Spread this mixture over the cooled crust and refrigerate.

4. Mix the gelatin and water until dissolved. Add the strawberries and let cool a bit.

5. Spoon the gelatin mixture over the cream cheese mixture.

6. Refrigerate about 4 hours, or until completely set.

Peach Bavarian

Erma Martin,
East Earl, PA

Makes 8–10 servings
Prep. Time: 30 minutes
Chilling Time: 8 hours, or overnight

16-oz. can sliced peaches

2 3-oz. pkgs. peach, or apricot, gelatin

½ cup sugar

2 cups boiling water

1 tsp. almond extract

8-oz. container frozen whipped topping, thawed

additional peach slices, *optional*

1. Drain peaches, reserving ⅔ cup juice. Chop peaches into small pieces. Set aside.

2. In a large mixing bowl, dissolve gelatin and sugar in boiling water.

3. Stir in reserved peach juice. Cover and chill in the fridge until slightly thickened.

4. Stir almond extract into whipped topping. Gently fold into gelatin mixture. Fold in peaches.

5. Pour into 6-cup mold. Cover and chill overnight.

6. Unmold when ready to serve. Garnish with additional peach slices, if you wish.

Mandarin Orange Sherbet Dessert

**Lori Lehman,
Ephrata, PA
Mary Ann Bowman,
East Earl, PA**

Makes 8 servings
Prep. Time: 2 hours
Chilling Time: 8 hours

3-oz. pkg. orange gelatin

1 cup boiling water

1 pt. orange sherbet

16-oz. can mandarin oranges, drained

1 cup frozen whipped topping, thawed

1. Dissolve gelatin in water. Place in mixing bowl.

2. Add sherbet and oranges. Place in fridge until mixture begins to thicken, about 20 minutes.

3. Fold in whipped topping.

4. Spoon into serving dish. Cover and chill 8 hours before serving.

Variation:
Instead of folding the whipped topping into the dessert, use it as a topping just before serving.
—Mary Ann Bowman, East Earl, PA

Vanilla Pudding

Rhonda Freed,
Croghan, NY

Makes 8–10 servings
Prep. Time: 15 minutes
Cooking Time: 25 minutes
Chilling Time: 2–4 hours

8 cups whole milk, *divided*

¾ cup cornstarch

1¼ cups sugar

2 eggs

2 tsp. vanilla extract

1. In a 3- or 4-qt. microwave-safe bowl, heat 6 cups milk in microwave on High until scalded, approximately 8–10 minutes.

2. Meanwhile, blend remaining milk, the cornstarch, sugar, and eggs in blender until smooth.

3. Whisk blended ingredients into scalded milk.

4. Microwave on High for 5 minutes. Remove carefully with potholders and mix with whisk.

5. Microwave on High for 4 minutes and stir. Decrease cooking time by a minute each time until the pudding is a bit thinner than you want. (It will continue to thicken as it cools.)

6. Remove from microwave. Stir in vanilla.

7. While still hot, cover with plastic wrap, pressing plastic against the surface of the pudding to prevent a skin from forming.

Variation:
Pour the finished pudding into ice pop molds. Freeze for pudding pops.

NOTE

I am at least the fourth generation (that I know of and remember) to make this recipe. My mom adapted it for the microwave, which saves standing and stirring over a double boiler on a hot stovetop!

Desserts

Caramel Pudding

Esther S. Martin,
Ephrata, PA

Makes 16 servings
Prep. Time: 10 minutes
Cooking Time: 15-20 minutes
Chilling Time: 2-3 hours

1 stick (8 Tbsp.) butter

2 cups brown sugar

½ cup water

2 qts. milk

pinch of salt

6 eggs

5 rounded Tbsp. cornstarch

5 rounded Tbsp. flour

1 Tbsp. vanilla extract

whipped topping or whipped cream

1. In heavy saucepan, melt butter. Add brown sugar. Bring to a boil and continue simmering until mixture browns. Stir occasionally so it doesn't stick and burn.

2. Remove from heat and add water. Stir in milk and salt. Return pan to stove over low heat.

3. In a blender, mix eggs, cornstarch, and flour.

4. Add to caramel-milk mixture and heat until boiling, stirring constantly or whisking as mixture thickens.

5. Remove from stove and add vanilla.

6. Pour into two serving dishes.

7. Chill 2–3 hours. Top with whipped topping or whipped cream just before serving.

Desserts

Rice Pudding

Judy Koczo,
Plano, IL

Makes 6 servings
Prep. Time: 30 minutes
Cooking Time: 25–30 minutes
Chilling Time: 2–3 hours

1⅓ cups uncooked, converted rice

½ cup sugar

pinch of salt

½ tsp. nutmeg

2 Tbsp. butter

1 tsp. vanilla extract

5 cups milk

5-oz. can evaporated milk

2 egg yolks

3 Tbsp. milk

whipped topping, *optional*

cinnamon, *optional*

1. Combine all ingredients (except egg yolks, 3 Tbsp. milk, and optional ingredients) in a pan. Cover and cook over low heat. After it comes to a slow boil, cook for 20 minutes.

2. While rice is cooking, beat egg yolks with 3 Tbsp. milk in a small bowl.

3. When rice is cooked, remove rice from heat. Add egg-yolk mixture immediately.

4. Refrigerate until chilled and then serve. Garnish with whipped topping and sprinkles of cinnamon, if you wish.

Award-Winning Ice Cream

Monica Leaman Kehr,
Portland, MI

Makes 6 servings
Prep. Time: 10 minutes
Chilling Time: 1–2 hours
Churning and Freezing Time (in an electric ice-cream maker): 30–40 minutes

12-oz. can evaporated milk

14-oz. can sweetened condensed milk

1½ cups milk (2% works well)

1½ cups heavy whipping cream

2 Tbsp. vanilla extract

1 cup sugar

1. Mix all ingredients very well. Chill.

2. Mix again before pouring into your ice cream freezer.

3. Follow your ice-cream freezer's directions for churning and freezing.

Desserts

Ice Cream in a Bag

**Annabelle Unternahrer,
Shipshewana, IN**

Makes 2 cups or more
Prep. Time: 10 minutes
Shaking Time: 10-15 minutes

2 cups skim milk

⅓ cup sugar

1 tsp. vanilla extract

5 cups ice

¾ cup rock salt

¼ cup water

1. In a 1-qt. resealable bag, combine milk, sugar, and vanilla.

2. In a 1-gallon resealable bag, combine ice, salt, and water. Then place bag with ice cream mix inside it.

3. Close gallon bag very securely. Wrap with a heavy towel.

4. Shake 10–15 minutes, or until ice cream is frozen. Kids ages 3–90 love to make this recipe.

Chocolate Ice Cream Syrup

Christine Weaver,
Reinholds, PA

Makes 2½–3 cups
Prep. Time: 5 minutes
Cooking Time: 30 minutes

¾ cup semisweet chocolate chips, or
   6 squares unsweetened chocolate

3 Tbsp. butter (no substitutes)

2 cups sugar

12-oz. can evaporated milk

1. Microwave the chocolate and butter in a microwave-safe dish, stirring a few times, for approximately 3–4 minutes.

2. Transfer chocolate to a heavy saucepan. Add sugar and milk alternately, stirring until blended.

3. Cook 15 minutes over low heat, stirring frequently.

4. Serve warm over ice cream. Refrigerate leftovers.

Blueberry Sauce

Jeannine Dougherty,
Tyler, TX

Makes 2½ cups
Prep. Time: 5 minutes
Cooking Time: 15–20 minutes

¼–½ cup sugar, according to your taste
  preference

2 tsp. cornstarch

pinch of salt

½ cup water

2 cups fresh or frozen blueberries

2 tsp. lemon juice

1. In a medium-sized saucepan, combine sugar, cornstarch, and salt. Mix well.

2. Add water and blueberries. Mix well.

3. Bring mixture to a boil, stirring constantly. Cook until thick and translucent.

4. Remove from heat and stir in lemon juice.

TIP

Here's a great dessert—or quick meal: place a waffle or a couple of thin pancakes on a plate. Add a scoop of good ice cream and cover with warm blueberry sauce. When cold, this sauce is also very good over plain ice cream, yogurt, or cottage cheese. Or serve it as a topping for pound cake or angel food cake.

Peanut Butter Fudge

Jamie Schwankl,
Ephrata, PA

Makes 16 servings
Prep. Time: 10 minutes
Cooking Time: 5–8 minutes

2 sticks (16 Tbsp.) butter or margarine

1 tsp. vanilla extract

1 cup peanut butter

pinch of salt

3 cups confectioners' sugar

1. Melt butter in a medium saucepan over low heat.

2. Add vanilla, peanut butter, and salt. Mix with a spoon until smooth. Remove from heat.

3. Add confectioners' sugar. Stir until well blended.

4. Spread mixture in an 8x8-inch pan to cool.

5. Refrigerate 1 hour. Cut into small squares.

TIPS

1. A 7x9-inch pan also works well.
2. Do not use a mixer.

Desserts

Peanut Brittle

Lois Niebauer,
Pedricktown, NJ

Makes 3 cups
Prep. Time: 5 minutes
Cooking Time: 9 minutes
Cooling Time: 1 hour

1½ cups raw Spanish peanuts

1 cup sugar

½ cup light corn syrup

⅛ tsp. salt

1 tsp. butter

1 tsp. vanilla extract

1 tsp. baking soda

1. In an 8-cup glass bowl or measuring cup (works well because of handle), mix peanuts, sugar, corn syrup, and salt.

2. Microwave on High for 3 minutes. Stir.

3. Microwave for 3 more minutes. Add butter and vanilla and stir.

4. Microwave 3 more minutes.

5. Working quickly, add baking soda and stir rapidly.

6. Quickly pour into a buttered 9x13-inch pan.

7. Let cool.

8. When completely cool, break into pieces and store in an airtight container.

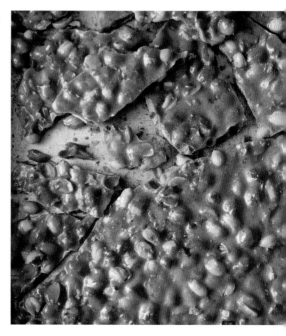

Taffy Apple Pizza

**Lauren Eberhard,
Seneca, IL**

Makes 12 servings
Prep. Time: 15 minutes
Baking Time: 10-20 minutes
Cooling Time: 30 minutes

16½-oz. tube peanut butter cookie dough

8-oz. cream cheese, softened

¼ cup sour cream

¼ cup brown sugar

2 crisp apples, Gala or Braeburn

¼ cup chopped peanuts

¼–½ cup caramel sauce or ice cream topping

¼–½ cup chocolate sauce or ice cream
   topping

1. Roll out cookie dough to a 12x14-inch circle. Place on a pizza stone or baking sheet.

2. Follow package directions for baking. Cool at least 30 minutes.

3. Mix cream cheese, sour cream, and brown sugar together in a small mixing bowl.

4. Spread on cooled cookie.

5. Slice unpeeled apples thinly. Layer in a decorative pattern on top of cream cheese mixture.

6. Sprinkle peanuts over apple slices.

7. Drizzle with caramel sauce and chocolate sauce.

8. Refrigerate until ready to serve.

Strawberry Dessert

**Glenda Weaver,
Manheim, PA
Joyce Nolt,
Richland, PA**

Makes 6-8 servings
Prep. Time: 15-20 minutes
Cooking Time: 25 minutes
Chilling Time: 4-8 hours

4 cups water

⅔ cup granulated tapioca

1-1½ cups sugar, according to your taste
preference

2 qts. crushed strawberries

8-oz. container frozen whipped topping,
thawed

1. Place water and tapioca in a large
saucepan. Stir. Bring to a boil.

2. Cook until mixture is clear and slightly
thickened.

3. Stir in sugar.

4. Cool.

5. Add crushed strawberries, mixing well.

6. Fold in whipped topping.

7. Refrigerate until thoroughly chilled and
thickened.

Snickers Apple Salad

Jennifer Archer,
Kalona, IA

Makes 10-12 servings
Prep. Time: 15-20 minutes

3-oz. pkg. instant vanilla pudding

1 cup milk

8-oz. container frozen whipped topping, thawed

6 apples, peeled or unpeeled, diced

6 Snickers bars, diced or broken

1. Mix pudding with milk in a large mixing bowl.

2. Fold in whipped topping.

3. Fold in chopped apples and Snickers.

4. Cover and refrigerate until ready to serve.

Butter Rum Bananas

Shari Jensen,
Fountain, CO

Makes 4 servings
Prep. Time: 5 minutes
Cooking Time: 10 minutes

2 Tbsp. butter

½ cup sugar

2 Tbsp. water

2 Tbsp. light rum

½ Tbsp. lemon juice

grated rind of half a lemon

½ tsp. vanilla or rum extract

4 small bananas, peeled and halved

whipping cream or ice cream

1. Melt butter in a large skillet. Add sugar and water. Stir well. Cook until reduced to heavy syrup, stirring occasionally so the mixture doesn't stick to the bottom of the pan.

2. Add rum, lemon juice, rind, and your choice of flavoring. Cook 2 minutes, or until golden in color.

3. Remove from stove and add banana pieces. Plunge them into the syrup, covering them as well as possible.

4. Serve warm, not hot, topped with a dollop of whipped cream or alongside scoops of ice cream.

Snacks, Candies, and Beverages

Snacks, Candies, and Beverages

Puppy Chow

**Lena Sheaffer,
Port Matilda, PA**

Makes 15 servings
Prep. Time: 20 minutes
Cooking Time: 5-7 minutes

1 stick (8 Tbsp.) butter

1 cup peanut butter

1 cup chocolate chips

9 cups cereal (Chex, Cheerios, or a mixture)

2 cups confectioners' sugar

1. Melt butter, peanut butter, and chocolate chips together in a medium-sized saucepan.

2. Place cereal in a large bowl. Pour sauce over cereal, stirring it in as you pour to make sure cereal is well coated.

3. When cereal is cool, put cereal and confectioners' sugar in a ziplock bag.

4. Make sure bag is securely locked. Coat cereal evenly by shaking it together with the sugar.

5. Store in airtight container or ziplock bags.

Party Mix

**Kayla Snyder,
North East, PA**

Makes 30 cups
Prep. Time: 30 minutes
Baking Time: 1¼–2 hours

4 cups Cheez-Its or cheese curls

4 cups Corn Chex

4 cups Rice Chex

4 cups Cheerios

4 cups Kix

10-oz. thin pretzel sticks

1½ lb. salted peanuts

1 lb. assorted nuts

1 lb. (4 sticks) butter, melted

1½ Tbsp. onion salt

1½ Tbsp. seasoned salt

3 Tbsp. Worcestershire sauce

1. Mix Cheez-Its, cereals, pretzels, peanuts, and nuts together.

2. Mix melted butter, onion salt, seasoned salt, and Worcestershire sauce together.

3. Pour over dry ingredients. Mix until all the cereal is totally covered.

4. Spread mix evenly on 2 cookie sheets.

5. Bake at 225°F for 1¼–2 hours, stirring every 15 minutes until toasted and crispy.

Seasoned Pretzels or Crackers

Eileen Eash, Carlsbad, NM
Marie Raber, Millersburg, OH
Trudy Kutter, Corfu, NY
Ruth Shank, Monroe, GA
Karen Kay Tucker, Manteca, CA
Barbara Gautcher, Harrisonburg, VA

Makes 15 servings
Prep. Time: 15 minutes
Baking Time: 1 hour

20-oz. bag large thick pretzels, or nuggets, or oyster crackers

1 envelope, or 2 Tbsp., dry ranch dressing mix

½ cup canola oil

1½ tsp. dill weed

1½ tsp. garlic powder

1. Break large pretzels into bite-sized pieces. Place in large mixing bowl.

2. Mix remaining ingredients in another bowl and pour over pretzels. Stir well.

3. Pour mixture into jelly-roll pan or cookie sheet with 1-inch sides.

4. Bake at 200°F for 1 hour, stirring every 15 minutes.

5. Allow to cool. Keep in tightly closed container until ready to serve.

Natalia's Soft Pretzels

Laura R. Showalter,
Dayton, VA

Makes 8-10 servings
Prep. Time: 60-70 minutes
Rising Time: 20-30 minutes
Cooking Time: 5-7 minutes

2¼ cups warm water

2 Tbsp. yeast

6-6½ cups unbleached flour, *divided*

½ cup brown sugar

1 tsp. salt

6 cups very hot water

¼ cup baking soda

pretzel salt, *optional*

melted butter, *optional*

1. Dissolve yeast in 2¼ cups warm water. Pour into a large mixing bowl.

2. Stir in 2 cups flour. Add sugar and salt.

3. Continue adding flour, stirring, until dough is too stiff to stir. Then roll out onto counter and knead until dough is smooth and soft.

4. Place dough in large, lightly greased mixing bowl. Cover with a tea towel. Leave in a warm place.

5. Let dough rise 20–30 minutes.

6. While dough is rising, grease 2 large baking sheets, or cover them with parchment.

7. Just before the end of the dough's rising time, bring 6 cups water to a boil in a large stockpot. Stir baking soda into water until dissolved. Pour into a wide bowl.

8. When dough has finished rising, divide dough in half. Divide each half into 6 portions.

9. Roll each portion into a 16-inch-long rope. Form each into a pretzel shape.

10. Dip each pretzel into hot soda water. Lay briefly on bread cloth or towel to absorb excess moisture.

11. Place on greased, or parchment-covered, baking sheets.

12. Sprinkle with pretzel salt if you wish.

13. Bake at 400°F for 5–7 minutes, or until golden brown.

14. Brush with melted butter if you wish. Serve warm.

15. You can freeze any extra pretzels after they're baked.

TIPS

1. The pretzels are best if you replace 2 cups white flour with 2 cups freshly ground whole wheat flour.
2. The possibilities for serving these soft pretzels are many: Serve with cheese sauce or hot mustard. Sprinkle with cinnamon sugar, or sour cream and onion powder. Form them into breadsticks and sprinkle them with herbed Parmesan cheese when they come out of the oven. Then dip in pizza sauce. Add raisins to the dough and drizzle with icing when they've cooled a bit from baking.

Caramel Popcorn Crunch

Jamie Schwankl, Ephrata, PA
Deb Martin, Gap, PA

Makes 8 servings
Prep. Time: 5 minutes
Baking Time: 60–90 minutes

2-4 qts. popped corn

1 cup brown sugar

1 stick (8 Tbsp.) margarine or butter

¼ cup corn syrup or molasses

½ tsp. salt

½ tsp. baking soda

½ tsp. vanilla extract, *optional*

1. Pour popped corn into a large roasting pan.

2. Sort through the popcorn to remove kernels that are unpopped.

3. In a medium sauce pan, combine sugar, margarine, corn syrup, and salt over medium heat, stirring frequently. Bring to a boil.

4. Boil for 5 minutes. Remove syrup from heat.

5. Stir in baking soda and optional vanilla until mixture becomes foamy.

6. Pour syrup over popcorn, stirring quickly and thoroughly to coat.

7. Bake at 200°F for 1–1½ hours, stirring every 15 minutes.

8. Allow to cool, stirring occasionally to keep kernels from sticking together.

9. Store in an airtight container.

Variation:
Add 1 cup nuts.

—Renee Hankins,
Narvon, PA

Sugared Pecans

**Janet Derstine,
Telford, PA**

Makes 6 cups
Prep. Time: 15 minutes
Baking Time: 30 minutes
Cooling Time: 30 minutes

1 egg white, beaten

1 Tbsp. water

1 lb. pecan halves

1 cup sugar

1½ tsp. salt

1 tsp. cinnamon

1. Preheat oven to 300°F.

2. Beat egg white until stiff in a good-sized mixing bowl.

3. Fold water and pecans into egg white.

4. In a small bowl, mix sugar, salt, and cinnamon together. Sprinkle over pecan mixture and mix well.

5. Spread on a nonstick cookie sheet. Bake for 30 minutes, stirring once or twice.

6. Remove from oven. Stir and separate pecans. Cool before serving or storing in an airtight container.

Fiddle Sticks

Cova Rexroad,
Kingsville, MD

Makes 20 servings
Prep. Time: 15 minutes
Baking Time: 10 minutes

2 cups pretzel sticks, broken in half

1½ cups raisins

1½ cups lightly salted peanuts

½ cup pecans, *optional*

12-oz. pkg. white chocolate chips

2 Tbsp. butter

1. Mix together pretzels, raisins, and nuts in a large mixing bowl or 9x13-inch baking pan.

2. Place in a warm 200°F oven for about 10 minutes.

3. Melt the white chocolate chips and butter in a double boiler over hot water, or in the microwave (50% power for 1 minute; stir; 50% power for 30 seconds; stir. Continue microwaving at 50% for 30-second time periods, stirring between each one, until the mixture is melted).

4. Pour melted chocolate and butter over the warmed pretzel mixture. Stir well to coat.

5. Spread out on a baking sheet to cool.

6. Break up and serve or store.

Salted Peanut Squares

John D. Allen,
Rye, CO

Makes 20–24 servings
Prep. Time: 5 minutes
Cooking Time: 5 minutes
Chilling Time: 1 hour

16-oz. jar salted peanuts, *divided*

3 Tbsp. butter

10-oz. pkg. peanut butter chips

2 cups miniature marshmallows

14-oz. can sweetened condensed milk

1. Cover the bottom of a greased 9x13-inch baking pan with half the salted peanuts.

2. In a saucepan, melt butter and peanut butter chips.

3. Stir in marshmallows and milk. Heat until melted.

4. Pour over peanuts.

5. Top with remaining peanuts.

6. Chill. Cut into squares.

Peanut Butter Clusters

Ruth Ann Gingrich,
New Holland, PA

Makes 4-5 dozen pieces
Prep. Time: 5-10 minutes
Cooking Time: 3-5 minutes
Cooling Time: 1 hour

2 cups light corn syrup

2 cups peanut butter

2 cups sugar

1 12-oz. box cornflakes, or 12 cups cornflakes

1. Mix corn syrup, peanut butter, and sugar in a large saucepan.

2. While stirring constantly over medium heat, bring to a boil.

3. Immediately remove from heat and stir in cornflakes until coated evenly.

4. Drop by spoonfuls onto waxed paper.

5. When fully cooled, store in airtight container, placing a sheet of waxed paper between each layer.

TIP

You must stir constantly in Step 2 so the mixture doesn't burn. As soon as it reaches the boiling point, remove from heat!

Cranberry Clusters

Edwina Stoltzfus,
Narvon, PA

Makes 24 clusters
Prep. Time: 5–10 minutes
Cooking Time: 2–4 minutes
Standing Time: 1 hour

2 cups (12-oz. pkg.) semisweet chocolate chips

²/₃ cup Craisins

²/₃ cup peanuts

1. Place chocolate chips in a microwave-safe bowl. Microwave at 50% for 1 minute. Stir. Microwave at 50% for 15 seconds. Stir. Continue microwaving at 50% for 15-second periods, followed by stirring, until the chips are melted.

2. Stir in Craisins and peanuts.

3. Drop by teaspoonfuls onto waxed paper. Let stand until set.

Variations:
Use white chocolate chips instead of chocolate chips, cashews instead of peanuts, and raisins or dried cherries instead of Craisins.

Creamy Popsicles

**Joyce L. Moser,
Copenhagen, NY**

Makes 15 servings
Prep. Time: 10–15 minutes

1 qt. vanilla ice cream, softened

2 pts. orange sherbet, softened

16-oz. bottle lemon-lime soda

1 qt. milk

fresh orange slices, *optional*

1. Combine softened ice cream, sherbet, and soda in a large bowl or pitcher.

2. Gradually add milk and stir vigorously until mixture is smooth.

3. Serve in a punch bowl.

4. Garnish with orange slices if you wish.

Strawberry Refresher

**Helen R. Goering,
Moundridge, KS**

Makes 1 gallon
Prep. Time: 20 minutes

10-oz. pkg. frozen strawberries

6-oz. can frozen lemonade concentrate

8-oz. can crushed pineapple, undrained

3 qts. ginger ale

fresh strawberry slices, if available

1. Place frozen strawberries, frozen lemonade concentrate, and crushed pineapple into blender. Blend on high speed.

2. Pour into punch bowl.

3. Add ginger ale just before serving.

4. If serving in a punch bowl, garnish with fresh strawberry slices.

Piña Colada Punch

Melissa Raber,
Millersburg, OH

Makes 20 cups
Prep. Time: 20 minutes
Chilling Time: 2–4 hours

½ gallon vanilla ice cream

20-oz. can crushed pineapple

16-oz. can coconut cream or coconut milk

46-oz. can pineapple juice

2-liter bottle lemon-lime soda

1. Combine ingredients except soda in bowl.

2. Freeze until slushy, 2–4 hours.

3. Combine with soda and serve in punch bowl.

TIP

Put the crushed pineapple in the blender for a smoother texture.

3-2-1 Lemonade

Tabitha Schmidt,
Baltic, OH

Makes 1 gallon
Prep. Time: 15 minutes

3 lemons

2 cups sugar

water and ice to make 1 gallon

1. Thinly slice lemons, discarding tips.

2. Place in a one-gallon pitcher and add sugar. Stir thoroughly until lemon slices are well-covered with sugar. Let stand for 10 minutes.

3. Add ice and water to make 1 gallon.

4. Serve immediately or within hours, putting a lemon slice in each glass if desired.

TIPS

1. If you have leftover lemonade, remove the lemons if you won't be using it within 24 hours. The rinds can turn bitter if left in too long.
2. To get the maximum flavor from the lemons, mash the sugar and lemon slices together (Step 2) until well blended.

Iced Tea (Brewed or Sun)

**Stacy Stoltzfus,
Grantham, PA**

Makes 16 servings
Prep. Time: 5 minutes
Cooking Time: 20 minutes, or 6–8 hours

4 cups, or 1 gallon, water

3 regular, or decaf, tea bags

3 flavored tea bags (mint, raspberry, peach, etc.), or 1 pt. tightly packed fresh mint leaves and stems, washed thoroughly

⅓ cup sugar, or to taste

To make Brewed Tea:

1. Bring 4 cups water to a boil in a large saucepan.

2. Place tea bags, or fresh mint tea, in a 1-gallon pitcher or non-reactive large bowl (non-breakable when heated quickly).

3. Pour boiling water over tea.

4. Cover. Steep approximately 10 minutes.

5. Remove tea bags, or tea, and stir in sugar. Stir until sugar is dissolved.

6. Add enough water to make 1 gallon.

7. Pour over ice or refrigerate until cold.

To make Sun Tea:

1. Place tea bags in a gallon jar. (I haven't had good luck with fresh tea using this method.) Cover with water to make 1 gallon.

2. Cover jar. Place in the warm sun for several hours (6–8) until tea is the strength you like.

3. Add sugar and stir to dissolve.

4. Pour over ice or refrigerate until cold.

Sauces, Seasonings, Marinades, and Dressings

Sauces, Seasonings, Marinades, and Dressings

Phyllis's Homemade Barbecue Sauce

**Phyllis Barrier,
Little Rock, AR**

Makes 16 (2-Tbsp.) servings

2 8-oz. cans tomato sauce, no added salt

¼ cup cider vinegar

brown sugar substitute, to equal 2 Tbsp. sugar

½ cup minced fresh onions

1 tsp. garlic powder

½ tsp. dry mustard powder

6 tsp. chili powder

⅛ tsp. Tabasco sauce

½ tsp. black pepper

6 tsp. Worcestershire sauce

1 tsp. paprika

1 tsp. liquid smoke

¼ tsp. salt

1. Mix all ingredients together and cook in microwave until minced onion is tender and sauce has thickened.

Marinade for Grilling

**Samuel and Sadie Mae Stoltzfus,
Bird-in-Hand, PA**

Makes 3⁄4 cup
Prep. Time: 2–3 minutes

1⁄4 cup low-sodium soy sauce

1⁄3 cup water

2 Tbsp. olive oil

1 tsp. lemon juice

1 clove garlic, minced

2 Tbsp. brown sugar

1⁄2 tsp. black pepper

1 tsp. vinegar

1. Mix ingredients together in a small bowl.

2. Use as marinade for turkey fillets, turkey cutlets, boneless and skinless chicken breasts, or beef steaks.

Teriyaki Steak Marinade

Marsha Sabus,
Fallbrook, CA

Makes enough for 2 lbs. steak
Prep. Time: 5 minutes

¾ cup oil

2 Tbsp. chopped green onions

¼ cup soy sauce

¼ cup honey

1 clove garlic, chopped

2 Tbsp. cider vinegar

1½ tsp. ground ginger

1. Mix the marinade ingredients thoroughly in a long, shallow container.

2. To use: add the meat and submerge it as well as you can in the marinade.

3. Cover the container and refrigerate it for 2–24 hours (or overnight). If you're home and available to do so, flip the meat several times as it marinates to allow the whole piece to have contact with the sauce.

4. Cook to your liking.

Carne Asada Marinade

**Judy Gonzalez,
Fishers, IN**

Makes enough for 2 lbs. steak
Prep. Time: 5 minutes

½ cup olive oil

½ cup red wine vinegar

½ cup lemon juice

1 Tbsp. salt

1 tsp. cumin

1 tsp. garlic salt

1 tsp. chili powder

1 tsp. dried oregano

1. Mix the marinade ingredients thoroughly in a long shallow container.

2. To use: add the beef and submerge it as well as you can in the marinade.

3. Cover the container and refrigerate it for 2–24 hours (or overnight). If you're home and available to do so, flip the meat several times as it marinates to allow the whole piece to have contact with the sauce.

4. Cook to your liking.

Pear Honey

Alta Metzler,
Willow Street, PA

Makes 7½–8 cups
Prep. Time: 1 hour
Cooking Time: 30–45 minutes

17-18 medium-large fresh pears

20-oz. can unsweetened crushed pineapple in
    natural juice

1½ cups sugar

1. Peel and core pears. Grind in food
chopper. Place in large kettle. Add pineapple
and mix sugar in gradually.

2. Cook until thickened, about
30–45 minutes, stirring frequently to prevent
burning.

3. Pour into jars and seal or freeze.

Blueberry Apple Butter

**Willard E. Roth,
Elkhart, IN**

Makes 1⅓ cups
Prep. Time: 15 minutes
Cooking Time: 15 minutes

1 lb. cooking apples, cored and quartered

½ cup fresh, or frozen, blueberries

2 Tbsp. apple juice

½ tsp. ground cinnamon

1 Tbsp. butter, softened

1 Tbsp. fresh lemon juice

1. Toss apples, blueberries, and apple juice in large saucepan.

2. Cook over high heat until fruit is soft, 12–15 minutes.

3. Cool.

4. Blend in processor or blender until smooth.

5. Add cinnamon, butter, and lemon juice halfway through.

6. Use as spread for breads and muffins. Store in refrigerator up to two weeks.

Taco Seasoning

**Hope Comerford,
Clinton Township, MI**

Makes 4 (2½-Tbsp.) servings, or 4 store-bought pkgs.

4 Tbsp. chili powder

2 Tbsp. cumin

1½ Tbsp. garlic powder

1½ Tbsp. onion powder

2 tsp. salt

1 tsp. oregano

1 tsp. red pepper flakes

1. Mix all of the ingredients together and store them in an airtight container, in a dark place.

2. Use 2½ Tbsp. of this mix in place of 1 store-bought pkg. of seasoning.

Salt Substitute Herb Mixtures

**Ann Bender,
New Hope, VA**

Makes about ¼ cup of each mixture
Prep. Time: 5 minutes

Mixture #1:

1 Tbsp. onion powder

1 Tbsp. paprika

1 Tbsp. parsley

1 tsp. garlic powder

1 tsp. dried basil

Mixture #2:

2½ tsp. dried marjoram

2½ tsp. dried savory

2 tsp. dried thyme

2 tsp. rosemary

1½ tsp. dried sage

1. Mix each mixture together in separate small bowls.

2. Transfer each mixture to a separate herb shaker.

3. Remember, use an herb shaker instead of a salt shaker. These are both good on meats and vegetables.

Italian Seasoning Mix

Madelyn Wheeler,
Zionsville, IN

Makes 13 (1-Tbsp.) servings

6 tsp. marjoram, dried

6 tsp. thyme leaves, dried

6 tsp. rosemary, dried

6 tsp. savory, ground

3 tsp. sage, dry, ground

6 tsp. oregano leaves, dried

6 tsp. basil leaves, dried

1. Combine all ingredients.

2. Store leftover mix for future use.

Herb Salad Dressing

Renita Denlinger,
Denver, PA

Makes ⅔ cup
Prep. Time: 10 minutes or less

2 Tbsp. powdered fruit pectin (Sure-Jell)

½ tsp. (or more to taste) dried herb (choose one: basil, thyme, tarragon, savory, or dill weed)

4 tsp. sugar

¼ tsp. ground mustard

¼ tsp. pepper

½ cup water

4 tsp. vinegar

2 garlic cloves, minced

1. In a small bowl or jar with tight-fitting lid, combine first five ingredients.

2. Stir in water, vinegar, and garlic. Chill.

3. Serve over greens and vegetables of your choice.

Raspberry Vinaigrette

Colleen Heatwole,
Burton, MI

Makes 1–1½ cups dressing
Prep. Time: 5–10 minutes

1 cup raspberries, fresh or frozen and thawed

¼ cup raspberry vinegar

2 Tbsp. olive oil

1 Tbsp. honey

¼ tsp. dry mustard

1. Blend all ingredients in food processor or blender.

2. Refrigerate.

Favorite Balsamic Dressing

Ann Bender,
Fort Defiance, VA

Makes about ½ cup dressing
Prep. Time: 5 minutes

¼ cup olive oil

2 Tbsp. balsamic vinegar

1 tsp. prepared mustard

1 clove garlic

2 Tbsp. sugar

⅛ tsp. salt

⅛ tsp. pepper

1. Combine olive oil, vinegar, mustard, garlic, sugar, salt, and pepper in blender.

2. Blend until smooth.

3. Store in refrigerator.

Ranch Dressing

**Pat Unternahrer,
Wayland, IA**

Makes ¾ cup dressing
Prep. Time: 5 minutes

²/₃ cup cottage cheese

2 Tbsp. milk

1 Tbsp. tarragon vinegar

1 garlic clove, minced

1 Tbsp. sliced green onions

1. Blend cottage cheese, milk, vinegar, and garlic in blender or food processor.

2. Add green onions and blend just to combine.

3. Store in refrigerator.

Zesty French Dressing

Erma Rutt,
Newmanstown, PA

Makes about 2 cups dressing
Prep. Time: 5–10 minutes

1 small onion, chopped

⅔ cup vegetable oil

½ cup white sugar

⅓ cup vinegar

2 Tbsp. ketchup

1½ tsp. Worcestershire sauce

1 tsp. salt

1 tsp. prepared mustard

1 tsp. paprika

½ tsp. garlic powder

½ tsp. celery seed

1. Combine all ingredients in blender.

2. Blend until smooth.

3. Store in refrigerator.

Country Sweet and Sour Dressing

**Annabelle Unternahrer,
Shipshewana, IN**

Makes about 3¼ cups
Prep. Time: 5 minutes
Chilling Time: 1 hour

1½ cups sugar

½ cup light mayonnaise

1½ cups olive oil

½ tsp. pepper

1½ tsp. celery seed

¾ cup cider vinegar

2 Tbsp. dry mustard

2 Tbsp. chopped onions

1. In a blender, combine all ingredients.

2. Blend on High for 2 minutes.

3. Refrigerate 1 hour before serving. Refrigerate any leftover dressing.

Abbreviations, Assumptions, and Equivalents

Abbreviations used in *Welcome Home Cookbook*

lb. = pound
oz. = ounce
pkg. = package
pt. = pint
qt. = quart
Tbsp. = tablespoon
tsp. = teaspoon

Assumptions

flour = unbleached or white, and all-purpose
oatmeal or oats = dry, quick or rolled (old-fashioned), unless specified
pepper = black, finely ground
rice = regular, long-grain (not instant)
salt = table salt
shortening = solid, not liquid
spices = all ground, unless specified otherwise
sugar = granulated sugar (not brown and not confectioners')

Equivalents

dash = little less than $\frac{1}{8}$ tsp.
3 tsp. = 1 Tbsp.
2 Tbsp. = 1 oz.
4 Tbsp. = $\frac{1}{4}$ cup

5 Tbsp. plus 1 tsp. = ⅓ cup
8 Tbsp. = ½ cup
12 Tbsp. = ¾ cup
16 Tbsp. = 1 cup
1 cup = 8 oz. liquid
2 cups = 1 pt.
4 cups = 1 qt.
4 qts. = 1 gallon
1 stick butter = ¼ lb.
1 stick butter = ½ cup
1 stick butter = 8 Tbsp.
beans, 1 lb. dried = 2–2½ cups (depending on the size of the beans)
bell pepper, 1 large = 1 cup chopped
cheese, hard (for example, cheddar, Swiss, Monterey Jack, mozzarella), 1 lb.
    grated = 4 cups
cheese, cottage, 1 lb. = 2 cups
chocolate chips, 6-oz. pkg. = 1 scant cup
coconut, 3-oz. pkg., grated = 1 cup, lightly filled
crackers, graham, 12 single crackers = 1 cup crumbs
crackers (butter, saltines, snack), 20 single crackers = 1 cup crumbs
herbs, 1 Tbsp. fresh = 1 tsp. dried
lemon, 1 medium-sized = 2–3 Tbsp. juice
lemon, 1 medium-sized = 2–3 tsp. grated rind
mustard, 1 Tbsp. prepared = 1 tsp. dry or ground mustard
oatmeal, 1 lb. dry = about 5 cups dry
onion, 1 medium-sized = ½ cup chopped
pasta: macaroni, penne, and other small or tubular shapes, 1 lb. dry = 4 cups
    uncooked; Noodles, 1 lb. dry = 6 cups uncooked
spaghetti, linguine, fettucine, 1 lb. dry = 4 cups uncooked
potatoes, white, 1 lb. = 3 medium-sized potatoes = 2 cups mashed
potatoes, sweet, 1 lb. = 3 medium-sized potatoes = 2 cups mashed
rice, 1 lb. dry = 2 cups uncooked
sugar, confectioners', 1 lb. = 3½ cups sifted
whipping cream, 1 cup un-whipped = 2 cups whipped
whipped topping, 8-oz. container = 3 cups
yeast, dry, 1 envelope (¼ oz.) = 1 Tbsp.

Index

Recipe and Ingredient Index

Index

Index

Metric Equivalent Measurements

If you're accustomed to using metric measurements, I don't want you to be inconvenienced by the imperial measurements I use in this book.

Use this handy chart, too, to figure out the size of the slow cooker you'll need for each recipe.

Weight (Dry Ingredients)

1 oz		30 g
4 oz	¼ lb	120 g
8 oz	½ lb	240 g
12 oz	¾ lb	360 g
16 oz	1 lb	480 g
32 oz	2 lbs	960 g

Slow Cooker Sizes

1-quart	0.96 l
2-quart	1.92 l
3-quart	2.88 l
4-quart	3.84 l
5-quart	4.80 l
6-quart	5.76 l
7-quart	6.72 l
8-quart	7.68 l

Volume (Liquid Ingredients)

½ tsp.		2 ml
1 tsp.		5 ml
1 Tbsp.	½ fl oz	15 ml
2 Tbsp.	1 fl oz	30 ml
¼ cup	2 fl oz	60 ml
⅓ cup	3 fl oz	80 ml
½ cup	4 fl oz	120 ml
⅔ cup	5 fl oz	160 ml
¾ cup	6 fl oz	180 ml
1 cup	8 fl oz	240 ml
1 pt	16 fl oz	480 ml
1 qt	32 fl oz	960 ml

Length

¼ in	6 mm
½ in	13 mm
¾ in	19 mm
1 in	25 mm
6 in	15 cm
12 in	30 cm

About the Author

Hope Comerford is a mom, wife, elementary music teacher, blogger, recipe developer, public speaker, ALM Zone fitness leader, Young Living Essential Oils essential oil enthusiast/educator, and published author. In 2013, she was diagnosed with a severe gluten intolerance and since then has spent many hours creating easy, practical, and delicious gluten-free recipes that can be enjoyed by both those who are affected by gluten and those who are not.

Growing up, Hope spent many hours in the kitchen with her Meme (grandmother) and her love for cooking grew from there. While working on her master's degree when her daughter was young, Hope turned to her slow cookers for some salvation and sanity. It was from there she began truly experimenting with recipes and quickly learned she had the ability to get a little more creative in the kitchen and develop her own recipes.

In 2010, Hope started her blog, *A Busy Mom's Slow Cooker Adventures*, to simply share the recipes she was making with her family and friends. She never imagined people all over the world would begin visiting her page and sharing her recipes with others as well. In 2013, Hope self-published her first cookbook, *Slow Cooker Recipes: 10 Ingredients or Less and Gluten-Free*, and then later wrote *The Gluten-Free Slow Cooker*.

Hope became the new brand ambassador and author of Fix-It and Forget-It in mid-2016. She is excited to bring her creativeness to the Fix-It and Forget-It brand. Through Fix-It and Forget-It, she has written *Fix-It and Forget-It Lazy and Slow, Fix-It and Forget-It Healthy Slow Cooker Cookbook, Fix-It and Forget-It Favorite Slow Cooker Recipes for Mom*, and *Fix-It and Forget It Favorite Slow Cooker Recipes for Dad*.

Hope lives in the city of Clinton Township, Michigan, near Metro Detroit. She's been a native of Michigan her whole life. She has been happily married to her husband and best friend, Justin, since 2008. Together they have two children, Ella and Gavin, who are her motivation, inspiration, and heart. In her spare time, Hope enjoys traveling, singing, cooking, reading books, spending time with friends and family, and relaxing.

Also Available from Good Books

FIX-IT and FORGET-IT®

Fix-It and Forget-It® NEW COOKBOOK — 250 new delicious slow cooker recipes! — Phyllis Good

New York Times bestselling author Phyllis Good — Fix-It and Forget-It® BAKING with your SLOW COOKER — 150 Slow Cooker Recipes for Breads, Pizza, Cakes, Tarts, Crisps, Bars, Pies, Cupcakes, and More!

Fix-It and Forget-It® Lazy and Slow COOKBOOK — 365 Days of Slow Cooker Recipes — Hope Comerford — NEW YORK TIMES BESTSELLING SERIES

Fix-It and Forget-It® Healthy SLOW COOKER COOKBOOK — 150 Whole Food Recipes for Paleo, Vegan, Gluten-Free, and Diabetic-Friendly Diets — HOPE COMERFORD

NEW YORK TIMES BESTSELLING SERIES — Fix-It and Forget-It® FAVORITE SLOW COOKER RECIPES FOR MOM — 150 recipes Mom will love to make, eat, and share! — HOPE COMERFORD

NEW YORK TIMES BESTSELLING SERIES — Fix-It and Forget-It® FAVORITE SLOW COOKER RECIPES FOR DAD — 150 recipes Dad will love to make, eat, and share! — HOPE COMERFORD

Fix-It and Forget-It® SLOW COOKER Champion Recipes — 450 of our very best recipes — PHYLLIS GOOD

By the New York Times bestselling author — FIX-IT and FORGET-IT® BOX SET — A $47.85 VALUE! — PHYLLIS GOOD

Fix-It and FORGET-IT® Slow Cooker Magic — 550 Amazing Everyday Recipes — Phyllis Good

Fix-It and FORGET-IT® Vegetarian Cookbook — 565 Delicious Slow-Cooker, Stove-Top, Oven, and Salad Recipes, plus 50 Suggested Menus — Phyllis Good

Fix-It and FORGET-IT® Slow Cooker Diabetic Cookbook — REVISED & UPDATED — 550 Slow Cooker favorites—to include Everyone! — Phyllis Good — American Diabetes Association

Fix-It and FORGET-IT® Cooking Light for Slow Cookers — REVISED & UPDATED — 600 Healthy, Low-Fat Recipes for Your Slow Cooker — Phyllis Good

By The New York Times bestselling author — FIX-IT and FORGET-IT® 5-ingredient favorites — Comforting Slow-Cooker Recipes — Phyllis Pellman Good

#1 New York Times bestseller! — FIX-IT and FORGET-IT® Cookbook — REVISED & UPDATED — 700 Great Slow Cooker Recipes — Phyllis Pellman Good

Fix-It and FORGET-IT® kids' Cookbook — 50 Favorite Recipes to Make in a Slow Cooker — Phyllis Pellman Good

By the New York Times bestselling author — FIX-IT and FORGET-IT® BIG COOKBOOK — 1400 Best Slow Cooker Recipes! — Phyllis Pellman Good